ACQUISITIONS

ACQUISITIONS

Jane Chappell and Marie-Anne Denicolo

Published by

College of Law Publishing,
Braboeuf Manor, Portsmouth Road, St Catherines, Guildford GU3 1HA

© The College of Law 2009

British Library Cataloguing-in-Publication Data

A catalogue record for this book is available from the British Library.

ISBN 978 1 905391 60 8

Typeset by Style Photosetting Ltd, Mayfield, East Sussex

Printed in Great Britain by Ashford Colour Press Ltd, Gosport, Hampshire

Preface

This book is designed to provide an introduction to the legal and taxation implications of buying and selling a business enterprise either by purchase of a business as a going concern by purchasing all of its assets, or by acquiring the entire issued share capital of a private company. The book highlights the various areas of the law that may fall to be considered during an acquisition transaction, focusing on the issues and legislative provisions which are most commonly relevant. Legislative references have been updated to include, where relevant, the new provisions of the Companies Act 2006, and recent changes to the capital gains tax regime.

This year the book has a new structure, with Part I dealing with factors relevant when planning an acquisition and Part II providing detailed explanations of the main terms of agreement, and how those terms may vary according to the type of transaction. Part III examines the particular concerns specific to an asset purchase and a share purchase, as well as issues relevant where the target is, or is to become, part of a corporate group. There is also a new chapter highlighting the main implications for an acquisition transaction of private equity funding.

Although many of the principles described are of general application to all acquisition transactions, it is worth noting that this book does not attempt to deal with the different procedures and additional obligations involved where the seller, the buyer, or the target company is a public company listed on the Stock Exchange. For a detailed explanation of those further issues, the reader is referred to *Public Companies and Equity Finance*.

This work is primarily written as a complement to the Legal Practice Course elective 'Acquisitions', to assist law students who will already have completed the compulsory business course. In the light of this, some references are made to *Business Law and Practice* to offer a helpful reminder of some of the underlying principles of, for example, company law. In addition, it is hoped that as an illustration of the main principles of acquisitions work this book will prove a useful guide for trainee solicitors in corporate seats, and for lawyers and advisers in other areas of commercial practice who may find themselves called upon from time to time to form part of an often extensive acquisitions team.

Although this edition of the book has a new structure, the authors have nonetheless benefitted from the industry of the original author, Denis Heshon. The original work was a clear, accurate and helpful guide, and we have endeavoured to maintain the same standards with the current edition. If this aim is achieved, it is due in no small part to the support of our colleagues at the College of Law who have been kind enough to offer helpful suggestions as to the content of the book. Marie Calleja read the manuscript and provided feedback, Chris Morris advised on taxation, and Karen Scott and Gillian Phillips provided material on TUPE. We would also like to thank colleagues practising in the acquisitions field for their much appreciated practical insights.

The law is stated as at 1 October 2008.

JANE CHAPPELL
MARIE-ANNE DENICOLO
The College of Law

Contents

Table of Cases

Table of Statutes

EC primary legislation

Table of Seconday Legislation

Table of Abbreviations

ACAS	Advisory, Conciliation and Arbitration Service
ACT	advance corporation tax
BATNEEC	'best available techniques not entailing excessive cost'
CA 1985	Companies Act 1985
CA 1989	Companies Act 1989
CA 2006	Companies Act 2006
CGT	capital gains tax
EA 2002	Enterprise Act 2002
EIS	Enterprise Investment Scheme
EPA 1990	Environmental Protection Act 1990
ERA 1996	Employment Rights Act 1996
ETO reason	economic, technical or organisational reason
FII	franked investment income
FSA 1986	Financial Services Act 1986
FSMA 2000	Financial Services and Markets Act 2000
HMRC	Her Majesty's Revenue & Customs
ICTA 1988	Income and Corporation Taxes Act 1988
IPC	integrated pollution control
LAAPC	local authority air pollution control
MBO	management buy-out
MCT	mainstream corporation tax
MTF	Merger Task Force
OFT	Office of Fair Trading
PAYE	pay as you earn
RPB	recognised professional body
SDLT	stamp duty land tax
SDRT	stamp duty reserve tax
SLC	substantial lessening of competition
SRO	self-regulating organisation
TCGA 1992	Taxation of Chargeable Gains Act 1992
TUPE 2006	Transfer of Undertakings (Protection of Employment) Regulations 2006
UCTA 1977	Unfair Contract Terms Act 1977
VAT	value added tax
VATA	Value Added Tax Act 1994
VCT	Venture Capital Trust

Part I
PLANNING AN ACQUISITION

Chapter 1

Types of Acquisitions

1.1 Introduction

The term 'acquisition' is used to describe a wide variety of transactions involving the sale and purchase of either the underlying assets of an operational business, or the ownership and control of a corporate entity that operates a business. The same major concerns are common to all acquisitions, whatever the size or nature of the parties involved or the entity being acquired. The buyer must ensure that it acquires exactly what it wants (and no more than that) for the best possible price. The seller will try to minimise its continuing obligations whilst aiming for the highest realistic price. In order to achieve those aims, the terms of the proposed acquisition will be carefully negotiated. Although in a complex acquisition those negotiations may cover a whole series of smaller transactions including many different parties, the basic principles explored in this book will apply throughout. It should be noted, though, that this book does not cover the additional regulations that apply to a transaction involving the acquisition of control of a public company ('takeovers'), nor those that apply to transactions involving companies whose shares are listed on The Stock Exchange. Public company takeovers are governed by the City Code on Takeovers and Mergers (on a statutory footing since April 2007, when Pt 28 of the Companies Act 2006 (CA 2006) came into force), while the Stock Exchange Listing Rules apply to transactions concerning listed companies. Details of these regulations and of the typical structure of a public company takeover are dealt with in *Public Companies and Equity Finance*.

In this book, the two most common types of acquisition are considered: (i) the sale and purchase of the underlying assets of an operational business (an asset acquisition); and (ii) the sale and purchase of a private company (the 'target company') by share transfer (a share acquisition). In either case, the seller may be an unlisted company or a group of private individuals.

An asset acquisition involves the buyer acquiring the assets (and certain agreed liabilities) that make up the business. The contract is made between the buyer and the owner of the assets of the business, who may be an individual, a partnership or a company. The assets of the business may include tangible assets, such as land, machinery and stock, as well as intangible assets, such as intellectual property and goodwill. After the acquisition, the buyer will own the business and will continue to operate it using the assets acquired.

A share acquisition is where the buyer acquires the shares in the company that owns and operates the business. The contract is made between the buyer and the owners of the shares. In such a transaction the ownership of the company is transferred to the buyer, but there is no change in ownership of the business. The business, with all its assets and ongoing liabilities, remains in the hands of the company.

1.2 Types of acquisition

Both an asset acquisition and a share acquisition will achieve the same commercial objective of acquiring a target business. However, the legal and tax consequences of the two forms of acquisition are very different, as highlighted below.

1.2.1 Shares

In a share acquisition where the buyer acquires all or the majority of the shares in the target company, it is the ownership of the company itself that is transferred. The sale and purchase agreement is made between the buyer and the owner(s) of the shares (the seller(s)). The target company otherwise remains in exactly the same shape as it was prior to the acquisition and, in particular, it still owns and runs the business. The target company will continue to have whatever assets, liabilities, rights or obligations it had before the acquisition.

The sellers may be individual shareholders, corporate shareholders, or a mixture of both. Many companies are owned by other companies and the businesses are therefore operated through a group structure (see **11.1**). If all the shares in the target company are owned by another company (its 'holding company'), the target company is called a 'wholly-owned subsidiary'. In this case, there is only one seller – the holding company.

However, a company need not hold all the shares in another company to be its holding company. If one company effectively controls over half the voting rights in another company, the two companies are classified under the CA 2006 as holding company and subsidiary (see **11.1.2.2**). Although a sale of this controlling shareholding would transfer effective control, the buyer will usually want to acquire the entire share capital of the company. The holding company in this case will therefore be joined as seller in the acquisition transaction by the holders of the remaining shares. The sellers may thus comprise a mixture of both corporate and individual shareholders. The buyer of the shares may be an individual (or individuals) or, perhaps more commonly, a company. If all the shares of the target company are acquired by another company, it becomes a wholly-owned subsidiary of the buyer.

Example 1

Steve and Andy are equal shareholders in Street Printers Limited, a small print and design company. They are approached by Big Limited, a much larger printing company, with a generous offer for the company. Steve and Andy sell all their shares in Street Printers Limited to Big Limited, so Street Printers Limited becomes a wholly-owned subsidiary of Big Limited.

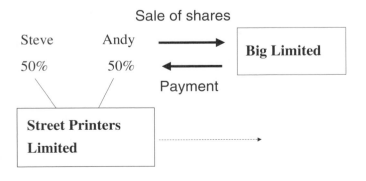

A buyer will usually want to acquire all the shares of the target company; but if this is not possible, for example because a small number of shares are held by an individual who refuses to sell, the buyer may still go ahead and acquire most of the target's shares, thereby giving the buyer control, though it will have the inconvenience of a dissenting shareholder within the company.

If the target company itself owns shares in another company, ie it has a subsidiary, then ownership of that subsidiary will transfer along with the other assets of the target.

Example 2

Street Printers Limited has a subsidiary company, Greet Limited, specialising in greeting cards. When Steve and Andy sell their shares in Street Printers Limited, the shareholding in Greet Limited will transfer to Big Limited as an asset of the target company. After the acquisition, Big Limited becomes the holding company of Street Printers Limited, which continues to be the holding company of Greet Limited.

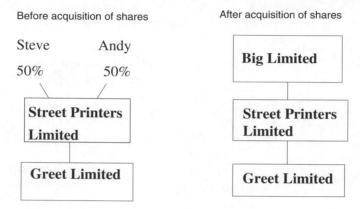

1.2.2 Assets

In an asset acquisition the buyer acquires the underlying assets needed to carry on the business, such as premises, plant and machinery, and intellectual property. Each of these assets must be transferred in accordance with the specific form of transfer required for that asset. For example, a conveyance is needed to transfer land. If the assets will be used to carry on the business after completion of the acquisition, part of the purchase price will be attributed to the goodwill, which usually includes customer details and the right to use the business's trading name. The buyer will also be concerned to acquire important contracts that the business has concluded with third parties (for the supply of goods and services, for example). The sale and purchase agreement will specify the assets to be transferred, which may include transfers for which third party consents are required.

1.2.2.1 Acquiring assets from an unincorporated seller

A business may be operated by a sole trader or a partnership. If so, the assets required to run that business, such as the premises, stock and goodwill, are owned by that individual or partnership.

Example 3

Marco Barr is a sole trader. He owns a motor repair business and trades under the name 'MB Motors'. He agrees to sells the business lease, tools, outstanding orders, customer details and the continued use of the trade name 'MB Motors' to Patrick Cook for £50,000. The acquisition of these assets will enable Patrick Cook to continue the trade of 'MB Motors'.

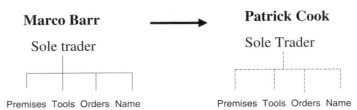

Example 4

Guy and Kate Holdsworth are partners in a grocery business trading under the name of 'Best Fresh'. They sell the assets of the business to BettaBuy Limited, and the proceeds from that sale will be divided between them in accordance with any partnership agreement. After the acquisition, BettaBuy will own the 'Best Fresh' business and will choose either to continue it in the same form, or to absorb it into its existing corporate structure.

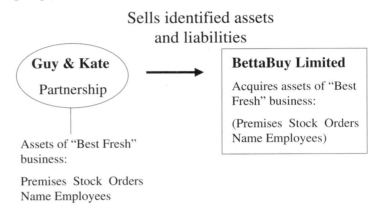

1.2.2.2   Acquiring assets from a company

It is possible to acquire the underlying assets of a business from a company in much the same way as from a sole trader or partnership.

A business may be operated by a company either as the sole concern of that company, or as one of many businesses, or 'divisions', run by it.

Example 5

Computers R Us Limited is a medium-sized company which manufactures computers and also produces a wide range of software packages. In view of the prevailing economic climate, the board of directors decides to concentrate on the software business. The board arranges for Computers R Us Limited to sell the computer manufacturing division to Avaricious Limited.

If the sale of assets involves the assets of the only business operated by the selling company then that company will usually distribute the proceeds of the sale to its shareholders post-acquisition, and the empty shell of the company will be dissolved. On the other hand, where the sale of assets relates to only one of a number of businesses operated by the selling company, the parties must be particularly careful in choosing the assets that will transfer under the sale and purchase agreement, and, once the sale has completed, the company must decide whether to distribute the proceeds of sale to the shareholders or reinvest them in new projects within the company.

Sells identified assets
and liabilities

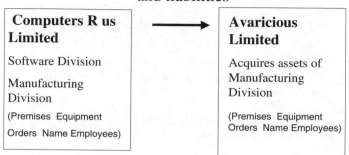

1.2.2.3   Transfer of assets that comprise a 'business'

In this book it is assumed that a buyer on an asset purchase will want to acquire all the assets it needs to be able to continue to run an ongoing business after completion. However, in practice there may be circumstances where the proposed sale is in relation to only some of the assets used in the business, and as such those assets would not be sufficient to enable the business to continue to operate. This would be a mere sale of assets. It is important to distinguish transfer of most of the assets of a business, enabling that business to continue to trade, and a transfer of just a few assets used in a business, since the rules on taxation and employment protection are quite different in each case. This distinction can be difficult to make in practice, however, not least because the precise terms of the tests under the relevant legislation do vary.

Employees

The Transfer of Undertakings (Protection of Employment) Regulations 2006 (SI 2006/246) (TUPE 2006) may protect employees on an asset sale. These Regulations apply to a sale of assets if that sale represents a transfer of 'an economic entity which retains its identity'. The phrase 'economic entity' is defined in the Regulations and has been considered in a number of cases (see **8.3.1.1**). In general terms, if the transfer of the assets enables an identifiable business to be continued by the buyer in essentially the same form, TUPE 2006 will apply. The effect of TUPE 2006 is that the rights and obligations of the employees working in that identifiable economic entity will automatically be transferred to the buyer. In other words, full responsibility for the employees may pass to the buyer of the assets of an identifiable business, whether the parties intend this or not.

If the sale of the specified assets does not represent the transfer of an 'economic entity' then TUPE 2006 do not apply and the rights and obligations of the employees remain with the seller. If the sale of the assets means that the seller can no longer continue its own business then, unless the seller redeploys its employees, the employees' contracts will be terminated and the seller will be open to all potential claims arising from the termination of their employment, notably wrongful dismissal, unfair dismissal and redundancy.

Tax reliefs for unincorporated seller

Two reliefs, one from capital gains tax (CGT) and the other from income tax, are potentially available where the assets of an unincorporated business (whether a sole trader or a partnership) are transferred to an existing company in return for shares in that company. These reliefs are not available on a mere sale of assets (see **8.4.2**).

Value added tax

Another important factor for both seller and buyer to take into account is value added tax (VAT). If the sale involves a 'transfer of a business as a going concern' (as defined in art 5 of the Value Added Tax (Special Provisions) Order 1995 (SI 1995/ 1268)), the transfer is treated as a supply neither of goods nor of services (see **8.4.4**) and VAT is therefore not chargeable. On a mere transfer of assets though, VAT will be chargeable on the assets that are transferred, such as plant and machinery and stock.

The remainder of this chapter concentrates on a comparison of asset acquisition and share acquisition, and does not consider further a mere sale/purchase of assets.

1.3   Factors affecting choice of acquisition

Where a business is owned and operated by a company, the parties can choose whether to transfer the business either by transferring all of the shares in the company or by transferring the underlying assets that comprise the business. The parties may have opposing views on the form that the acquisition should take. This stems from the fact that, in relation to many of the factors which influence the decision as to how to proceed, what is an advantage to one party is a disadvantage to the other and vice versa. Although this is very much a generalisation, the owners of a company will often prefer to sell their shares, whereas a buyer will often prefer to acquire the assets of the business from the company. In these circumstances, the relative bargaining power of the parties is likely to dictate the outcome.

Before analysing the advantages and disadvantages of both types of acquisition, it is worth pointing out that there will be situations where the choice may not realistically be available to the parties. This will be the case if, for example, a company has a number of different businesses (perhaps run as separate 'divisions'), only one of which the buyer wishes to buy. In this situation, the deal must progress as an asset sale unless the parties are willing to use a hive-down structure (see **1.4.2**).

1.3.1   Comparison between share sales and asset sales: seller

1.3.1.1   Clean break from business

Shares

Following the disposal of shares, the seller loses its connection with the company. The company itself continues to exist and, in particular, liabilities (hidden or otherwise) continue to be enforceable against it. It is the buyer who will now have a close eye on the state of the company and, thus, the value of its investment.

Too much can be made, however, of the share sale advantage of a clean break. The very nature of a share sale means that the buyer will make detailed investigations about the company and will seek wide protections from the seller in the acquisition agreement. The buyer will take every action possible to ensure that it has a right of comeback against the seller if the target company turns out to be riddled with undisclosed problems. Additionally, where the seller has guaranteed obligations of the target company, by, for example, offering a personal guarantee on bank lending or by standing as a surety on a business lease, a clean break will be possible only if the seller is able to negotiate releases from such obligations on completion.

Assets

It is a feature of any asset sale that legal liability to third parties for debts and obligations of the business remains with the seller company. Even where the buyer has contracted to assume responsibility for certain liabilities in the acquisition agreement, this will not affect third parties, who can still take action against the seller unless they have expressly released it from liability. Although the seller would have a right of indemnity from the buyer in these circumstances, this may be difficult to enforce, particularly if the buyer is insolvent. In addition, the buyer may have expressly excluded responsibility for certain specific matters for which the seller will, accordingly, remain 'on the hook', as indeed it will for any unforeseen liabilities which may materialise.

1.3.1.2   Scope of warranties and due diligence

Although the acquisition agreement will invariably contain warranties and indemnities by the seller in favour of the buyer, whether it is an asset sale or a share sale, it follows from what has been said above that the scope of these protections should be wider in the context of a share sale. For example, on an asset sale, there is no need for complex taxation warranties and indemnities, for the simple reason that most contingent tax liabilities will remain with the seller. For the same reasons, the investigation into the affairs of the target company will usually be more extensive on a share sale.

1.3.1.3   Transfer of title

Shares

Although the pre-contract investigation and the contract documentation will invariably be more extensive on a share sale, the actual mechanics of transferring title are much simpler – a stock transfer form is all that is necessary to transfer title to shares. However, the terms of the company's contracts should still be checked to determine whether any of them will terminate on a change of control of the company, or whether third party consent to the change is required.

Assets

On an asset transfer, on the other hand, each separate asset of the business must be transferred, and this can involve complications, particularly where consents are required from third parties. Where, for example, leasehold property is involved, the landlord's consent to assignment may be required, and this can often delay the transaction significantly. Some assets, such as stock and loose plant and machinery, are transferable by delivery, but formal transfers of assets such as land and certain intellectual property rights will be necessary to transfer title.

1.3.1.4   Restrictions in the Financial Services and Markets Act 2000

Shares

The requirements of the Financial Services and Markets Act 2000 (FSMA 2000) are more onerous on a share sale than on an asset sale. For example, s 21 of the FSMA 2000 restricts the issue of 'an invitation or inducement to engage in investment activity'. The definition of 'investment activity' in this context includes advising on or arranging the purchase or sale of shares, so any communication in relation to an agreement to buy and sell shares could be caught by this restriction. Importantly, breach of the restriction is an offence rendering the sale agreement unenforceable. This provision does not apply when considering the purchase of assets. A potential seller of shares who has yet to find a buyer must therefore be made aware of this legislation, though specific exemptions exist for financial promotions in the context of share acquisitions (see **9.2**).

Solicitors (or other professional advisers) who give advice in relation to a proposed sale of shares must also ensure either that they comply with the FSMA 2000 requirements for authorisation to carry out a 'regulated activity', or that the transaction falls within a number of possible exclusions under the Financial Services and Markets Act 2000 (Regulated Activities) Order 2001 (SI 2001/544) (see **9.2**).

Assets

Although the provisions of the FSMA 2000 do not extend to the sale of the assets of a business, it should be appreciated that, in relation to a target company, the decision to dispose of the assets rather than the shares may be taken at a fairly late stage in the negotiations. In other words, compliance with the provisions of the FSMA 2000 may be necessary even if the transaction ultimately proceeds as an asset sale.

1.3.1.5   Employees

Shares

On a share sale, there is no change of employer; the target company is the employer before and after the change of control, which has no direct effect on the contracts of employment of the workforce. The share sale itself will not, therefore, give rise to any potential claims by the employees, and it is the buyer, as the new owner of the company, who will be affected (at least indirectly) by any liabilities and obligations of the target company which arise in the future in relation to those employees. The seller no longer has a direct interest, except in relation to warranties given to the buyer in the acquisition agreement.

Assets

The application of TUPE 2006 on the transfer of assets that form a continuing economic entity has already been noted (see **1.2.2.3**). The effect of TUPE 2006 is that the transfer does not operate to terminate contracts of employment. The rights and obligations in respect of any employee working in the economic entity are transferred automatically to the buyer, who takes on responsibility for those employees. As with a share acquisition, the seller no longer has a direct interest, except in relation to warranties given to the buyer in the acquisition agreement.

Employees' claims

In both types of acquisition, actions by the seller or the buyer, before or after the acquisition, may result in claims by the employees. For example, it may be part of the deal that certain employees are dismissed prior to the transfer, or there may be a substantial change in the terms and conditions of employment imposed on the workforce after the transfer. These issues are explored in full in **Chapter 8** (asset sales) and **Chapter 9** (share sales).

1.3.1.6   Taxation factors

Shares: direct receipt of consideration

Where the company is owned by individual shareholders, a sale of the shares ensures that the consideration is received by them directly. The taxation consequences of a sale of shares by individuals are relatively straightforward. Shares are chargeable assets for CGT purposes and any disposal which realises a gain will involve (subject to exemptions) a charge to tax at the disposing shareholder's marginal income tax rate. The seller may be able to exempt some or all of the gain if he qualifies for reliefs.

Where the company is owned by another company, a sale of shares results in the selling company receiving the consideration directly. Any capital gain realised by the selling company is likely to be exempt from corporation tax, however, provided the seller is disposing of a substantial shareholding in a trading company. The availability of this exemption (see **9.4.2.4**) will clearly be an important consideration where ownership of the shares of the target company is in corporate hands.

Assets: two-tier taxation

On an asset sale, if the company owns the assets of the business then it, as the seller, receives the purchase price. For the benefit to accrue to the shareholders of the selling company further steps have to be taken, such as the company declaring a dividend or, if the sale is of all the assets of the company, the shareholders liquidating the company. Apart from the administrative inconvenience involved, this also complicates the tax position, since there are effectively two separate charging points.

First, the selling company suffers corporation tax on the sale of the assets. The disposal of the capital assets of the business may give rise to a chargeable gain; proceeds from the disposal of stock are chargeable as income receipts; and the sale of assets in respect of which capital allowances have been claimed, such as plant and machinery, may trigger balancing charges (treated as income receipts) if the assets are sold for more than their tax written-down value.

Secondly, there will be a further charge when the proceeds of sale of the assets, as reduced by the above tax charges, are distributed to the shareholders. How this distribution of the proceeds is taxed will depend on whether the shareholder is an individual or a company. If the shareholder is an individual and the net proceeds are distributed in a winding up, there is a disposal by the shareholders of their shares for CGT purposes. The alternative possibility of distribution by dividend involves an income tax charge (Income Tax (Trading and Other Income) Act 2005, Pt 4) on the shareholders (although they will have a tax credit). By contrast, a corporate shareholder is unlikely to incur a charge to tax. A distribution on a winding up is likely to attract the benefit of the substantial shareholder exemption, and a distribution by way of dividend will be covered by group relief on intra-company dividends.

Reinvesting the proceeds

Assets   Roll-over relief from CGT/corporation tax under s 152 of the Taxation of Chargeable Gains Act 1992 (TCGA 1992) is available on the disposal of qualifying assets (including land, fixed plant and machinery) used in the trade where the disposal proceeds are applied in the acquisition of replacement qualifying assets (see **8.4.2.1**). The relief operates to roll the gain into the replacement asset, thus postponing any charge to CGT or corporation tax until the replacement asset is disposed of (without itself being replaced). This relief often makes an asset sale look attractive from a tax point of view for a company which is selling a division and planning to acquire new assets to develop other businesses operated by it.

Shares: individual sellers   Shares are not qualifying assets for the purpose of the above roll-over relief. However, an individual shareholder who reinvests a chargeable gain from the disposal of shares (or indeed any gain) in subscribing for shares which qualify for the Enterprise Investment Scheme (EIS) would be able to claim a deferral relief. (See **8.4.2.1**, 'Deferral relief on reinvestment in EIS shares', and **9.4.4.2**.)

Shares: corporate sellers   Deferral relief on reinvestment in EIS shares is not available to a corporate seller which reinvests a chargeable gain in shares. However, as mentioned above, capital gains arising on the disposal by companies of substantial shareholdings in trading companies are exempt from tax.

Taxation considerations are dealt with in more detail in **Chapter 8** (asset sale) and **Chapter 9** (share sale).

1.3.2 Comparison between share sales and asset sales: buyer

Many of the points mentioned above are equally relevant when considering the matter from the buyer's standpoint. Set out below are some additional considerations for a buyer contemplating whether to proceed with an acquisition as an asset or a share purchase.

1.3.2.1 Trade continuity

The main advantage of acquiring the entire issued share capital of the target company is the lack of disruption to the trade which results. From an outsider's point of view, very little will appear to have changed, and customers and suppliers will usually be content to carry on dealing with the company as before. An asset sale, on the other hand, is more likely to prompt them to review their dealings with the new owners, who may have to work harder to build up confidence again.

Assets

The benefit of existing contracts entered into by the seller will not be transferred to the buyer automatically on a sale of the assets of the business. These contracts must be transferred to the buyer either through assignment or novation, and the terms of many contracts require the consent of the third party for an assignment of the benefit to be effective. There may be certain contracts which the buyer sees as crucial to the continued well-being of the business, and it may be reluctant to rely on the third party continuing to honour the contract despite the change in ownership of the business. There is always the danger that, if a formal approach is made, the third party may feel inclined to seek to renegotiate the terms of the contract as a price for consenting to the assignment.

Where the assets of the business include leasehold property, it will usually be necessary to obtain the consent of the landlord to the assignment of the lease. The landlord will wish to ensure that it is not taking any greater risk by having the new owner as tenant, and will often agree to the assignment only if the buyer is able to arrange suitable guarantees. Obtaining a landlord's consent may considerably delay completion of the transaction.

The buyer must also remember that, on an asset sale, it must arrange either for all appropriate insurances to be transferred, or for fresh cover to be taken out.

Shares

On a share purchase the assets of the company and outstanding contracts remain unaffected legally by the change in ownership of the company. However, the buyer of shares does need to be careful on two counts. First, it has no guarantee that those third parties who are accustomed to dealing with the company, but who are not contractually obliged to do so, will continue to deal with it after the change in ownership. Secondly, some contracts contain clauses which permit a party to terminate the contract where control of the company changes hands. Change of control clauses are quite common, for example, in distribution and franchise agreements.

1.3.2.2   Choice of assets and liabilities

Assets

On a share sale, all the underlying assets of the company are indirectly acquired by the buyer, whether they are wanted or not. An asset purchase provides greater flexibility, in the sense that the buyer is able to pick and choose the assets it wishes to buy. For example, the buyer may already have some perfectly adequate plant and machinery and may, therefore, wish to exclude certain items of the seller's plant and machinery from the sale.

Liabilities

Perhaps the major advantage to a buyer of acquiring the assets of a business relates to liabilities. On a share purchase, all the liabilities of the company (hidden or otherwise) remain with it and indirectly become the responsibility of the buyer. Extensive investigations and wide-ranging warranties and indemnities are insufficient to protect the buyer in full. The seller may not, for example, be able to meet a warranty claim, or it may prove difficult (and costly) to establish that a particular matter is covered by a warranty.

On an asset acquisition, on the other hand, the buyer acquires a bundle of identified assets and liabilities. Subject to a few statutory exceptions (notably obligations in relation to employees and environmental matters), a buyer can select those liabilities for which it agrees to take responsibility in the acquisition agreement. In this way the buyer can avoid the risks associated with unknown or unquantifiable liabilities.

1.3.2.3   Integration

A buyer should consider how the new business will fit into its own commercial and organisational objectives. This will be particularly important if the buyer expects to make cost savings by integrating the new business into its existing companies. The buyer must decide whether it prefers to acquire a stand-alone operational company, or whether a collection of assets will be more readily absorbed into its existing operations.

1.3.2.4   Securing finance

The buyer's arrangements for financing the acquisition may have a bearing on whether the matter proceeds as a share purchase or an asset purchase.

If the buyer is proposing to finance the acquisition through some borrowing, it may wish to offer the assets of the business being acquired as security for the loan. If the acquisition proceeds as a share acquisition and the buyer is a public company, however, such a charge over the target company's assets would be prohibited under the CA 2006 as constituting financial assistance by a company for the purchase of its own shares (see **9.2.2**).

1.3.2.5   Taxation factors

From a buyer's perspective, most of the taxation advantages lie with an asset purchase.

Base costs for CGT

On an asset acquisition, chargeable assets, such as land, will have a higher base cost for capital tax purposes on their subsequent disposal. In an arm's length transaction, the buyer will acquire these assets at market value. When the buyer comes to dispose of them at market value in the future it will be charged to capital tax, based on any increase in value since the date it acquired the asset.

Contrast this with the position on a share acquisition. Although the buyer acquires the shares at market value, the base cost of the assets which the company owns is the cost at which they were originally acquired by the company. It follows that on a subsequent arm's length disposal of any of these assets by the company, corporation tax will be charged, based on the increase in value of the asset since originally acquired by the company. There is, in effect, a deferred tax liability, in respect of which a prudent buyer should seek a discount on the price of the shares. The importance of this consideration to the buyer will depend on its future plans for the company and, in particular, whether it is contemplating imminent disposals of any assets by the company (perhaps in an attempt to rationalise the business).

Capital allowances

On an asset acquisition, the purchase of certain assets, such as plant and machinery and (until 1 April 2011) industrial buildings, will enable the buyer to obtain tax relief (as an income deduction) in the form of writing down allowances on the price paid for them. However, there may be a corresponding disadvantage to the seller if the actual price paid exceeds the tax written-down value. In that case the seller will be subject to a balancing charge – the amount by which the actual price paid exceeds the tax written-down value is treated as income profit (see **8.4.2**).

Apportionment of the purchase consideration

On the acquisition of the assets of a business, it will be necessary to apportion the total consideration between the various assets acquired (see **8.4.1**). This must be done on a fair and reasonable basis, but there is some flexibility here which can be used to gain tax advantages as the different types of assets transferred will be subject to different tax rules depending on the nature of the asset being acquired. For example, it will usually be in the buyer's interest to weight the consideration in favour of:

(a)   plant and machinery qualifying for capital allowances;
(b)   trading stock which will form a deduction against income profits for the buyer;
(c)   capital items qualifying for capital tax roll-over relief on replacement of business assets.

The apportionment is a matter of negotiation with the seller, and inevitably the parties may be pulling in different directions. For example, a high allocation to plant and machinery qualifying for capital allowances may result in a balancing charge on the seller, thus increasing his tax liability on income profits. A similar result flows from an allocation in favour of stock.

Acquiring the tax position of the company

A feature of a share acquisition is that the tax identity of the company continues. This means that, after the sale is completed, potential tax liabilities may arise in relation to activities that occurred in the company before the sale. The buyer generally seeks indemnity against such costs, usually provided by the seller in the Tax Deed of Covenant which forms a schedule to the main sale agreement.

Although the buyer must seek protection in relation to potential liabilities, a share acquisition can also enable it to take advantage of tax credits within the company. In particular s 393 of the Income and Corporation Taxes Act 1988 (ICTA 1988) permits trading losses of a company to be carried forward and set against trading profits from the same trade in the future. This enables accumulated tax losses of the target company to be carried forward and set against profits generated after the buyer has acquired the shares (although see **9.4.2** for certain restrictions on this carry forward). This may be a significant factor for a buyer who is confident that it will be able to change the company's fortunes and make it profitable, as it will view the accumulated losses as an asset.

The carry forward of losses is not generally possible on an asset acquisition.

Value added tax

A charge to VAT may arise on the disposal of business assets alone but not on the disposal of sufficient assets to enable the business to continue as a going concern (see **1.2.2.3**). Value added tax is not normally chargeable on a share sale.

Stamp duty

On the acquisition of shares, the buyer pays stamp duty at 0.5% of the purchase price to the nearest £5 (see **9.4.4**).

On the acquisition of a business, the buyer pays stamp duty on dutiable assets only (chiefly land and shares). On commercial land, no stamp duty is payable if the value of the property does not exceed £150,000. The buyer pays stamp duty land tax at 1% where the value is more than £150,000 but does not exceed £250,000; 3% where it is more than £250,000 but does not exceed £500,000; and 4% where it exceeds £500,000 (see **8.4.4**).

1.4 Pre-sale restructuring

As indicated at the start of this chapter, acquisition transactions do not always neatly fit the description of only one type of acquisition or the other. The commercial objectives of the parties to the transaction may mean that either a mixture of both asset and share acquisition, or even a whole series of related transactions, is required.

1.4.1 Creating a discrete unit

If the target company is part of a group of companies, it may use assets owned by other members of the group or hold assets that are used by other group members. The buyer may require that these assets be transferred into the company prior to any purchase of its shares or, conversely, that certain assets be transferred out of the target company prior to its purchase. Care must be taken with such pre-sale transfers as they may trigger tax charges (see **11.2**).

1.4.2 A hive-down

If the target business is one of a number of divisions but for various tax and commercial reasons the parties do not wish to proceed on the basis of an asset sale, the parties may agree that the business is first 'hived down'. This is the process whereby the target company sells some or all of its assets and undertaking to a brand new company, usually set up as a wholly-owned subsidiary of the target company. The buyer then acquires the shares of this new company. See **Figure 1.1** below.

Figure 1.1   Hive-down

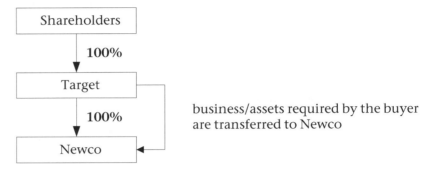

Following the hive-down (that is, the transfer) of the assets to the newly-formed subsidiary Newco, Target will sell all its shares in Newco to the buyer, resulting in:

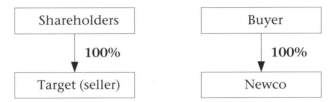

The feature of a hive-down which makes it similar to an asset transfer is that only those assets (and liabilities) which the seller wishes to sell and which the buyer wishes to buy will be hived down. Unlike a normal share sale, the buyer will not need to worry about liabilities or other 'skeletons in the cupboard' cropping up unexpectedly; the company it is buying will be 'clean' as it will have no history. It is principally for this reason that hive-downs are popular with receivers, liquidators and administrators of insolvent companies; they are able to attract buyers by hiving down only the profitable parts of the business to be passed on to the buyer, who need not be unduly worried about the past troubles of the insolvent company. Hive-downs are by no means restricted to this situation, however. Where a buyer wishes to buy one of several businesses owned by a company, and a straightforward share sale is therefore not possible or desirable, a hive-down structure can prove a viable alternative which may suit both parties.

Chapter 2

The Acquisition Process

2.1 Role of advisers

At the outset of a proposed acquisition, the buyer, the seller, and even the target company, will consider the appointment of a group of professional advisers to assist in the proposed transaction. This team usually includes at least legal advisers and accountants, but often also other professional advisers such as financiers and business advisers, and specialist advisers such as patent agents and actuaries. This acquisition team must work as a cohesive body, and it is often the legal advisers who undertake to co-ordinate matters whilst translating specialist advice into appropriate legal documentation.

2.1.1 Solicitor's role

The extent of a solicitor's involvement in an acquisition is dependent upon the instructions of the client and varies from case to case. The objective which the parties' solicitors will be expected to achieve is the legal transfer of ownership from seller to buyer either of the shares or of the assets of the business, as appropriate. The client will also expect his solicitor to identify risks of a legal nature and to seek to protect him from those risks as far as possible.

It is the solicitor's input into the commercial (as opposed to purely legal) aspects of the transaction which varies enormously in practice. The stage at which the client instructs the solicitor tends to be equally variable. These two factors are often linked, in that if the client sees the solicitor's role as excluding the commercial side of the transaction, he may instruct the solicitor only at a relatively late stage in proceedings, perhaps after the substance of the deal has been negotiated.

The reality is, however, that it is difficult to isolate the legal aspects from the commercial aspects, and it is for this reason that most solicitors prefer to be involved as early as possible in the parties' negotiations. This is particularly so where the solicitor is asked to give taxation advice in relation to the acquisition. The way the acquisition is structured can have a significant bearing on the parties' tax position; if the client delays in instructing the solicitor, it may be too late to choose the most tax-effective method. The solicitor will also wish to ensure that his client does not enter into any binding commitments and that all negotiations are subject to contract. Lastly, there is a danger that, if the solicitor is not instructed at an early stage, the client may inadvertently commit a breach of the FSMA 2000 (see **9.2**).

2.1.2   Accountant's role

The precise roles of accountants acting for the parties in an acquisition vary considerably. Indeed, the client may instruct more than one firm of accountants and assign a different role to each firm. Accountants will often be instructed by the buyer at an early stage of a proposed acquisition to help determine the value of the target and the cost of undertaking the acquisition. In addition they will be asked to identify any potential financial and taxation risks, and may also offer advice on the most efficient way to structure the proposed acquisition from a finance and tax point of view.

2.1.2.1   Valuing the target

The seller's accountant may be asked to put a value on the assets of the target business or company, which can be used as a starting point for negotiations with potential buyers. The buyer's accountant will go through a similar exercise on behalf of his client, and his valuation will determine the parameters within which the buyer is prepared to negotiate.

The value of the business is, of course, what a buyer is prepared to pay for it, which itself depends on the buyer's motives for acquiring it. For example, the buyer's principal motive may be to prevent the target from being acquired by a competitor; or the buyer may wish to acquire a competitor in order to reduce competition, or to acquire a supplier in order to protect the source of supply. In these instances, a valuation based on established principles is unlikely to coincide with the worth of the business to the buyer. Similarly, the seller may have his own special reasons for selling which may impact more on the negotiations than a formal valuation.

A detailed analysis of the principles of valuation is outside the scope of this book. However, it is important that the parties' solicitors understand the basis on which any valuations have been undertaken, as this can have an important effect on the provisions which are included in the main sale and purchase agreement.

The two main categories of valuation are assets-based valuations and earnings-based valuations.

Assets-based valuation

A valuation based on the net assets of the target is rare as it will not usually reflect the true value of the target as a going concern. It is appropriate on an asset sale only in so far as the valuation includes a figure for goodwill, and the valuation of this intangible asset is itself likely to be earnings based (see below).

An assets-based valuation of a company may be appropriate where a company is in financial difficulty or has been making consistently low profits. In these circumstances, the 'break up' value of the business may be more than its value as a going concern. Also, certain types of companies lend themselves more easily to this method of valuation, for example property and investment companies.

Earnings-based valuation

The potential of the target to generate profits in the future is the crucial factor in an earnings-based valuation. The main pointer towards this potential is the level of profit achieved by the target in the years leading up to the proposed earnings. Appropriate adjustments to the profit figures appearing in the accounts will be necessary, however, when using these historical figures to forecast future profits. For example, the profits may be significantly understated for this purpose if the award of large salaries to directors, who are also shareholders, has been used as the main method of extracting profits from the company. On the other hand, profits may be overstated where, for example, goods or services have been supplied to the target on favourable terms by connected persons and these arrangements will discontinue after completion.

The next stage is to apply a multiplier to the figure reached above in an attempt to capitalise the future profit-generating capacity of the target. Sometimes, in determining the appropriate multiplier, the valuer will have recourse to information published about comparable quoted companies in the same industry.

There are several other methods of valuing the target which will be appropriate in specific circumstances, and there are additional factors involved when valuing holdings of shares of less than 100%.

Valuations for auction bids – debt free/cash free

Where the target is being sold at auction, accountants may also be asked to prepare a valuation for an indicative bid (see **2.4.2.3**). The bids on an auction often have to be put forward on the basis that the buyer will have to refinance any of the company's existing borrowings that remain after all available cash in the company has been applied to the repayment of those borrowings. This is known as a 'debt free/cash free' price, and means that the auction bids will be based chiefly on the inherent value of the target as derived from profit forecasts and cash flow statements.

2.1.2.2 Completion accounts

Where the price of the target has been arrived at on the basis of either net assets or profits, the parties may not wish to rely on out-of-date audited accounts or unaudited management accounts containing this information. In these circumstances, the sale and purchase agreement will usually provide for the drawing up of completion accounts following completion and, if the 'net assets' or 'earnings' are not as anticipated, for appropriate adjustments to be made to the price (see **4.3.4**). In addition, if a price has been agreed on a debt free/cash free basis for an auction, an adjustment will need to be made to reflect the actual amount of net debt in the company when the acquisition is completed.

The seller's accountant, who will probably be the target company's auditor, will prepare the completion accounts on the basis set out in the sale and purchase agreement. The seller's accountant will then try to agree the accounts with the buyer's accountant. If they cannot reach agreement, it is usually provided that the dispute is to be referred to an independent accountant.

Where the valuation of the target is based on its future profit-generating capacity, the parties may agree that some of the consideration will be deferred until after completion, the amount then payable being calculated by reference to profits actually achieved for specified periods after completion (this is called an 'earn out' agreement and is discussed in detail in **4.3.4**). These arrangements will again involve input from both parties' accountants in advising on the details of the scheme to be included in the sale and purchase agreement and, once again, in preparing and agreeing accounts for the periods concerned.

2.1.2.3   Investigation and report

The prospective buyer will often commission a full accountant's investigation and report into the affairs of the target business or company before committing itself to the acquisition. This aspect is dealt with in **Chapter 3**.

2.1.3   Engagement letters

In larger transactions, professional advisers are often appointed through 'engagement letters' clarifying the terms of their appointment. Accountants have been using engagement letters for large transactions for many years, and the practice has now extended to legal advisers, financial advisers and banks. Engagement letters may also be required by other advisers who are involved in investigating the target, such as patent agents, actuaries and environmental specialists.

An engagement letter usually has three main purposes, as set out below.

2.1.3.1   Identify areas of responsibility

The letter will usually specify the scope of the work the adviser has agreed to undertake, together with agreed procedures for co-ordinating this with the work of other advisers. There is usually a reference to one group of advisers (often the solicitors) having been appointed to co-ordinate the advice.

2.1.3.2   Agreement on fees

The letter will also set out the agreement as to fees. If the advice is being given in relation to an auction bid (see **2.4.2**), there may be an adjustment of fees if the bid proves to be unsuccessful.

2.1.3.3   Statement as to liability

An indemnity in favour of the adviser for losses arising from its appointment other than as a result of its negligence will also form part of the letter. This is to avoid the potentially high claims that may arise if the acquisition proceeds without a particular problem having been identified.

2.2   EC and domestic merger control

At the outset of an acquisition transaction, consideration should be given to whether there are any potential legal barriers to the proposed sale or purchase. In particular, both parties' solicitors must consider whether the proposed acquisition is likely to be affected by the provisions of EC or UK law which seek to control 'mergers'. The term 'merger' in this context covers share sales and asset sales, but it is generally only large-scale transactions which are affected. This is not to say, however, that merger control is limited to listed companies; it may well apply to acquisitions of sufficient importance involving private companies.

The parties to a merger can notify the relevant authorities either in advance of completion or post-completion. In practice they often notify in advance if referral, for example to the Competition Commission, is a real possibility.

2.2.1   UK merger control

Mergers are regulated in the UK by the Enterprise Act 2002 (EA 2002). However, where EC Regulation 139/2004 applies (ie where the merger has a 'Community dimension', see **2.2.2.3**) this overrides the UK legislation, or that of any other Member State.

2.2.1.1   **When will an acquisition be controlled by the EA 2002?**

The merger control provisions of the EA 2002 will apply to a transaction if:

(a)   it is not caught by the EC Merger Regulation (see **2.2.2** below);

(b)   two or more enterprises cease to be distinct;

(c)   the time limit for a reference to the Competition Commission has not yet expired; and

(d)   either:

    (i)   the market share test, or

    (ii)   the turnover test,

is fulfilled.

Not caught by the EC Merger Regulation

If the merger constitutes a *concentration* with a *Community dimension* then, subject to limited exceptions, the Regulation will apply to the exclusion of any national competition law rules. It is only if the merger falls outside the EC Merger Regulation that the provisions of the EA 2002 may apply.

Two or more enterprises cease to be distinct

Enterprise   Section 129(1) of the EA 2002 provides that an 'enterprise' is the activities, or part of the activities, of a business. 'Business' in this context includes an undertaking carried on for gain or reward, or in the course of which goods or services are supplied otherwise than free of charge.

At least one of the enterprises must be carried on in the UK (or by, or under the control of, a body corporate which is incorporated in the UK).

Ceasing to be distinct   Enterprises cease to be distinct if either:

(a)   they are brought under common ownership or control; or

(b)   one of the enterprises ceases to be carried on at all pursuant to some arrangement entered into to prevent competition between the enterprises.

Most typical share sale and asset sale arrangements clearly come within this definition.

The time limit for a reference has not expired

If more than four months have elapsed since the merger took place then normally no reference to the Competition Commission will be possible (EA 2002, s 24).

The market share test and turnover test

For a merger to be caught by the legislation, either of the following must apply:

(a)   the merger will result in at least 25% of all goods or services of a particular description which are supplied in the UK, or a substantial part of it, being supplied by or to the same person (or, if this was already the case before the merger, then after the merger the enterprise acquires an even greater share of the market) (the 'market share' test); or

(b)   the value of the turnover in the UK of the enterprise being taken over exceeds £70 million (the 'turnover' test).

The 'market share' test involves an assessment of when goods or services are of a separate description and, accordingly, form a distinct market. This makes it very difficult for the parties' advisers to be certain when the criterion is met. Where the market for particular goods or services is small, acquisitions which are relatively minor in terms of overall value may, nevertheless, be the subject of regulation.

2.2.1.2   Pre-notification procedure and undertakings

The Office of Fair Trading (OFT), acting through the OFT Board (and the Secretary of State in cases relating to national security), can refer a proposed or a completed merger to the Competition Commission, which may decide to take action if it feels (after carrying out a full investigation) that the merger has resulted, or may be expected to result, in a substantial lessening of competition. Although there is no definition of 'substantial lessening of competition' in the EA 2002, the OFT and the Competition Commission do produce guidance for determining whether this has occurred, or is likely to occur.

If the parties consider that a referral is likely, they may seek what is known as 'clearance' by serving a 'merger notice' (containing prescribed information) on the OFT giving it advance notice of a merger. This is designed to elicit formal confirmation that the merger will not be referred to the Competition Commission. The effect of serving the notice is that, unless the OFT refers the merger to the Competition Commission within a specified time period, it loses the right to make such a reference. The time limit is 20 days from receipt of the notice (although this may be extended by a maximum of 10 days). This is a useful device which enables parties who are concerned about the possibility of a reference, with all the attendant uncertainties and delays that it would bring, to force the hand of the OFT. It is, however, a requirement that the proposed merger must be made public before the notice is served.

For mergers which have not been published, on the other hand, prior to December 2005 it was possible for the parties to seek confidential guidance from the OFT as to the likelihood of clearance. However, the increased workload created by references under the EA 2002 has led the OFT to limit this advice service for the time being. Currently, it will provide informal guidance for confidential merger transactions only where there is a good faith intention to proceed, and where there is a genuine issue as to the OFT's duty to refer to the Competition Commission. The confidential nature of the merger means that the OFT must give its opinion based only on information provided by the parties to the transaction, and therefore the informal guidance given is not binding. The OFT is still at liberty to make a reference to the Competition Commission once the merger becomes public knowledge and the views of other interested parties can be ascertained.

Lastly, the OFT has the power to accept undertakings from the parties (eg providing for parts of the business or undertaking to be sold off after completion) rather than making a merger reference, if such undertakings will effectively avoid a substantial lessening of competition.

2.2.2   EC merger control

2.2.2.1   Council Regulation 139/2004

The EC Merger Regulation will apply if the merger constitutes a *concentration* with a *Community dimension*. If the merger fulfils these criteria then, subject to limited exceptions, the Regulation will apply to the exclusion of any national competition law rules and the merger will fall within the exclusive jurisdiction of the European Commission. This is intended to relieve the burden on the parties to the merger, by reducing the number of regulatory authorities to which they are subject. For this reason the Regulation is often referred to as 'the one-stop shop'. If the merger does not fulfil these criteria then it falls outside the scope of the EC Merger Regulation, but it may still be caught by domestic merger control rules (see **2.2.1**).

2.2.2.2   Concentration

Article 3 of the EC Merger Regulation provides that a concentration can arise on:

(a)   the merger of two or more independent undertakings; or

(b)   the acquisition of direct or indirect control of the whole or part of an undertaking or undertakings.

'Control', in the context of the EC Merger Regulation, is widely defined and means more than just voting control. It includes, for example, the situation where one party can exercise 'decisive influence' over another. A 25% holding may, therefore, constitute control for the purposes of the EC Merger Regulation.

2.2.2.3   Community dimension

Article 1 provides that a concentration will have a Community dimension if, subject to the two-thirds rule (see below), it fulfils certain turnover criteria. There are two alternative sets of criteria, namely:

(a)   the aggregate worldwide turnover of all parties exceeds €5,000m; and

(b)   the aggregate Community-wide turnover of at least two of the parties exceeds €250m

or

(a)   the aggregate worldwide turnover of all parties exceeds €2,500m;

(b)   the aggregate Community-wide turnover of at least two of the parties exceeds €100m; and

(c)   in at least three Member States:

    (i)   the aggregate turnover of all the parties exceeds €100m, and

    (ii)   the aggregate turnover of at least two of the parties exceeds €25m.

Note that even if the merger does not have a Community dimension, the EC Merger Regulation provides that the parties can request the European Commission to take jurisdiction over the transaction if the merger is capable of being reviewed under the national competition laws of at least three Member States.

The two-thirds rule

A concentration will not have a Community dimension if each of the parties achieves more than two-thirds of its Community-wide turnover within the same Member State. This means, practically, that if the main impact of the merger is within one Member State, it will not have a Community dimension. It may, of course, still be caught by the national competition rules of that Member State.

Practically, it can be helpful, when calculating whether a merger falls within the jurisdiction of the Commission, to check whether the two-thirds rule applies *before* applying the Community dimension test above. If the two-thirds rule applies, the Commission will not have jurisdiction, and so there is no need to apply the other test.

2.2.2.4   Notification

If the merger constitutes a concentration with a Community dimension then the EC Merger Regulation provides that the parties must notify the European

Commission before completion. The merger cannot complete until the European Commission clears it. The notification should answer the Commission's questionnaire, Form CO, which requires considerable information about the parties and the transaction. Form CO is annexed to Regulation 802/2004/EC, which implements the EC Merger Regulation.

From notification the Commission has 25 working days to decide that:

(a)   it does not have jurisdiction because the merger does not fall within the scope of the EC Merger Regulation; or

(b)   it will clear the transaction (because it does not create or strengthen a dominant position in any relevant Community market); or

(c)   it will investigate the transaction further (because it has serious concerns that it may create or strengthen a dominant position in any relevant Community market).

If the Commission decides to investigate the merger then, after a further period of time for that investigation, it must decide either;

(a)   to clear the merger; or

(b)   to allow the merger to proceed subject to certain conditions; or

(c)   to block the merger.

2.2.2.5   Exceptions

As mentioned at **2.2.2.1** above, the EC Merger Regulation is intended to be a 'one-stop shop' and applies to the exclusion of any national competition laws. However, a Member State can intervene to request repatriation of a case if it can demonstrate to the Commission that a reference back to the national authorities is necessary:

(a)   to protect legitimate interests (such as national security); or

(b)   because the merger threatens significantly to affect competition in a distinct market within that Member State (art 9).

2.3   Procedural overview

No two acquisitions are the same. However, a typical acquisition – whether of assets or shares – can be broken down into the same five distinct stages: pre-contract; contract; pre-completion; completion; and post-completion. In practice, though, contract and completion often take place simultaneously so that the pre-completion stage disappears. The requirements for conditional contracts are covered in detail in **Chapter 7**.

2.3.1   Pre-contract

Very few acquisitions will proceed immediately to an exchange of contracts. The buyer will usually make thorough investigations of the target business and the terms of the proposed purchase will be negotiated. The parties will follow accepted procedures for the investigations and negotiations, and often will agree preliminary documentation that governs their relationship during this pre-contract stage.

2.3.1.1   Heads of agreement (exclusivity and terms)

Before committing to the time and expense of detailed negotiations, the buyer and seller may wish to record the main points on which they have agreed and the basis on which they are prepared to proceed with the transaction. The principal commercial terms of the proposed acquisition may therefore be set out in a 'heads of agreement' (sometimes also called a 'letter of intent'), and this document may also provide for an agreed period of exclusive negotiation. The agreement as to commercial terms is not intended to be legally binding but will serve as an outline of the parties' intentions and as a starting point for negotiation of the sale and purchase agreement (see **2.5.2**).

2.3.1.2 Confidentiality agreement

Both parties will usually want to keep the terms of the deal (and even the existence of it) confidential. In addition, the seller must also protect any confidential information passed to the buyer during its investigation of the target. To this end, the parties will enter into a confidentiality agreement specifying the parties' obligations in relation to the confidential information, procedures for handling it, and remedies for breach (see **2.5.1**).

Even with a confidentiality agreement in place, the seller is well advised to restrict the disclosure of commercially sensitive information. The extent to which the seller is prepared to disclose such information and the timing of the disclosure depends on the nature of the business, the type of information requested and the identity of the buyer.

2.3.1.3 Due diligence

Before the buyer enters into a contractual commitment to buy the assets or the company, it should acquire as much information about the business as is possible in the circumstances (time constraints and expense being the main limiting factors). The process by which detailed information about the target is obtained and assessed is called due diligence and is considered in detail in **Chapter 3**. The information obtained through due diligence will help the buyer to decide whether it wants to proceed with the purchase and, if so, at what price and on what terms. On larger transactions the buyer's solicitors will prepare a due diligence report highlighting the main areas of risk identified by the investigations and how such risks may be minimised by the inclusion of appropriate terms in the sale and purchase agreement (see **3.6**).

2.3.1.4 Drafting and negotiation of contract terms

The draft documents implementing the sale and purchase of the target will be negotiated between the parties until a final form of each agreement is settled. Understandably, the initial draft is likely to favour heavily the party producing it. For example, the main sale and purchase agreement, prepared by the buyer's solicitor, is unlikely to contain limitations on the seller's liability for breaches of warranty; it will be for the seller's solicitor to draft this section of the agreement and to negotiate its inclusion.

Negotiation of the various transaction documents may involve other advisers from the acquisition team. For example, detailed amendments to taxation warranties may be made by tax specialists within the solicitor's firm, or by the accountant member of the team, or both.

2.3.2 Contract

When both parties are prepared to commit themselves contractually to effect the acquisition, they will enter into a sale and purchase agreement. At the same time, the seller will hand over a disclosure letter to the buyer.

2.3.2.1 Sale and purchase agreement

The first draft of the sale and purchase agreement is prepared by the buyer's solicitor and is then submitted to the seller's solicitor for approval/negotiation. In the agreement, the parties will agree to transfer title to the shares (share acquisition) or the assets of the business (asset acquisition). This aspect of the agreement tends to be short; nevertheless, the agreement will invariably be very lengthy (particularly on a share transfer) as a result of the protections sought by the buyer in the form of warranties and indemnities from the seller. On a share acquisition the whole company is acquired, including its tax liabilities, and there will usually be a separate Tax Covenant by which the seller agrees to indemnify the buyer for any tax costs which arise as a result of events occurring prior to the sale of the company.

2.3.2.2 Disclosure letter

The disclosure letter, which is closely linked to the sale and purchase agreement, is prepared by the seller's solicitor. The purpose of this document is to disclose matters relating to the target and its affairs which, were they to remain undisclosed, would result in the seller being in breach of warranty. The seller attaches copies of documents referred to in the letter (the 'disclosure bundle') and this can make it a lengthy document.

The disclosure letter may be written by the seller or by the seller's solicitor. In the latter case it should incorporate an appropriate disclaimer that all information has been provided by the client and that the solicitor accepts no responsibility for its contents. The letter is handed to the buyer at the same time as the parties enter into the sale and purchase agreement. It has such an important bearing on the seller's potential liability under the agreement that the seller's solicitor should send it to his opposite number in draft form well in advance of this; a final version will be negotiated and agreed by the parties' solicitors in much the same way as the sale and purchase agreement itself. Indeed, the disclosures may prompt the buyer to renegotiate the deal (perhaps asking for a reduction in the price), or to seek to include further protections in the main agreement, usually by way of specific indemnities.

2.3.3 Pre-completion

Completion normally – and indeed ideally – takes place immediately after the sale and purchase agreement has been signed (simultaneous exchange and completion). However, there may be a gap between exchange of contracts and completion where, for example, the parties enter into the sale and purchase agreement with completion conditional upon the happening of certain events (see **7.1**). After exchange of contracts, the parties will chiefly be concerned with satisfaction of the completion conditions and confirmation that the intervening period has seen no change in the general state of the assets or the company (see **7.2**).

2.3.4 Completion

On completion, title to the assets which are the subject of the acquisition is formally transferred by the seller to the buyer in return for the buyer providing the purchase price or consideration. On a share sale, the seller's solicitor will hand over duly signed stock transfer forms, and there will be a completion board meeting of the target company to deal with such matters as the resignation and appointment of directors and the approval of the share transfers (see **9.4**). The method by which completion takes place will normally be included as a clause of the sale and purchase agreement itself. Provisions dealing with what is to happen on completion are, therefore, negotiated by the parties at the pre-contract stage as described at **2.3.1** above. In addition, completion board meeting minutes (and, if necessary, general meeting minutes) of the target company will also have been negotiated and agreed by the parties. They will usually be referred to in the sale and purchase agreement as being in the 'agreed form', and will often be annexed to or contained in schedules to that agreement.

On an asset sale, the individual assets must be transferred in the manner appropriate for that asset. Any land which is included in the sale must be transferred by deed (assignment, transfer or conveyance as appropriate). Assignment of certain intellectual property rights (eg copyrights, patents and trademarks) is necessary. Goodwill and the benefit of contracts may also be formally assigned. On the other hand, no formal documentation is required to transfer title to assets such as loose plant and machinery and stock – title to these passes on delivery (see **8.2**).

2.3.5 Post-completion

On a share sale, the buyer's solicitor will ensure that stock transfer forms are duly stamped; that the internal registers of the target company are updated, to reflect, for example, the change in members and directors; and that the appropriate information (eg on a change of director) is filed at the Companies Registry. On an asset sale involving the transfer of land, the buyer's solicitor must make appropriate registrations at HM Land Registry or the Land Charges Department.

The buyer may also need to take further steps to incorporate the acquired assets or company into its existing business organisation. Those steps may involve changes to the constitution of the target company, or transfer of ownership or licences in respect of particular assets.

2.4 Methods of sale

In some acquisition transactions the buyer and seller will already be known to one another. Usually, however, a seller will seek out buyers, or a buyer may seek out a company or business that meets its particular requirements. A seller of shares or assets must decide which is the more appropriate method of sale, there being essentially two options:

(a) *Private arrangement.* A buyer for the assets or shares may be sought by an intermediary such as a financial adviser, bank or accountant.

(b) *Auction sale.* The seller can hold an auction sale, and is likely to do so if it believes it will receive a number of competing bids. The use of the auction procedure often leads to a higher price for the seller, who may also find it has greater control over the terms on which it will sell. However, if there are only one or two potential buyers, or if the structure of the proposed acquisition is complicated, an auction sale may not be appropriate. In addition, it is clearly more difficult to keep the transaction confidential where there will be a sale by auction.

In recent years, auction sales have become increasingly popular and protocols have arisen as to how such auctions should proceed. The accepted auction procedure is just a variation of the traditional private sale procedure. The essential elements of the pre-contract stage, such as agreeing confidentiality, investigating the target and negotiating favourable terms within the sale and purchase agreement, all remain the same, regardless of the method of sale.

2.4.1 Private sale

Where the buyer and seller are already known to each other, they will often have agreed the main commercial terms of the proposed acquisition, and possibly an agreed period of exclusive negotiations, before instructing solicitors. These main terms and any rights as to exclusivity of bargaining may be included in a heads of agreement, often prepared by the buyer or its solicitor (see **2.3.1.1**).

The buyer will also initiate enquiries about the target company or assets, often by issuing a comprehensive, and sometimes lengthy, questionnaire to the seller. Before the seller will provide the information requested, an agreement as to confidentiality of both information and of the negotiations themselves will be concluded between the parties to the transaction. As the protection of confidential information is primarily of concern to the seller, the seller or its advisers will usually prepare the first draft of the confidentiality agreement.

On a private sale, the buyer's solicitor will usually provide the first draft of the contract documentation. Negotiation of the sale and purchase agreement will often run alongside the investigations into the target, with adjustments being made to it to provide for any risks identified during the investigation. The usual procedure for negotiating the contract documents on a private sale is as follows:

(a) The buyer's solicitor prepares the draft sale and purchase agreement. He submits this to his client and, with his client's agreement, forwards it to the seller's solicitor.

(b) The seller's solicitor considers the draft sale and purchase agreement with his client and amends it, returning the amended draft to the buyer's solicitor.

(c) The seller's solicitor prepares a draft disclosure letter based on information provided by the seller which, after the seller has approved it, will be sent to the buyer's solicitor.

(d) The buyer's solicitor considers the draft disclosure letter with his client, and amends it appropriately, returning it to the seller's solicitor.

(e) Both parties' solicitors agree final versions of the sale and purchase agreement and the disclosure letter (there may have been many drafts before getting to this stage).

Each stage in the process will involve discussions with the other members of the acquisition team and will take into account further information ascertained through the buyer's due diligence investigations.

2.4.2 Variations for auction sale

On an auction sale the seller has greater control of the sale process, as it is the seller who will set out the terms on which it is offering the company or assets for sale. Although there is no set procedure for the auction process and the timing or order of events may vary, most auctions will tend to follow the following format.

2.4.2.1 Advertisement of sale

When a seller has decided that it wishes to proceed by way of an auction sale, the sale will be advertised to prospective buyers. The seller must decide to whom the proposed sale will be advertised. A private company is not permitted to offer its shares for sale to the general public (CA 2006, s 755(1)). However, an advertisement issued to prospective purchasers identified by the seller falls within an exception under CA 2006, s 756(3), as the advertisement is not regarded as resulting in the shares becoming available to persons other than those receiving the offer. The FSMA 2000 must also be taken into account in drafting the advertisement of the proposed auction, if the auction relates to a possible sale of shares.

The advertisement, or notice of sale, is a key disadvantage of the auction process as it will inevitably make the proposed sale public knowledge. This may be disruptive to the target's business, and the seller may face embarrassment if the auction does not lead to a sale.

A period of time will usually be fixed in the notice of sale by which notifications of interest in the proposed sale are to be received. The seller may also require prospective buyers to provide some form of confirmation of credible interest. The seller will respond to the notifications of interest either by admitting the relevant party to the auction, or by rejecting it. The parties who are admitted to the auction process will be sent confidentiality agreements to be signed. On an auction sale there is usually little negotiation of the confidentiality agreement, which will be signed in the seller's format provided that it does not contain any unreasonable or unworkable restrictions (see **2.5.1**).

2.4.2.2   Provision of information memorandum

On receipt of the signed confidentiality agreement, the seller will send out an 'information memorandum' together with a letter detailing the auction process. This 'process letter' will be drafted carefully to ensure it does not create a legally binding contract and will invite the recipients to submit indicative offers. The basis on which bids are to be made will be outlined to ensure that meaningful comparisons between the bids will be possible. In auction sales the seller will often require that bids are made on the basis that the target will be sold without finance. In other words, valuations for the bid will be made on an artificial assumption that the target has neither debt nor cash, giving what is commonly known as a 'debt free/cash free' price (see **2.1.2.1**). The process letter may also request information from the prospective buyers to enable the seller to assess whether any regulatory problems, such as merger clearance or other conditions, may inhibit the conclusion of the transaction with particular bidders.

The information memorandum is prepared by the seller's advisers and outlines key information about the target assets or company. It will usually contain details of the corporate structure, the main assets, methods of finance, the tax position, and may even identify potential liabilities. The kind of information included is usually that which would be requested by a buyer at the outset of its due diligence investigations (see **3.4**).

As well as providing information about the target, the information memorandum is a sales document identifying the strengths and weaknesses of the target business. Its strengths will be emphasised to demonstrate that the target is an attractive purchase, and its weaknesses may be presented as opportunities for a potential buyer to add value.

When preparing the information memorandum, the seller and its advisers must consider the consequences of including misleading or incorrect statements. The buyer will often seek a warranty in the final sale and purchase agreement as to the accuracy of any statements of fact or forecasts contained in the information memorandum. Although the seller may resist this on the basis that the information memorandum is a sales document and therefore only generally descriptive, such resistance is not always successful.

If the information memorandum relates to the sale of shares, it will be subject to s 21 of the FSMA 2000 as an invitation to engage in an investment activity. However, where an invitation relates to the proposed acquisition of control of the company, an exemption is likely to be available under the FSMA 2000 (Financial Promotion) Order 2005 (SI 2005/1529).

2.4.2.3 Indicative bids and preferred bidders

Based on a review of the information memorandum, potential buyers will put in an 'indicative bid' to the seller by a stated deadline. On the basis of these indicative bids the seller will select a small number of preferred bidders. These are not always selected purely on the basis of price, as the seller will take into account such additional factors as the proposed methods of payment and the likely speed and success of the transaction.

As on a private sale, the group of preferred bidders may be given some reassurances as to exclusivity of negotiations for a set period of time (see **2.5.2**). Preferred bidders may also be given an assurance as to break fees, whereby certain costs of the preferred bidder will be reimbursed in the event that its bid is not successful. Bidders may not be prepared to pursue the potential acquisition without some protection as to costs in the event that they are not selected as the final bidder.

2.4.2.4 Further investigations and terms of purchase

Preferred bidders will be given access to additional information about the target assets or business, often through access to a data room set up by the seller (see **3.4**). In some transactions, preferred bidders may be given the opportunity to ask further questions of the seller, and will often be subject to further selection before any access to confidential information is permitted. One of the main advantages of the auction process for the seller is that the due diligence process is under its control, whereas on a private sale it is usually driven by the buyer's enquiries.

On some auctions the seller will also take control of the terms of the sale and purchase agreement. Preferred bidders may be sent a first draft of the agreement prepared by the seller, setting out the terms on which it wishes to proceed with the sale. In contrast to the buyer's first draft on a private sale, this will be drafted in the seller's favour, and preferred bidders must indicate any required amendments. As part of the bidding process, preferred bidders may be asked to propose draft amendments to the seller's contract to give the seller an idea of the contractual terms upon which the bidders may be prepared to make a final offer.

2.4.2.5 Selection of buyer

The preferred bidders will be asked to submit a final bid based on the results of their further investigations and an outline of the contractual terms of the purchase. A single bidder will then be selected and the final negotiations, exchange of contractual documentation and completion of the acquisition will proceed as for a private sale.

2.5 Pre-contractual documentation

Whether the transaction proceeds as a private sale or an auction, the target company or assets must be investigated and the terms of the proposed purchase contract negotiated. As already discussed in this chapter, the parties will seek the reassurance of some preliminary documentation governing their respective obligations during this process.

2.5.1 Confidentiality agreement

At the outset of an acquisition transaction, the parties will enter into an agreement to try to protect confidential information that will inevitably pass between them during the negotiations. Indeed, the parties may wish to keep even the existence of the proposed acquisition itself a secret.

When the buyer undertakes its due diligence investigations, the seller will be expected to provide a wide variety of often commercially sensitive information. If the buyer is a competitor, the seller will be particularly concerned about revealing information such as customer lists and important contracts which the buyer may be able to use to its own advantage if the acquisition falls through. The seller is therefore advised to require the buyer to enter into a confidentiality agreement before any sensitive information is released. As it is the seller who is most at risk from any potential misuse or release of information, the initial draft of the agreement is usually prepared by the seller or its advisers.

A confidentiality agreement will usually follow a standard format, but there may be some scope for negotiations as to the precise terms. From the seller's point of view, the agreement should cover as much information as possible, and should provide precise procedures for the use and safe-keeping of that information. By contrast, the buyer will seek to reduce restrictions imposed, particularly those with a cost implication. Accordingly, the buyer may prefer that the restrictions apply only to the most sensitive information, and it may not wish to agree to extensive procedures for tracking information in its possession.

In general terms a confidentiality agreement will usually include:

(a) a definition of confidential information (this is likely to exclude information in the public domain and information already known to the proposed buyer). The definition will include information obtained from the seller and its advisers, and should extend to any document prepared on the basis of this information by the buyer;

(b) an obligation on the buyer not, without the seller's consent, to disclose or use such information except for authorised purposes (as defined) in connection with the acquisition. A list of authorised persons entitled to receive the information, such as certain employees and professional advisers of the buyer, may be included (with an assurance by the buyer that it will notify them of the terms of the confidentiality agreement). In addition, the seller may prevent the buyer from soliciting customers, suppliers or employees of the target for a specified period (although care needs to be taken that these provisions are not void as being in restraint of trade);

(c) an undertaking by the buyer to return or destroy such information (including copies) if the acquisition does not proceed. If the information is particularly sensitive, agreed procedures for tracking it may also be included;

(d) an agreement that the parties will not, without the written consent of the other party, make any announcement or disclosure of the fact that negotiations are taking place.

The various undertakings of the buyer may be contained in a formal agreement between the parties or, quite commonly, in a letter to the seller. Whichever form is chosen, consideration must be given for this agreement to be enforceable, the usual consideration being the provision, by the seller, of the confidential information.

A confidentiality agreement provides comfort to a seller who is in a commercially sensitive position. Nevertheless, it may prove extremely difficult for the seller to monitor breaches and, indeed, to assess the loss where it can be proved that breaches have occurred. It is therefore important that the contractual obligations are supported by monitoring the buyer's procedures for handling the confidential information. In addition, wherever possible the release of sensitive information should be restricted. Some commercial information may be so sensitive that it should not be divulged to the buyer until the moment of exchange of contracts.

2.5.2   Heads of agreement/letters of intent

Once negotiations have reached a certain point, the parties may wish to record the main points on which they have agreed and the basis on which they are prepared to proceed with the transaction. The parties often feel more confident that the whole exercise will not prove to be a waste of time, money and effort if they are able to point to a document setting out at least some of the fundamental issues (eg price). Drawing up the document may serve to focus the minds of the parties and establish whether there is a sufficient measure of agreement between them to make it worthwhile continuing with the proposed acquisition. In practice, the heads of agreement may serve as a useful guide to the transaction for the various professional advisers involved and for those who may have been approached by the buyer to finance the deal.

Heads of agreement (often also called a 'letter of intent') are by no means universally employed in acquisitions. The parties' solicitors often take the view that the time involved in producing them can be more usefully employed in drafting and negotiating the main agreement, which – unlike the heads of agreement – will incorporate appropriate protections for their clients. Regrettably, it is relatively common for the parties to enter into heads of agreement before taking any professional advice.

Two considerations will often arise in connection with heads of agreement: first, whether the terms (or some of them) are to be legally binding; and, secondly, whether the buyer is to be granted an exclusive right to bargain with the seller.

2.5.2.1   'Subject to contract'

It is extremely unlikely that the buyer, in particular, will want all the heads to be binding. The signing of heads of agreement will invariably precede the buyer requisitioning a detailed investigation of the target, the outcome of which may prompt it to seek to withdraw from the transaction or to renegotiate the price. The buyer will not wish to be fully committed until it has completed the investigation and is satisfied that adequate protection by way of appropriate warranties and indemnities is included in the main agreement. Indeed, if the heads were fully binding, there would be little incentive for the seller to sign a further agreement.

Normal practice is for the document containing the heads of agreement to be marked 'subject to contract' and (because of the uncertainty as to the precise effect of this phrase) for it to include a statement that the provisions are not intended to be legally binding.

The parties may, however, want some of the provisions which are included in the heads of agreement to be legally binding, in which case this needs to be stated expressly. For example, provisions relating to confidentiality, exclusivity of bargaining (see **2.5.2.2** below) and liability for costs in the event of an abortive transaction, should be legally binding from the outset.

2.5.2.2 Exclusivity

A buyer who is considering acquiring the target may be reluctant to spend the time and money necessary to undertake a full investigation into the target's affairs unless it is granted an exclusive bargaining right for a certain period, ie it is agreed that, during this period, the seller will not enter into or continue negotiations for the sale of the target with anyone else.

It is clear from the House of Lords case of *Walford v Miles* [1992] 2 WLR 174 that such a clause (commonly known as an 'exclusivity' or 'lock-out' clause) is enforceable provided it is sufficiently certain. Some doubt had been thrown on this by the Court of Appeal, which found a lock-out agreement to be void on the grounds that it was no more than an agreement to negotiate (it being a long-established contractual principle that an agreement to agree is unenforceable).

In the House of Lords, Lord Ackner concurred with the view that an agreement to negotiate is void for uncertainty, pointing out that the essence of negotiations is that the parties are entitled to withdraw from those negotiations at any time and for any reason. He described these sort of agreements as 'lock-in' agreements. Lord Ackner, on the other hand, saw no such difficulty with 'lock-out' agreements, ie agreements not to negotiate with anyone else for a fixed period, provided they are sufficiently certain. The House of Lords decided unanimously that the lock-out clause in question was not sufficiently certain because it did not specify how long it was to last.

The exclusivity clause should include a remedy in the event of a breach, usually the recovery of costs incurred in pursuing the acquisition. There is some doubt over whether costs incurred before the execution of the lock-out agreement would also be covered by such a provision, significant if the agreement was entered into at a late stage of the negotiations. *Radiant Shipping Co and Sea Containers* [1995] CLC 976 provided that costs incurred before the execution of the agreement could be recovered if this was expressly provided for, as long as it did not amount to a penalty. A well-drafted provision for a remedy for breach of exclusivity should therefore allow for the recovery of all expenses, whether incurred before or after execution of the exclusivity agreement.

Lastly, consideration must be given in order to render the exclusivity clause enforceable. The usual consideration is the buyer's commitment to finance the due diligence investigation.

2.6 Summary of procedure for conditional contracts by private sale

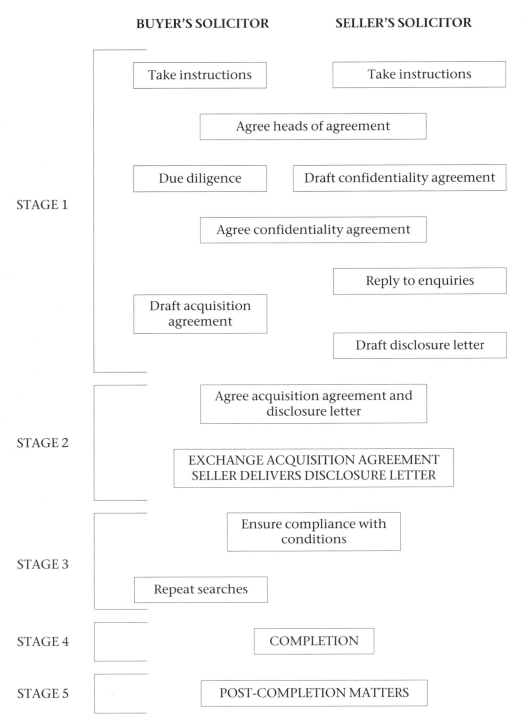

If the parties are able to exchange and complete simultaneously, Stage 3 above is not necessary, although repeat searches should be carried out prior to Stage 2.

Chapter 3

Investigating the Target

3.1 What are the buyer's objectives?

During the initial negotiations on the terms of the proposed acquisition, the buyer may not have any detailed knowledge of the target. It will often be relying in these early stages on information received from the seller, what is publicly known about the target, any sales information released by the seller, any knowledge of the target's business acquired from previous dealings, perhaps as a supplier or even a competitor, and a search of the company's file at the Companies Registry.

The parties or their advisers may draw up heads of agreement to record the results of their preliminary discussions and to provide a helpful basis on which to proceed to the signing of the main agreement (see **Chapter 2**). The buyer, however, will not want to enter into a binding commitment to acquire the target until it has as much information as possible about it, and this information-gathering stage is often known as 'due diligence'. The aim of due diligence is to furnish the buyer with essential management information, to enable it to decide whether or not to go ahead with the proposed acquisition and, if so, on what terms. In particular, the results of the investigation may prompt the buyer to renegotiate the price for the target. In addition, the due diligence investigation can help to identify any consents or preconditions that may need to be obtained or satisfied.

Whilst the due diligence process can provide the buyer with an enormous insight into the business it is planning to buy, it is important to remember the basic common law principle of *caveat emptor* ('let the buyer beware'). Due to the harshness of this principle, the buyer will seek to protect itself in two ways: first, like any prudent buyer, by obtaining as much information as possible on the target; and, secondly, by backing that up with extensive warranties and indemnities in the sale and purchase agreement. The purpose of the warranties and indemnities is to provide the buyer with contractual protection should the target not turn out to be as expected (see **Chapter 5**). It is important to remember that the two are not mutually exclusive and, indeed, that a thorough investigation of the target is essential to reveal areas where the buyer is at risk and needs, therefore, to protect itself by including warranties and indemnities.

3.2 Types of due diligence

Depending on the size of the proposed acquisition, the investigation of the target may be undertaken by a variety of professional advisers, including general business advisers, accountants and lawyers.

3.2.1 Business advisers

When considering whether to undertake a possible acquisition, the buyer will usually want to carry out a preliminary commercial assessment of the target business. This may include a consideration of the market position of the target, its financial position and any business plan to which the buyer may have obtained access. This business assessment will often be undertaken by the buyer itself or, if the buyer is a company, by the senior management of that company. If the buyer lacks sufficient expertise in the relevant market, it will approach professional business advisers to carry out the business analysis. If the buyer is seeking to raise finances to fund the proposed acquisition, there may also be a business review by its financial advisers.

3.2.2 Accountants

The buyer may instruct a firm of accountants (if the buyer is a company, its auditors will often be appointed) to investigate the target and produce a report. Normally, this is done when negotiations are far enough advanced for the buyer to feel that the expense is justified.

3.2.2.1 Accountants' report

The accountants' report is often central to the conduct of negotiations between the parties and plays an important role in the framing of the acquisition documentation, particularly the warranties and indemnities (although it is likely that the buyer will have produced the first draft of the main agreement before the report is available). It is important that the buyer's professional advisers liaise with their client and with each other on the precise scope of the various investigations to be carried out. An early meeting between the buyer's solicitor and the reporting accountants should serve to define areas of responsibility, avoid duplication and determine a timetable which ensures that the report is produced early enough to be useful in negotiations.

The buyer should instruct the firm of accountants formally by a letter of engagement, which should set out clearly the matters on which the accountants are required to report (the initial draft of the letter is often produced by the firm of accountants after discussions with their client). The accountants will need to be in direct contact with the proprietors or management of the target, and must be informed of the terms of any confidentiality agreement between the parties.

3.2.2.2 Matters covered by the report

The matters on which the accountants may be asked to report include the commercial activities of the target, management structure and employees, taxation, profitability, balance sheet strength, accounting systems and policies, and premises.

Commercial activities

The report may include the following:

(a) details of the past, present and planned activities of the target;

(b) an analysis of the market in which the target operates and a description of its main customers, geographical coverage, market share and principal competitors;

(c) details of pricing policy, terms of trade (including credit arrangements) and significant agreements with suppliers, customers, agents, etc.

Management structure and employees

The information requested may include the following:

(a)   management structure and details of the ages, qualifications and service records of the directors and senior management;

(b)   details of the service contracts of the directors and senior management, including remuneration, commission, fringe benefits, pensions, profit-sharing and share option schemes, etc;

(c)   the number of other employees (broken down into departments and locations) and details of pay structure and staff relations;

(d)   staff training schemes and recruitment policies.

Taxation

The buyer will usually want detailed information about the tax affairs of the target (particularly on a share acquisition). The tax due diligence will usually cover the following main areas:

(a)   the current tax position of the target – details of current tax liabilities, the adequacy of provisions made for tax in the accounts of the target, VAT and PAYE compliance, and whether the target's tax affairs are up to date;

(b)   if relevant, what effect the acquisition will have on the tax affairs of the target and of the buyer, for example whether the transaction will itself create any charges to tax;

(c)   the likely future tax position of the target;

(d)   the warranties and indemnities that should be obtained, including any specific indemnities to cover known problem areas.

Profitability

The accountants will usually conduct a detailed review of the audited results of a target company for the previous three or four accounting periods and any unaudited information which may be available (eg management accounts), with a view to providing a detailed breakdown of turnover, overheads and profit (perhaps in relation to each activity of the target) and analysing relevant trends.

Balance sheet strength

The accountants will report on the assets and liabilities of the target, and may include details of (and comments on) the following:

(a)   borrowing commitments, both long-term and short-term, including details of any security provided;

(b)   recent capital expenditure, outstanding capital commitments, long-term contracts and contingent liabilities;

(c)   debtors and provision for bad debts;

(d)   insurance policies (and adequacy of cover).

Accounting systems and policies

A report on the accounting systems and the accounting policies adopted by the target will assist the buyer in understanding the accounts and in determining whether changes will be necessary after completion (eg to integrate with the buyer's systems).

Premises

The buyer will usually be relying on its solicitor to provide detailed information about the properties owned or occupied by the target, but the accountant's report will often contain brief details, including location, use and tenure of each property.

3.2.2.3   Use of the report

The final section of the report, which usually sets out the accountants' summary of the strengths and weaknesses of the target, any recommendations and their conclusions on the reasonableness of the price, is often of greatest interest to the buyer, who may use the report as a lever for lowering the price.

Practice on allowing the seller to have a copy of the report is variable (although, if it is given a copy, the summary and conclusion will often be omitted). The seller's disclosure letter may deem matters contained or referred to in the accountants' report to have been disclosed by the seller (thus potentially reducing the seller's exposure under the warranties). In these circumstances the buyer may insist on a warranty by the seller as to the accuracy of the contents of the accountants' report. These are all matters for negotiation between the parties.

The buyer will, of course, have claims against the reporting accountants if the report is negligently prepared (both in contract for breach of the implied duty of reasonable skill and care, and in tort for negligent misstatement). It should be noted that if the buyer does not commission its own report but merely relies on the audited accounts of the target company, it will not normally have any remedy against the company's auditors if they act to its detriment.

3.2.3   Legal advisers

The buyer will expect its legal advisers to carry out an investigation into any legal issues that may affect the value or prospects of the target. Such an investigation should also identify any preconditions that must be satisfied, or consents that may be required, effectively to transfer ownership of the shares or assets of the target business. This investigation is known as 'legal due diligence' (see **3.3**) or a 'legal review' and is usually undertaken by the buyer's legal advisers.

Legal due diligence will generally focus on the constitutional framework of the target company, the terms on which the target does business, ownership of its assets and any restrictions on the free use of them, and the extent of any potential liabilities. Much of this information will be examined by junior lawyers, though the more complex areas will be reviewed by lawyers within specialist departments or other professional advisers with particular expertise, such as pensions actuaries.

On a relatively small transaction the results of the investigation will be informally communicated to the client and to those negotiating the acquisition documentation. However, on larger transactions, more formal procedures may be required to avoid overlap of investigation and to ensure efficient reporting of the results to the client and those lawyers charged with negotiating the contractual terms of the deal (see **3.2.2.1**).

Whatever the reporting process, the results of the due diligence investigation should directly inform the negotiation of the acquisition documentation.

3.3 Scope of legal due diligence

The scope of a legal due diligence investigation can be extremely wide. In practice, the extent of the investigation will be dictated by the nature of the target business, and by the requirements and concerns of the particular buyer. A number of factors will influence both the scope and focus of a legal due diligence review, as discussed below.

3.3.1 Commercial aims

The scope and focus of the investigation will depend to a certain extent on the buyer's position and on the commercial aims underlying the transaction. If the buyer is already familiar with the target, extensive due diligence will be less important, as the buyer will be aware of the potential strengths and weaknesses of the business.

The reason for the purchase may also influence the focus of the investigations. If the acquisition is intended to allow expansion into a new market, the buyer is likely to focus on existing trading contracts for example; but if the purchase is for investment purposes, the financial stability of the target and how the investment may be realised will be of more interest to the buyer.

3.3.2 Identified areas of risk

During the due diligence process, consideration must be given to the typical risks inherent in the market in which the target business operates. For example, if the target operates in a heavily regulated sector, the buyer must carefully explore the grant of, and any conditions attached to, any necessary consents, licences or approvals.

Any particular risk factors within the target itself must also be explored. For example, if the target has been in financial difficulties, the terms of its loan agreements should be checked carefully to ensure that no events of default have occurred which may result in claims over the target's assets.

3.3.3 Types of transactions

3.3.3.1 Shares

The scope of the investigation will usually be more extensive on the acquisition of the entire share capital of a company than on an asset acquisition. This is because the buyer of shares acquires a 'live' company with all its assets and, perhaps more significantly, its liabilities, whether actual or contingent, fixed or unquantified. There is far more involved than checking that the seller has title to the shares themselves; all aspects of the target company are of concern to a potential buyer and should, ideally, be examined.

3.3.3.2 Assets

The buyer of the assets of a target business does not assume the liabilities of the business (except as regards employees, see **Chapter 8**), which remain with the seller unless it is released from them by the third parties involved. The buyer will, however, often agree to accept responsibility for certain of these liabilities by giving the seller an indemnity in the sale and purchase agreement. The buyer will therefore direct its investigation at the specific assets which it wishes to acquire and at the liabilities which it is prepared to accept. It should be appreciated, however, that the goodwill of the business acquired by the buyer may be adversely affected by certain liabilities, even if these remain with the seller (eg a successful claim against the seller for manufacturing defective products). Information gained during the due diligence process will also be used after the transaction has closed by a buyer who must integrate the acquired entity into its existing business structure. Consequently, it is in the buyer's interest to discover as much about the business generally as is feasible in the circumstances.

3.3.4 Extent of contractual protection

In some circumstances, the seller may not be able (or prepared) to give much contractual protection to the buyer (see **Chapter 5**). For example, the sale may be by an insolvency practitioner, who may be prepared to give only very limited contractual reassurances about the target; or it may be by way of an auction sale, where the seller has indicated that very few contractual protections will be given. In such a case, the buyer should try to investigate as thoroughly as possible to ascertain the exact nature of the business it proposes to acquire. Conversely, if the buyer knows that it will have the benefit of extensive contractual protections, it may consider that the time and expense of a full investigation is not merited.

3.3.5 Limiting factors

Although the issues mentioned above may help to determine the scope of the due diligence investigation, the buyer is not always able to be as painstaking as it would like. A number of matters may, in practice, hinder a thorough scrutiny of the target business or company.

3.3.5.1 Time constraints

Time constraints are often the most significant factor in determining the scope of the buyer's enquiries. It is in the nature of commercial transactions that tight (and sometimes unrealistic) timetables are often agreed upon by the parties. Also, where the seller is in a strong bargaining position (perhaps because there are other interested parties), it may dictate a short timescale for the parties to enter into the contract.

3.3.5.2 Financial resources and manpower

The buyer may be unable to commit sufficient financial resources or manpower to a full-scale examination of the target. Saving money at this stage of the transaction may prove a false economy in the long term but, nevertheless, the buyer will inevitably be working within the constraints of a budget.

3.3.5.3 Confidentiality

The seller may be keen to keep the proposed sale a secret, not only from outsiders, such as competitors and suppliers, but also from its own workforce (see **2.3.1.2**). The practical limitation which this puts on the extent of the searches and enquiries of the buyer and its advisers is obvious. The seller will often insist that all communications are channelled through one person; that a code-name is used for all such contact; and that the true purpose of any visits to the seller's premises by the buyer or its advisers (eg a surveyor) is not disclosed.

It has also been seen that sellers may, understandably, be reluctant to pass on commercially sensitive information to the buyer, such as customer lists, in advance of exchange of contracts. This problem may, in some cases, be mitigated by a confidentiality agreement between the parties.

In addition, some of the documentation that the buyer may seek to review, such as joint venture agreements for example, may themselves be the subject of confidentiality obligations. This may mean that the consent of a third party will be necessary before the buyer is able to review the information.

3.4 Undertaking a due diligence investigation

3.4.1 Public searches

At the outset of the acquisition transaction, the buyer's lawyers will usually review all public records relating to the target business or company. This will include information about the company held at Companies House, property details held at Land Registry or the Land Charges Registry, and details of any registered intellectual property rights. In addition, the buyer may also seek information from relevant websites, the trade press, and from commercial organisations which specialise in providing corporate and financial information about businesses.

Although searching public records is a quick and inexpensive method of obtaining information, it should be remembered that the information sourced is not always up to date.

3.4.2 Questionnaire

The buyer's solicitor will often begin the due diligence process by forwarding a detailed request for information to the seller's solicitor, often known as a 'due diligence questionnaire'. The replies to these enquiries will form the buyer's main source of information on the target business. The questionnaire should not be a pro forma document but should be tailored to the particular business involved, thus avoiding burdening the seller's solicitor with unnecessary or irrelevant questions. In compiling the questionnaire, the buyer and its advisers should give particular thought to the typical risks inherent in the market in which the target operates and to the buyer's specific concerns. The buyer's solicitor should liaise with the other professional advisers representing the buyer in an attempt to avoid duplicating requests for information; he will often act as 'information controller'.

On a share sale, if any of the selling shareholders are not also directors, they may have little personal knowledge of the matters raised. Consequently, the seller's solicitor will have to obtain much of the information which is requested about the structure of the company and the running of the business from the management of the target company. Whatever the source of the information, the seller has little to gain from giving evasive replies (particularly if the replies are to be attached to the disclosure letter, thus qualifying the warranties). So, provided the seller is satisfied as to the confidentiality of any information passing to the buyer, it should give full and frank replies to the pre-contract enquiries.

The buyer's solicitor, in conjunction with his client and the rest of the team, should check the replies carefully and follow up any points which remain outstanding. As with the accountants' report, the replies are likely to have a significant bearing on the warranties and indemnities required by the buyer.

3.4.3 Data room

In transactions where information about the target business is highly sensitive, or where the sale is by way of an auction with a number of potential bidders, access to information provided by the seller may be by way of a secure data room. In the data room the seller, aided by its legal advisers, will make information about the target available to the buyer. The seller's advisers will carefully consider what information should be made available. This information will then be indexed and laid out in the room for review. In some transactions the data room is a physical room, but it is increasingly common for the seller to create, instead, a secure website through which the buyer's advisers can gain electronic access to the key documentation.

In setting up a data room, either real or virtual, the seller's advisers must try to ensure that the key documentation a potential buyer would want to review is included, whilst also attempting to protect any commercially sensitive material. When reviewing the information in the data room, the buyer's advisers must focus on the key areas of concern for the buyer; if the information provided seems insufficiently detailed, the buyer may need to make additional enquiries of the seller.

3.5   Common areas of investigation

3.5.1   Corporate information

As mentioned at **3.4.1** above, useful information about a target company can be obtained by making a search of the company's file at the Companies Registry. The buyer's solicitor will usually seek this information at the outset of the due diligence process, and repeat the search for confirmation purposes shortly before the sale and purchase agreement is concluded.

Where a company is selling the assets of a business or shares in a subsidiary, a search should be made against the selling company. Also, a seller is wise to search the file of a corporate buyer to satisfy itself that it is of sufficient substance to effect the acquisition and to fulfil any post-completion obligations, such as the payment of any deferred consideration.

The company search does have serious limitations, however, which means that the information it reveals may not be entirely reliable. The obligation to file information at the Companies Registry is placed on the company itself, and although the company and its officers are liable to fines on default, there is no provision for compensating a third party who suffers loss as a result of this information being incomplete or inaccurate. Indeed, the buyer of shares is not given any statutory assistance in these circumstances. In addition, even if the target has duly filed its returns on time, the information revealed by the search will in many cases be out of date.

3.5.1.1   Constitutional documents

Where the assets of a business are being acquired from a company, the buyer's solicitor should check that the company's constitutional documents give it the power to dispose of its assets, and that the articles enable the directors to exercise that power.

The buyer's solicitor will also study the constitution of the target company to check that the company has power to carry on the business and to discover what steps will need to be taken on completion. The buyer should also check whether the articles contain any restrictions on the transfer of shares. They may, for example, contain pre-emption provisions, obliging shareholders wishing to transfer their shares to offer them pro rata to existing members. In this event, the selling shareholders will usually waive their respective rights as a term of the sale and purchase agreement (although it may be safer to change the article, since pre-emption rights are sometimes triggered by an 'intention' to dispose of the shares). After it has acquired the shares, the buyer may, of course, wish to change provisions of the target company's constitution to suit its own specific needs.

3.5.1.2 Directors and shareholders

The annual return contains a list of the shareholders, directors and company secretary, and details of the nominal, issued and paid-up share capital of the company. This is a useful starting point for the buyer's solicitor in preparing the initial draft of the sale and purchase agreement, but he will need to ask the seller's solicitor to provide details of all changes since the return date because the information revealed may be out of date. The buyer's solicitor requires accurate information as to the existing shareholders, in order to ensure that the correct persons enter into the agreement, and as to the current directors, so that the buyer can consider what arrangements should be made with them on completion (the buyer may intend that some directors resign on completion and that others enter into new service contracts with the target company). The annual return will also reveal whether the target's directors hold any other directorships. This may be of interest to the buyer, particularly if it transpires that any of the target's directors are also directors of companies which have been trading with the target.

3.5.1.3 Internal registers and minutes

The buyer's solicitor will wish to inspect the internal registers of the target company (statutory books and otherwise). The register of members and the minute books will be of particular interest; the buyer's solicitor should check that allotments and transfers of shares have been carried out in accordance with statute (eg CA 2006, ss 550 and 561 on issues of shares) and with the articles of the company (eg in compliance with any pre-emption provisions). Copies of charges created by the company and copies of directors' service contracts should also be available for inspection.

Subject to any confidentiality restrictions, the buyer's solicitors may be able to look at any board minutes that are included in the statutory books. These minutes can be a very good source of information, as they will record important decisions made by the company and will evidence whether required company procedures have been followed correctly.

3.5.2 Financial information

3.5.2.1 Accounts

Whether or not a full accountants' report is commissioned, the buyer's solicitor should study the target's accounts. In the case of a company, copies of the audited accounts for the last three years should be requested, together with any recently produced management accounts. In conjunction with the accountants, the buyer's solicitor can then consider what warranties or indemnities should be included in the agreement as a result of information revealed in the accounts. For this reason, and for drafting and negotiating other aspects of the sale and purchase agreement, such as the provision of completion accounts, the solicitor must have a clear understanding of business and company accounts (see **4.3.4**).

3.5.2.2 Loans

On an asset acquisition, existing banking arrangements in relation to the target will generally cease and the buyer will need to organise its own facilities. The buyer should enquire whether any of the assets which are being transferred are the subject of a charge; any such charge will have to be removed on completion, or the consent of the chargee obtained for the asset to be transferred subject to the charge.

On a share acquisition, the buyer should request copies of all loan documentation in order to ascertain the nature and extent of the target's borrowing commitments and obligations. It should check whether any loans are repayable on demand (this is common with bank overdraft facilities) or entitle the lender to demand immediate repayment of the balance of the loan on a change of control of the target. In either case, unless the buyer can make satisfactory arrangements with the lender directly, it must be confident of securing funds from elsewhere.

A buyer of shares will also be interested in whether the seller has guaranteed any obligations of the target (eg repayment of a fixed-term loan). Although this is the primary concern of the seller, whose liability will continue after completion, the buyer should anticipate that it may be asked to try to procure the release of the seller from such guarantees and to indemnify the seller if the release is not obtained on completion. Whoever has the benefit of the seller's guarantee is likely to require at least equivalent pledges from the buyer before agreeing to release the seller.

Lastly, where the target company is a member of a group, it may have guaranteed various obligations of other members of the group. The buyer will insist that such guarantees do not continue in place after completion.

3.5.2.3 Charges

A search against a company disposing of a business will reveal whether there are any charges over the assets which are being transferred. The buyer will usually insist that these charges are released on completion.

Similarly, the buyer of shares will want to establish the extent to which a target company has charged its assets as security for loans. The information held on record may not be up to date, since the company may have recently created charges which have still to be registered within the statutory period of 21 days from creation. Even if such charges are not registered within the statutory period, they are, nevertheless, valid against the company itself, and thus the buyer of shares receives no protection against late registration or non-registration. Indeed, the target company is in a vulnerable position in relation to charges which have not been registered; not only is it the company's duty to register, in default of which it is liable to a fine, but, perhaps more significantly, the loan becomes repayable immediately.

3.5.2.4 Credit reports

A quick and easy method of obtaining general (and up-to-date) financial information about a target company is for the buyer to request a credit report from a reputable credit agency, such as Dun & Bradstreet. As well as commenting on the company's creditworthiness in general, such reports will also deal with specific aspects of its performance and financial position (eg average debt collection and payment periods, and the company's 'liquidity', ie its ability to pay off short-term liabilities out of realisable assets).

3.5.2.5 Checking the solvency of the seller

Bankruptcy searches at the Land Charges Department should be carried out against individual sellers of shares or of a business immediately before completion. Similarly, a search of the file at the Companies Registry of a corporate seller of shares or a business should be made prior to completion to ensure that no notice of insolvency procedures has been entered. As this information may not be up to date, a telephone enquiry should also be made to the Central Registry of winding-up petitions. This is important as any transactions entered into after the commencement of insolvency procedures may be void.

3.5.3 Key contracts

3.5.3.1 Contracts fundamental to the business

One of the main advantages of a share acquisition is the lack of disruption which it causes to the target's trade, since outstanding contracts generally remain unaffected by the change in ownership of the company. This contrasts with an asset acquisition, where the benefit of existing contracts entered into by the seller will not pass to the buyer unless the contracts are assigned or novated. In either case, however, the buyer will require full details (and copies) of all significant contracts which the target has entered into. On an asset sale, the buyer should examine those contracts which he considers vital to the well-being of the business, to see whether they require consent to assignment or contain other restrictions on assignment. The buyer of shares must check that none of these significant contracts will be affected by the change of control of the company.

Contracts which may be fundamental to the business (and which may account for much of its turnover) include long-term contracts for the supply of the target's goods or services, distribution and agency agreements, contracts for the supply of raw materials to the target, intellectual property licences, service contracts for key staff, leases for important plant and machinery, etc. The buyer of shares should check which contracts are due to expire in the near future so that it can investigate the chances of renewal, perhaps by contacting third parties directly (subject to confidentiality). Similarly, some of these contracts may be terminable on short notice, and the buyer will want to be satisfied that this is not likely to happen as a result of the change of control.

The buyer of shares faces a danger in relation even to long-term contracts entered into by the target company. Such contracts may include a term which entitles the other party to terminate the agreement if control of the target changes hands ('change of control' clauses). Such clauses are sometimes included in, for example, distribution agreements, franchise agreements and joint venture agreements.

The buyer of a target should also check that all of these fundamental contracts have been properly executed and that none contains provisions which infringe EC or UK competition laws.

In conducting the review of the target's contracts, it is important that the buyer's advisers bear in mind the buyer's post-completion plans for the business. The buyer must be satisfied that the terms of on-going contracts are appropriate and, where contracts are to be brought to an end after completion, any provisions on early termination, for example, must be closely considered.

3.5.3.2 Rights triggered by a change of control

Some examples of where 'change of control' clauses in contracts may be found have been given in **3.5.3.1** above. Clauses conferring rights on parties where a company changes hands may also be found in employment contracts. For example, directors' service contracts might contain a so-called 'golden parachute clause', which entitles the director to a payment if the company changes hands (usually on the basis that the director can treat himself as dismissed in such circumstances). Also in the employment context, the right of employees to exercise rights to buy shares at a favourable price under share option schemes are sometimes triggered by a change of control of the company.

3.5.3.3   Non-arm's length trading relationships

Where the target is a member of a group, the buyer should ask for information on all goods and services which have been supplied by or to other members of the group (including administrative and management services supplied by a parent company). As it is unlikely that such arrangements will continue once the group relationship is broken, the buyer should assess the impact of their ceasing on completion of the acquisition.

It is also possible that individual sellers of a target company may have been supplying goods or services to the target company (or receiving goods or services from the target company) either directly or through other companies in which they have an interest. The buyer's analysis of the profit figures of the target may be very different in the light of these sorts of arrangements. Past profits may be a poor indicator of future performance of the business if these sources of supply (to or from the target) are terminated after completion, or if the terms of supply are changed significantly.

3.5.4   Intellectual property rights

Depending on the type of business, the seller or target may own or use on licence trade marks, patents, registered designs, know-how, service marks or copyrights. These intellectual property rights may be crucial to the business, and a thorough review of this area is essential to ascertain whether rights are adequately protected, what agreements or licences are in place and, on a share purchase, whether a change in control will affect such arrangements. The buyer will also want details of the computer system and software packages used by the target (he may wish to integrate these with his own systems). On an asset acquisition, the buyer may have to approach third parties with a view to renegotiating licences or agreements entered into with the seller.

In addition to requiring full details of all intellectual property rights from the seller, the buyer should, in appropriate cases, carry out a search at the UK Intellectual Property Office and instruct a patent agent to conduct a patent search to establish not only that the target's patents are valid, but also that the target is not infringing any patents owned by others.

3.5.5   Employees and pensions

3.5.5.1   Terms of employment

The buyer's solicitor will want to obtain full details of the target's workforce, and in particular the contractual terms that apply to its directors and managers. The terms of employment should be checked even if the buyer is only acquiring the assets of the business, because the rights and obligations of the employees working in that business will usually transfer automatically to the buyer (see **8.3** for the application of TUPE 2006).

In particular, the buyer's solicitor will want to review the current employees' service contracts and acquire details of any discretionary or customary arrangements. Also, any recent disputes, dismissals or changes in the terms and conditions that may result in a potential claim by an employee should be investigated. The buyer should also ask for details of anyone who works in the business but who is not employed by the target. For example, where the target is a subsidiary company, some individuals working in the business may have contracts with the parent company and will not, therefore, be available to work in the target business after the acquisition.

It will be particularly important to obtain full information on the employees if the buyer intends to make major changes to the workforce, such as integration with its existing employees, general reorganisation of the business, or redundancies. In such a case, the target company, or the buyer on an asset acquisition, may be faced with contractual claims from the affected employees, so careful planning, including an assessment of the potential financial consequences of the action, will be required.

3.5.5.2 Collective agreements

The buyer's solicitor should also consider any collective arrangements that may apply to the target, such as trade union recognition agreements or workplace agreements. It is important to check whether there are any consultation requirements to be followed either in relation to the acquisition itself, or in relation to any reorganisation of the workforce that may result from the transaction.

3.5.5.3 Retaining directors and managers

If the buyer is keen to retain certain directors or managers of the target, it should consult with them as early as possible in the acquisition negotiations (subject to considerations of confidentiality). It may be able to negotiate a term in the acquisition agreement that certain key personnel enter into new service contracts on completion. However, if a director or manager chooses to leave the target, the rights of the parties will depend on the terms of any existing contract with the target company, or the seller, as appropriate.

3.5.5.4 Restrictive covenants

The buyer should check whether the service contracts of the target's key personnel contain effective restraints on their activities after termination of their contracts. This is, of course, particularly important in relation to senior personnel whose contracts will definitely come to an end on completion of the acquisition. Typical clauses include covenants by the employee not to work in a competing business and not to solicit or entice away customers of the target company. The employee may also be prohibited from using or disclosing confidential information about the business of the target. In the absence of express terms, few post-termination restraints are implied into an employment contract (there is an implied term, however, that the employee will not reveal highly confidential information).

Restraints of this nature are valid and enforceable at common law only if they protect a legitimate trade interest of the employer (eg they protect the goodwill of the business), are not against the public interest and are reasonable between the parties. A non-competition covenant, for example, is likely to be considered void as being in restraint of trade unless its scope is limited in terms of duration and the geographical area which it covers. Similarly, a non-solicitation clause should be limited to customers who have recently dealt with the target (eg within the previous 12 months). It is now well established that clauses preventing the disclosure of information after termination can only be effective in relation to highly confidential information or trade secrets (*Faccenda Chicken Ltd v Fowler* [1986] IRLR 69, CA).

If any of the directors who are leaving are also selling shares in the target, the buyer should ensure that they agree to restrictive covenants in the sale and purchase agreement (see **5.10**). The courts will more readily uphold restraints which have been freely negotiated between parties to an acquisition than those included in employment contracts.

Even if restrictive covenants are prima facie valid, they will not survive a repudiatory breach of contract by the employer. This is on the basis that, by committing such a breach, the employer is indicating that it no longer considers itself to be bound by the contract and cannot, therefore, hold the other party to obligations contained within it. There is a danger here for buyers proposing that the target dismisses some of the management team; if dismissals are carried out in breach of contract, this may discharge the former employees from compliance with restrictive covenants (*General Billposting Co Ltd v Atkinson* [1909] AC 118, HL). Even if the covenant purports to enable the employer to enforce the covenant whatever the reason for the termination of the contract, this will not be effective (*Briggs v Oates* [1991] 1 All ER 411). Some directors' service contracts, however, permit the company to pay them salary in lieu of notice. Since, in this event, the company is not in breach of contract in terminating the contract without notice, it should be able to rely on post-termination covenants.

3.5.5.5 Pensions

Where the employees of the target business are members of a pension scheme, the parties will need to give careful consideration to the pension aspects of the acquisition. This is a complex area and one where the potential costs may be very high. It will often be necessary to refer issues regarding the pension fund to specialist pensions lawyers and actuaries. Therefore, in undertaking the due diligence review it is important to obtain as much information as possible about any pension scheme.

The buyer's solicitor will require full details of any pension scheme, including copies of the trust deed and rules under which the pension fund is administered, a list of the members of the scheme, and confirmation that the scheme enjoys a privileged tax position.

The buyer should ascertain the type of pension scheme operated, the two main possibilities being a final salary scheme or a money purchase scheme. In a final salary scheme, the members are guaranteed a particular level of benefit on retirement, whereas the benefit received by the members in a money purchase scheme is entirely dependent on the return on the fund invested. Unlike a money purchase scheme, there is no direct correlation between the contributions made to the final salary fund (by employer and employee) and the benefits received by the employee. A final salary scheme may therefore be in surplus or deficit at the time of the acquisition, depending on the prevailing economic conditions and the amount of the claims. In recent years, final salary schemes have become increasingly difficult to manage, leading many companies to close them to new employees who are instead offered participation in a money purchase scheme. It is therefore possible that the target may operate both types of pension schemes.

The buyer will also want to establish whether the pension scheme is a stand-alone, discrete scheme that can be transferred at completion, or whether the target's employees are members of a larger scheme involving other employees. In the latter case, arrangements must be put in place to transfer out, at completion, appropriate funds for those employees transferring to the buyer. Whether the buyer adopts the pension scheme or takes a transfer payment, it must ensure that the fund is sufficient for the trustees to fulfil their obligations. Accordingly, the value of the fund will be assessed by actuaries and any deficit or surplus will be dealt with by, for example, an appropriate adjustment to the purchase price of the target.

3.5.6 Property

The buyer's solicitor will not always carry out comprehensive searches and enquiries in relation to all the properties owned and occupied by the target. The timetable agreed by the parties for the acquisition often rules out a full investigation of all the conveyancing aspects. It may also prove impractical for full structural surveys to be carried out, particularly when the seller is keen not to alert its workforce to the proposed sale. The risk to the buyer in these circumstances depends on the importance of the properties. If they are relatively insignificant in the context of the deal as a whole, limiting the scope of the investigation may be justified. Also, the buyer may be able to rely on other means of protection against title or other property-related problems. Apart from a full title investigation by the buyer's solicitor, the two main means of protection for the buyer are as follows:

(a) *A certificate of title given by the seller's solicitor.* The chief certification sought by the buyer is that the properties have good and marketable title. Although the precise wording and format of the certificate may be the subject of negotiation between the parties, a standard form of certificate, settled by the Land Law Committee of the City of London Law Society, is in use and is generally accepted in commercial transactions. The certificate is addressed to the buyer, who can sue the seller's solicitor if it has been prepared negligently. However, if a false statement or an omission in the certificate is a result of incorrect information supplied by his client, the seller's solicitor will not generally be liable, provided the certificate makes it clear that that statement or omission was based on information given by his client. In these circumstances, the buyer will be left without a remedy, unless it has obtained a warranty direct from the seller that the information on which the certificate is based is true and accurate.

(b) *Property warranties given by the seller in the sale and purchase agreement.* The buyer will usually seek warranty statements, including that the target company (or seller) has good title to all the properties, that they are free from any charge or encumbrance, that all relevant planning legislation has been complied with, that any restrictions, conditions and covenants affecting the properties have been observed and performed, that there are no outstanding disputes, and that the properties are in good repair and fit for their current use.

Where a full investigation is to be carried out, the buyer's solicitor will need to make all the usual conveyancing searches and enquiries in relation to the properties being transferred (asset acquisition) or owned or occupied by the target company (share acquisition). It is not intended to explore these in detail; however, a number of points may be of particular concern to the buyer.

3.5.6.1 Inspection/valuation/survey

The practical difficulties of the buyer and its representatives carrying out inspections and surveys of the target's premises have already been discussed. However, physical inspection of properties which are important to the target is advisable, as this may disclose obvious problems which ought to be addressed prior to completion or may prompt further enquiry of the seller (eg whether certain uses have planning permission). In the case of leasehold premises, one of the main purposes of making an inspection is to ascertain whether the repairing obligations under the lease have been complied with. Also, by requisitioning a valuation of the properties concerned, the buyer will be able to compare their actual values with the values which appear in the accounts of the target business or company, although this may not be necessary if the buyer has access to a recent valuation carried out on behalf of the seller.

A full structural survey (of leasehold and freehold property) is the ideal, but is often not feasible in the circumstances.

3.5.6.2 Landlord's consents

On an asset acquisition, the consent of the landlord will frequently be required for the assignment of any leasehold premises included in the sale, as a term of the lease. Even on a share transfer, where the properties do not change hands, the buyer's solicitor should check the terms of leases carefully. It is not unusual for the landlord's consent to be required on a share acquisition (the lease may, for example, define assignment as including a change in control of the tenant company).

The buyer's solicitor should also ascertain whether the seller has guaranteed the lease obligations. The seller is likely to ask for an undertaking from the buyer (as a term of the main agreement) that the buyer will use its best endeavours to obtain the release of the seller from such guarantees and, in the meantime, to indemnify the seller against any liability. The buyer's solicitor should ask the landlord (subject to confidentiality) whether it will agree to release the seller and, if so, on what terms (the landlord is likely to insist that the buyer enters into a similar guarantee).

3.5.6.3 Original tenants of leasehold property

For leases granted before 1 January 1996, the original tenant of leasehold premises is in an invidious position because it remains liable to the landlord for breaches of the terms of the lease even after it has assigned the lease to a third party. Although there is an implied indemnity by the assignee in favour of the original tenant, this will be of little use if the assignee becomes insolvent. Indeed, the present tenant's insolvency is likely to be the reason why the landlord is pursuing the original tenant for breach of covenant.

On an asset sale, the seller may, therefore, have a contingent liability after completing the assignment to the buyer of leasehold premises of which it was the original tenant. On a share sale, the buyer's solicitor should ask whether the target company has been granted a lease at any time. Since the target company will remain liable on any such lease, he should ask for a copy of the lease to establish the extent of the potential liability.

For leases granted on or after 1 January 1996, the concept of continuing original tenant liability has been abolished. An original tenant who lawfully assigns its lease is generally released from liability as from the date of assignment, but could be required by the terms of the lease to guarantee performance of the lease obligations by its immediate assignee under an 'authorised guarantee agreement'.

3.5.6.4 Problems of investigation on a share purchase

A buyer of shares will not obtain protection from searches of official registers in the same way as a buyer of a business. This is because protection is usually afforded to, inter alia, a buyer of an interest in land, whereas on a share acquisition there is no change in ownership of the target company's properties. It has already been seen that failure to register a charge at the Companies Registry does not render it void against the company itself. The position is similar with searches at Land Registry, the Land Charges Department and the Local Land Charges Registry.

Although pre-completion searches at Land Registry or the Land Charges Department will reveal most registered charges, etc, the buyer of shares does not have the benefit of any priority period within which it can safely complete the acquisition without further matters appearing on the register (this follows from the fact that unregistered charges are valid against the company in any case). In addition, the buyer of shares is not entitled to receive compensation from a local authority which fails to register a local land charge (the Local Land Charges Act 1975 provides for the payment of compensation to a person who acquires an interest in the land).

3.5.7 Environmental matters

3.5.7.1 The environmental problem in acquisitions

With both an asset acquisition and a share acquisition, the buyer does not know the nature and extent of the environmental liabilities. If the deal is to be undertaken by a share acquisition then the buyer would be directly liable for the past actions of the company as it is, in effect, taking over the identity of the target company. This situation is of greater concern than the alternative, an asset acquisition, but there are still significant concerns even in that situation – the state of the site(s) being the most obvious.

To illustrate the problems, consider the operations of a typical factory. In this case, the environmental problems for a buyer fall into three categories:

(a)   First, there is the buyer's requirement that the factory should continue to operate after completion of the deal, otherwise the whole thing is pointless and the solicitor could be sued for negligence! In order that the factory continues to operate, all relevant environmental licences must be in place and must be transferred to the buyer if necessary.

(b)   Secondly, the buyer will be concerned to know whether the operations of the factory have resulted in pollution of the site, or of anywhere else. The buyer will also need to consider the historical use of the site and whether this may have caused pollution. If the site owned by the target company is polluted then the target and/or its new owner could be liable for the costs of cleaning it up, whether the pollution was caused by the operations of the factory or by, for example, previous owners of the site.

(c)   Thirdly, any pollution caused by the factory may give or have given rise to third party claims against the target, for example claims for nuisance, negligence or trespass, and breaches of environmental legislation may result in criminal sanctions.

3.5.7.2 The legislation

The Environmental Protection Act 1990 (EPA 1990), as amended by the Environment Act 1995 and the Pollution Prevention and Control Act 1999, introduced a wide-ranging system of environmental control which impacts on a large number of businesses, and further controls are imposed by the Water Resources Act 1991. A detailed explanation of the system of environmental regulation is beyond the scope of this book. However, a number of points of particular relevance to a potential buyer of a target business or company are made below.

The EPA 1990, as supplemented by the Environmental Permitting Regulations 2007 (SI 2007/3538) (in force 6 April 2008), provides a regime of pollution control which regulates the release into any environmental medium of discharges from prescribed processes involving, inter alia, fuel and power, metals, minerals, waste, and chemicals. The regulatory body is the Environment Agency. There is also a system of local authority air pollution control.

The type of prescribed process will determine the type of licence that is required. If a licence is required, it will list the conditions to which it is subject. This will often include specific restrictions on the operation of the relevant process and requirements to upgrade production techniques, both of which may entail considerable expense.

3.5.7.3 Penalties, directors' liability and clean-up costs

Breach of various provisions of the environmental legislation, such as carrying on a prescribed process without a licence, will give rise to criminal liability involving stiff penalties. In addition, where the offence is committed by a company, an offence is also committed by any director, manager, secretary or other similar officer who is proved to have consented to or connived in the offence, or to whose neglect the offence is shown to have been attributable.

In addition, there are various regulatory authorities which have wide powers to require land to be cleaned up, and an individual or a company could also face liability in tort for any damage done to other property. Clean-up costs and any damages resulting from civil liability can prove to be extremely substantial.

3.5.7.4 Public information

One of the objectives of the EPA 1990 is to make information on environmental matters available to the public by obliging relevant authorities to compile and maintain registers. The buyer of a business or company is, therefore, able to obtain useful information on the environmental background of the target. The EPA 1990 imposes a duty on licensing authorities, such as the Environment Agency, to maintain public registers of information relating to authorisations. These should include details of the initial application, the grant of authorisation and any conditions attached, statutory notices served, and prosecutions brought. The only restriction on publicity is in relation to matters which are harmful to national security or commercially confidential.

In addition, following the enactment of the Environment Act 1995, local authorities are required to keep registers of any remediation notices served in respect of contaminated land.

3.5.7.5 Licences

When acting for the buyer, it is important to ask the seller's solicitor for copies of all the relevant licences. An environmental lawyer (or consultant) can advise on the types of licence which a particular target business should have. These will need to be checked to make sure that they:

(a)   cover all the operations of the business;

(b)   are still in force;

(c)   do not contain any requirements regarding future upgrading of pollution control equipment; and

(d)   are not due to expire in the near future, as further upgrading requirements could be imposed as a condition of renewal of the licence.

Transfer of licences is rarely a problem and is often treated by the relevant authorities as merely a bureaucratic exercise.

The main commercial problem with licences is usually costly upgrading requirements. However, there is always the problem of the seller who should have environmental authorisation and does not. It is likely that considerable expenditure on pollution control equipment would be needed before such an authorisation could be obtained.

3.5.7.6 Other searches and enquiries

The extent of the buyer's enquiries of the seller will depend on the nature of the target business. However, even the most environmentally friendly business may be occupying a site which has a contamination history. The seller should be asked to provide details of any applications for authorisation, any statutory notices served on it or the target, and any complaints made by third parties. The seller should also be asked whether an environmental audit has been carried out in relation to the target and, if so, to provide a copy.

Although in many transactions the buyer will be content with a site visit, or a 'desk-top survey' (ie a review of available information), where a target business or company is involved in environmentally sensitive operations, or where land sites may have a history of contamination, the buyer should also consider commissioning a full environmental audit prior to entering into the agreement. This is likely to prove expensive and will require the full co-operation of the seller. However, the extent of the buyer's potential liability in these circumstances will often make it a worthwhile investment.

3.6 Due diligence reports

In large transactions, the legal advisers may be expected to produce a legal due diligence report, either on an on-going basis during the investigation process or as a final report once the investigation of the target is complete. The information revealed in the report will then be used in negotiation of the acquisition documentation and, in particular, will have a significant bearing on the warranties and indemnities required by the buyer.

A number of specialist lawyers or other professional advisers may have been involved, exploring different aspects of the target business. In addition, if the target has overseas subsidiaries, due diligence investigations may also have been undertaken by lawyers in the relevant overseas jurisdictions. The results of all these investigations must be co-ordinated and the key points brought to the buyer's attention in the report. The type of report that is required will depend on the particular circumstances of the transaction.

3.6.1 Types of report

3.6.1.1 Interim

On very large transactions the due diligence process may be very lengthy and the buyer may require interim reports summarising any issues of key importance. This is intended to provide an early warning mechanism in relation to matters that may be so serious that the buyer will consider withdrawing from the deal, or at least renegotiating the main contract terms.

3.6.1.2 Full audit

A full audit is a complete audit of the target business, including an in-depth summary of all the target's legal obligations. This type of report is very rare because it is very expensive to produce, and is required only if the buyer is particularly concerned about the risks associated with proceeding with the acquisition.

3.6.1.3 By exception

The usual form of report is a 'by exception' report. This report focuses only on matters that are material to the proposed acquisition, or on matters that are unusual or unexpected. This type of report is probably the most difficult to write, as the buyer's solicitor must make an assessment of what is material or unusual, and he must therefore have a good understanding of the type of business being reviewed.

3.6.2 Format of report

3.6.2.1 Executive report

The due diligence report will usually start with an executive summary which sets out the key findings of the report. It may also include key proposals either in terms of consents or conditions that must be fulfilled before the acquisition can proceed, or in terms of key contractual protections that should be included on the buyer's behalf in the acquisition documentation.

3.6.2.2 Scope of investigation and statement on liability

As with the accountants' report, the buyer will have claims against the reporting legal advisers if the report is negligently prepared (both in contract for breach of the implied duty of reasonable skill and care, and in tort for negligent misstatement).

Statements by third parties

The buyer of shares or the assets of a business may have relied on statements, forecasts and opinions (in relation to financial matters, in particular) made by parties other than the seller. Will it have a remedy against these third parties if the information turns out to be false or misleading? The scope of negligent misstatement generally and its application to acquisitions in particular have been considered in several important decisions.

Caparo Industries plc v Dickman [1990] 2 WLR 358

Caparo, which was a shareholder in Fidelity plc, acquired control of the company relying on the audited accounts. Caparo claimed that the accounts were inaccurate and misleading in showing a pre-tax profit, when in fact the company had made a loss. It sued the company's auditors for negligence in auditing the accounts (and certifying them as 'true and accurate'). Caparo alleged that the auditors owed it a duty of care either as a potential investor, or as an existing shareholder. The Court of Appeal held that the auditors owed Caparo a duty of care as a shareholder but not as a potential investor.

The House of Lords emphasised that the imposition of a duty of care in economic loss cases required 'proximity' of relationship as well as foreseeability of loss (a third criterion being that it must not be unreasonable to impose a duty of care). In determining the question of proximity, there was no single general principle, and the court should be guided by established categories of negligence. A review of previous cases in this area led the House of Lords to identify three conditions for proximity to exist. It must be shown that the maker of the statement knew the following:

(a)   that the statement would be communicated to the person relying on it or to a clearly defined class of person to whom that person belonged; and

(b)   this would be done specifically in connection with a particular transaction or a particular type of transaction; and

(c)   the person would be very likely to rely on it in deciding whether to enter into the transaction.

The House of Lords decided that the auditors owed no duty of care to Caparo as an investor or a shareholder; their Lordships were not prepared to find a duty of care on auditors to members of the public at large as potential investors (or bidders). As for shareholders, they considered that the auditor's duty in relation to the accounts was owed to the shareholders as a body to enable them to exercise collective control of the company, and not to individual shareholders to assist in their decision whether to buy more shares.

Morgan Crucible plc v Hill Samuel and Co Ltd [1991] 2 WLR 665

Caparo was distinguished in the *Morgan Crucible* case. Following a takeover bid for a listed company by the plaintiffs (claimants), the chairman of the listed company incorporated various statements and profit forecasts in documents issued to shareholders and to the press as a defence to the bid. The plaintiffs increased their bid and successfully acquired control of the company. Some of the financial statements and forecasts were misleading and the company was not as valuable as this information had led the plaintiffs to believe. They sued the chairman, the auditors, and the merchant bank advising the board in negligence.

On an application to amend the statement of claim after the decision in *Caparo* (the original claim had also been based on financial statements made prior to the bid and the plaintiffs wished to restrict it to statements, etc made after the bid), the Court of Appeal granted leave on the grounds that the amended claim disclosed a reasonable cause of action. The Court was of the view that it was arguable that there was a sufficient degree of proximity since the defendants intended the plaintiffs to rely on the representations in deciding whether to make an increased bid (the case settled before reaching trial).

To limit any possible exposure to such claims, the due diligence report will usually include a section that sets out the agreed scope of the investigations and any limitations on the liability of the advisers who have prepared it.

3.6.2.3   Main report

The main report is usually divided into sections covering each area of the target business. Each issue investigated is identified, together with the results of that investigation and any possible impact there may be for the proposed acquisition. Lastly, wherever possible, the report will indicate how particular issues may be practically resolved, for example by measures such as an adjustment of the purchase price of the target or by acquiring an appropriate consent from a third party.

Part II
THE TERMS OF THE ACQUISITION

Chapter 4

The Sale and Purchase Agreement

4.1 Structure of the agreement

This chapter sets out the main elements of a typical agreement governing the terms of a share acquisition or an asset acquisition (where a business is acquired as a going concern).

The order of the agreement will usually be as follows:

(a)   parties and date;

(b)   operative provisions;

(c)   schedules;

(d)   execution by the parties.

4.2 Parties

The parties to the agreement will usually be the buyer and the seller. Where there is more than one seller, the details of all the sellers will usually be set out in a schedule to the agreement.

Usually, all of the sellers will give the warranties to the buyer. However, in some circumstances some of the sellers, such as trustee shareholders or private equity sellers, may be unwilling to give warranties (see **5.8**). In this case, the parties will be described in the agreement as the seller(s), the warrantor(s) and the buyer(s).

The parties may also include guarantors of the seller's or buyer's obligations. For example, the seller may be required to provide a guarantor in relation to its potential liability under the warranties (see **5.9.1**). Similarly, if some part of the purchase price is to be left outstanding on completion, the seller may require that the buyer's obligation to pay that amount is guaranteed.

When the parties execute the agreement it will be dated, so creating a binding contractual agreement to buy and sell either the shares of the target company or the assets of the business.

4.3 Operative provisions

The operative provisions set out the basis on which the buyer agrees to purchase the shares or assets of the business, and on which the seller agrees to sell. This can cover a wide variety of issues, including a description of the assets to be acquired, the price and payment terms, and any contractual reassurances being provided with the sale. The precise details are often set out in the schedules to the agreement.

4.3.1 Definitions and interpretation

As a matter of good drafting, the operative provisions should commence with a definitions and interpretations clause. This defines terms which are used throughout the agreement (including the schedules) and, consequently, avoids repetition and the need for cumbersome cross-references.

An aspect of interpretation clauses which sometimes proves controversial concerns references to statutory provisions. The buyer will usually want it to be provided expressly that references to statutory provisions are to be interpreted as including subsequent amendments to those provisions. This is dangerous for the seller, particularly in relation to its potential liability under the warranties, because, by agreeing to such a clause, it would take the risk of those liabilities increasing as a result of legislation enacted after completion which has retrospective effect. For example, this could be a significant factor in the context of environmental protection legislation which may well become more strict in the future.

4.3.2 Conditions precedent

Completion of an acquisition, whether of shares or of assets, is normally simultaneous with exchange of contracts. The parties usually try to avoid any gap between exchange and completion and the consequent problems connected with running a business during this period. However, this is not always possible. Sometimes the sale and purchase agreement may be entered into on the basis that it will be completed when a certain condition is fulfilled. If the agreement is conditional it is usual to include an obligation on the parties to seek fulfilment of the condition, a longstop date by which the condition must be fulfilled or waived, and a time frame within which the acquisition must complete once the condition has been fulfilled (see **7.1** and **7.2**).

4.3.3 Agreement to purchase

The agreement will set out exactly what is being bought and sold, by reference to a schedule detailing either the shareholdings (share purchase) or the assets (asset purchase) being acquired.

The agreement will also provide that the parties agree to sell and purchase the specified shares or assets, and will usually provide that the buyer is not obliged to buy any of the shares or assets unless it can purchase all of them simultaneously.

4.3.4 Consideration

The sale and purchase agreement will stipulate the agreed price, the form that it will take, and the timing of payment.

Where there are multiple sellers, the amount of the purchase price payable to each seller will usually be stated in a schedule to the agreement.

On an asset sale, the amount of the consideration which is attributable to each separate asset will be specified in the agreement (the agreed apportionment is usually set out in a schedule). The parties have some flexibility in making this apportionment, and are usually influenced heavily by taxation and stamp duty implications (see **8.4**).

The purchase price may be fixed, or provisions may be included in the agreement allowing for adjustments to the price, for example as a result of the preparation of completion accounts or the operation of an earn-out agreement (see below).

4.3.4.1   Completion accounts

When negotiating the price, the parties may have based their valuation of the target on dated information, such as the last audited accounts or estimates in unaudited management accounts. The buyer may want confirmation that the figures on which the valuation was based have not altered significantly since the date to which the original accounts were made up. This may be of particular concern if the target experiences significant fluctuations in its net assets, or if its supposed current earnings were an important factor in the price negotiations. In these circumstances, the parties may agree that the purchase price should be adjusted to reflect the actual net assets or earnings of the target on the completion date, as determined by a set of agreed accounts drawn up after completion.

The sale and purchase agreement will usually provide for a maximum amount of the purchase price to be paid on completion, with a further adjustment payment or repayment to be made once the completion accounts have been prepared. The actual adjustment made and how it is to be paid will depend upon what the parties have agreed. For example, the parties may agree that the buyer will be entitled to a repayment if the net assets fall short of amounts on which the valuation was based, but that the seller is not entitled to any further payment if the figure exceeds the original figure. Similarly, if the valuation consisted of applying a multiplier to the earnings of the target, the agreement may provide for the purchase price to be adjusted by applying the same multiplier to any shortfall in earnings identified by the completion accounts. There are many variations on this theme and, in all cases, the legal advisers must ensure that the relevant contractual provisions are drafted carefully so as to implement precisely what the parties have agreed.

An agreed mechanism for the drawing up of the completion accounts will be included in the sale and purchase agreement, usually within a schedule. As the results of completion accounts will determine any necessary price adjustment, the agreed mechanism must be drafted with care.

A typical provision on completion accounts will provide for the following:

(a)   the completion accounts to be drawn up within a specified period after completion (eg one month). The seller's accountant, who is likely to have been the target company's auditor until completion, is usually nominated to prepare the accounts and will be instructed to do so using a basis which is consistent with the latest set of audited accounts;

(b)   the buyer (or the seller if the buyer's accountant has prepared the accounts) and its accountant to have the right to dispute the accounts within specified time limits;

(c)   in the absence of agreement, the matter to be referred to an independent firm of accountants acting as experts.

4.3.4.2   Earn outs

The term 'earn out' is used to describe an arrangement whereby at least part of the consideration is determined by reference to the future profitability of the target for a specified period after completion (eg for the three accounting periods following completion). Earn outs are often considered appropriate where the sellers continue to manage the target company after completion. Typically part of the purchase price will be paid at completion, followed by a further payment or series of payments made depending on the profits made by the target within the period specified.

Determining part of the purchase price on the basis of future profits not only avoids the buyer having to pay 'over the odds' for a target which fails to perform as expected, but also acts as a motivating factor for the sellers/managers of the target who are staying on post-acquisition and on whom the business (particularly one that is 'employee-orientated') may be heavily reliant.

The earn-out provisions will usually provide for accounts to be prepared for the relevant periods by the buyer's accountant (ie the target's auditor after completion), with the adjustment to the purchase price dependent either on a certain level of profitability being achieved or on a multiple of the profits achieved. As with completion accounts, the parties will specify how the accounts determining those profits will be calculated and will also agree the precise definitions of those items which will determine the amount of the deferred consideration, such as 'net profit' or 'earnings'.

A difficulty with an earn-out arrangement is that the sellers who continue to manage the target after completion and the buyer may be pulling in different directions. The former will be keen to maximise profitability in the earn-out period, whereas the latter will often be more concerned that decisions are taken which will benefit the target in the long term, at the expense, perhaps, of short-term profits. The parties may try to limit this tension by defining the objectives of the company during the earn-out period and agreeing to certain limitations on the conduct of the business post-completion. The buyer may, for example, undertake not to dispose of the whole or part of the business, or not to permit any non-arm's length trading between the target and the buyer (or other members of an acquiring company's group) during this period.

4.3.5 Payment terms

Payment on an acquisition will often be by way of a fixed amount paid in cash on the completion date, but the parties are free to agree other payment terms. For example, it may be agreed that part of the purchase price is paid at a later date (known as 'deferred consideration'), or that some or all of the purchase price is satisfied by a corporate buyer issuing shares or debentures to the seller.

4.3.5.1 Deferred consideration

In certain circumstances, the seller may be prepared to allow part of the purchase price to remain outstanding on completion.

The seller may simply agree to receive payment by instalments, for example to assist the buyer in financing the acquisition, but in these circumstances the seller will usually demand interest on the outstanding amount and will insist on some form of security for the payment.

In addition, the purchase price is often subject to an adjustment dependent on completion accounts, so the final payment may be delayed and, where an earn-out arrangement has been agreed, a part of the purchase price will necessarily be deferred until the earn-out accounts have been prepared, as detailed at **4.3.4.2** above.

Alternatively, the buyer may insist on a retention of part of the purchase price as security in case a warranty claim arises in relation to the target (see **5.9.2**). Although such a retention will usually be resisted strongly by the seller, it may be appropriate where the parties are aware of a potential liability, or where the buyer expects a particular benefit to accrue from the sale, such as the continuance of trade with a valued customer.

Tax treatment of deferred consideration

The general rule is that the seller will be charged to tax as at the date of sale on the total amount of the consideration, regardless of whether that consideration has actually been received. If the consideration is certain, the fact that some of it is deferred will not affect the seller's tax position.

However, where the consideration cannot be ascertained at completion because it is dependent on future events, such as the profitability of the target after the sale (as with an earn-out arrangement), the rule set out in *Marren (Inspector of Taxes) v Ingles* [1980] 3 All ER 95 applies and tax is charged on the disposal of two separate capital assets. The first disposal is of the shares of the target company or assets of the target business. On this initial disposal, the seller is treated as having received as consideration both the consideration actually received at completion plus a valuable 'chose in action' – that is, the right to receive a further payment if future profits are attained. This right to receive further payment is given a value by HMRC. When the earn-out payment is actually received, this is treated as a second disposal by the seller – in this case, the disposal of the contractual right to receive the payment. If the payment exceeds the original valuation by HMRC, the seller is treated as having made a capital gain and charged to CGT or corporation tax accordingly. A loss in these circumstances will be an allowable loss for the seller's capital tax purposes (see **9.4**).

4.3.5.2 Security

Whatever the reason for the deferred consideration, where part of the purchase price does remain outstanding on completion, the seller may seek security for the outstanding sums in one of the following ways:

(a) by taking a charge over some or all of the assets transferred to the buyer;

(b) by requiring a guarantee of the buyer's obligation to pay the balance of the price from, for example, individual shareholders, directors or the parent company of a corporate buyer;

(c) by providing in the agreement that title to specified assets is to remain with the seller until the purchase price is paid in full;

(d) by obliging the buyer to place a specified sum in a joint deposit account on completion and defining the circumstances in which this (and accrued interest) can be released to the parties (though this will not be appropriate if the seller is simply allowing the buyer time to finance the acquisition).

4.3.5.3 Form

The most common form of consideration is cash. The buyer will rarely have sufficient cash reserves to pay for the acquisition, so will usually borrow at least part of the purchase money. The buyer's solicitor must ensure that all necessary financial arrangements for this borrowing are properly in place before the buyer enters into any commitment to pay the purchase price.

Where the buyer is a company, all or part of the consideration may be satisfied by the company issuing equity securities (shares) or debt securities (loan notes) to the seller. This is a very attractive option for a corporate buyer as it avoids the need to increase borrowing commitments or to make disposals of assets to fund the acquisition. The seller, on a share sale, may be attracted by the tax treatment of a securities exchange: if certain conditions are fulfilled, the seller is able to roll over any capital gain made on the disposal of shares in the target, thus deferring the capital tax which it would otherwise pay at this time until disposal of the securities in the acquiring company received in exchange (see **9.4.2**).

Shares

The seller will accept consideration in the form of shares only if the shares are readily marketable, ie they can in the future be realised for cash. This rules out shares in most private companies, which will rarely have a ready market and will often, in practice, be subject to restrictions on transfer. Shares in companies listed on The Stock Exchange may, on the other hand, be virtually equivalent to cash for the seller.

Where shares are issued as consideration, the agreement should specify how they rank with the other shares of the acquiring company and what rights the seller will have to any dividend declared in relation to a period in which completion falls.

If the buyer is worried that the market for its shares may be adversely affected by the seller disposing of all the consideration shares at once, it may insist on a clause in the agreement restricting the seller from, for example, disposing of more than a certain percentage of its allocation within a specified period after completion.

Where the acquiring company wishes to issue shares as consideration but the seller is only really interested in receiving cash for the target company, this can be achieved, albeit in a roundabout way, by what is called a 'vendor placing'. This is an arrangement whereby the acquiring company issues shares to the seller but arranges (through its financial advisers) for the shares to be sold on immediately to institutional investors. The acquiring company undertakes in the acquisition agreement that the sale of the consideration shares will yield a specified sum. For further reading, see *Public Companies and Equity Finance*.

Debt securities (loan notes)

An acquiring company may issue debt securities such as loan notes to the seller for the purchase price or part of it. These loan notes will usually be issued on terms that the seller can demand repayment of all or part at six-monthly intervals after a certain period from completion (eg 12 months). It may suit the seller to receive staggered payments in this way with interest on the balance outstanding, particularly as roll-over relief from capital tax is available on the same basis as for shares under a securities exchange (see **9.4.2**).

The loan note itself is usually a fairly straightforward document recording the grantor's indebtedness to the holder, the interest payable and the terms of the repayment. The form of the loan note will usually be agreed between the parties and set out in a schedule to the sale and purchase agreement (see **4.4**). A loan note may or may not be secured, and will usually be an acceptable form of payment for the seller only if the creditworthiness of the buyer can be assured. Accordingly, loan notes generally form part of the consideration only where the buyer is a substantial company.

4.3.6 Contractual protections

The remaining section of the operative provisions will set out the basis on which the seller will provide any contractual reassurances, or warranties, about the target business or company. The actual warranty statements will appear in a (usually lengthy) schedule to the agreement. However, the operative provisions will set out the basis on which the warranties are given and will usually include some agreed limitations on the seller's liability for breach of warranty.

Similarly, the agreement may provide for certain specific indemnities in relation to identified problems (see **5.6**). On a share purchase this will include tax indemnities, whereby the seller agrees to indemnify the buyer in respect of any tax liability which arises in the target in relation to activities occurring before the sale. Although these tax indemnities (or 'covenants') may be drafted as a separate deed, they are more usually incorporated into the body of the main agreement (see **9.3**).

In addition to the comfort provided by the warranties and indemnities, the buyer will seek to protect the goodwill of the business by including restrictive covenants restricting the activities of the seller after completion.

4.4 Schedules

Usually, much of the bulk of the sale and purchase agreement is attributable to the schedules. The issues covered by the schedules will be determined by the terms of the transaction and whether it is an asset or a share acquisition.

Although a totally comprehensive list of possible schedules would be very long indeed, in broad terms a sale and purchase agreement may include schedules detailing some of the following matters:

(a)   details of the assets or shareholdings to be transferred with appropriate price allocations;

(b)   details of any price adjustment mechanism, such as completion accounts or earn-out arrangements, together with provisions governing subsequent payment terms and the resolution of disputes;

(c)   warranty statements about the condition of the target business and its assets;

(d)   limitations on the seller's liability in relation to warranty claims (although this is sometimes placed within the body of the agreement);

(e)   specific indemnities agreed between the parties in relation to identified risks, eg the tax covenant on a share sale (see **9.3**);

(f)   agreed forms of documentation governing associated transactions, such as the transfer of a pension fund;

(g)   if the agreement is to be exchanged conditionally (ie there will be a gap between exchange and completion), agreed restrictions on running the target business or company pending completion and details of the documentation required to complete the transaction (see **Chapter 7** on conditional contracts);

(h)   details of the completion procedure, specifically the documents which each party must deliver to the other and the steps each party must take on completion. Agreed forms of minutes of board and general meetings of the target company to be held on completion may also be included.

The advantage of consigning much of the fine detail of the acquisition agreement to schedules is that the main body of the agreement is not broken up with long lists of detailed information, which makes the agreement as a whole easier to follow.

4.5 Execution

The agreement will provide for its execution by the respective parties, usually the buyer and the seller, though on occasion a third party may be a party to the agreement.

The sale and purchase agreement is purely a contract setting out the terms on which the acquisition will be undertaken, so it can simply be signed by the parties. However, to avoid any question about whether appropriate consideration has been given in relation to specific indemnities and restrictive covenants included in the agreement, the buyer may prefer the agreement to be executed as a deed.

As with any major contract, prior to exchange and completion the legal advisers will confirm the parties' capability to enter into the agreement (see **7.3**).

Chapter 5

Allocation of Risk: Buyer's Protection

5.1 Introduction

The buyer will want some reassurances about the nature and state of the company or business it is acquiring, and some possibility of recompense if the acquisition turns out to be other than expected. In the context of a share or asset acquisition, warranties and indemnities included in the sale and purchase agreement go some way towards providing the buyer with this comfort.

5.2 Protections implied into the contract

5.2.1 Shares

On a share acquisition neither common law nor statute protects the buyer by implying terms into the contract; the principle that applies is *caveat emptor*. It was noted in **Chapter 1** that there is indeed every reason for a buyer of shares to beware, because it will be inheriting indirectly all the liabilities of the target company, whether it knows about them or not. In the absence of express provisions, an aggrieved buyer has very little comeback on the seller unless a misrepresentation can be established (discussed at **5.5.1**). In order to protect itself from the many risks involved, the buyer must therefore make express provision in the acquisition documentation.

5.2.2 Assets

The buyer of the assets of a business is not in such an exposed position, as it does not assume automatically all the liabilities of the business. The buyer may also get the benefit of some limited warranties under the Sale of Goods Act 1979 for some of the assets being transferred. However, as on a share acquisition, there will be many safeguards which the buyer will wish to incorporate expressly into the sale and purchase agreement.

5.3 Full or limited title guarantee

Whether a transaction takes place as an asset or a share acquisition, there are two bases on which the agreement for sale can be made which will attract the benefit of covenants implied by law. The covenants are implied by the Law of Property (Miscellaneous Provisions) Act 1994, and the alternative dispositions are sale with full title guarantee and sale with limited title guarantee.

Where the sale is expressed to be made with full title guarantee, this implies that:

(a)   the seller has the right to dispose of the property;

(b)   the seller will do all it reasonably can, at its own expense, to pass to the buyer the title it purports to give; and

(c)   the property is free from all charges, encumbrances and third party rights, other than those of which the seller is unaware and could not reasonably be expected to be aware.

If the sale is said to be made with limited title guarantee, this implies the covenants mentioned at (a) and (b) above, and also that, since the last sale for value, the seller has neither created nor allowed to be created any subsisting charge or encumbrance, and is not aware that anyone else has done so.

Of course, the type of guarantee to be given, if any, is a matter for negotiation. The implied covenants can be, and often are, modified by express provisions in the sale agreement relating to the nature and perfection of title to the assets. In general, although a receiver or trustee selling assets may be prepared to offer no more comfort than limited title guarantee, in the context of most other acquisitions full title guarantee will be appropriate.

5.4   Warranties

Much of the acquisition agreement is usually taken up with specific warranties by the seller in favour of the buyer, covering a whole range of aspects of the target business or company, including the accounts, subsisting contracts, employees, pensions, intellectual property rights, etc (see **Chapters 8 and 9** for details of typical warranties in asset and share acquisitions respectively).

These warranties are contractual statements about what is to be acquired. On a share acquisition the warranties will include statements about the shares to be acquired, for example that the shares are not subject to any charges, as well as about the company which is being transferred.

As the warranties are terms of the contract, if they prove to be untrue, the buyer will have a claim for damages against the warrantor(s) for breach of contract. This provides a clear means of redress for the buyer after completion of the acquisition. However, during negotiation of the sale and purchase agreement, one of the purposes of including warranties is to elicit information about the business from the seller. The seller will try to avoid later liability for breach of warranty by disclosing relevant information (that is, information that, undisclosed, would put the buyer in breach of warranty) before the acquisition is completed (see **6.3**).

The warranties are made about the state of the target as at a specified point. Where exchange and completion are simultaneous, the warranties will be statements given at the moment of completion, ie statements about what is being acquired at the moment that it is acquired. Where there is a gap between exchange and completion, warranties are made at exchange when the parties become contractually bound, and may then be confirmed at completion. This can be problematic, as any changes in the condition of the target between exchange and completion must be addressed. The parties will negotiate specific terms in the sale and purchase agreement as to how they will deal with such changes (see **7.2**).

5.4.1   What damages are recoverable?

Under the rule in *Hadley v Baxendale* (1854) 9 Exch 341, loss will be recoverable if it is not too remote. It must fall within one of the two following categories:

(a)   loss which flows naturally from the breach – in other words, it is a natural consequence of the breach, the type and extent of which a reasonable person would expect in the circumstances;

(b)   loss which was fairly and reasonably in the contemplation of both parties, at the time they entered into the contract, as the probable result of the breach. This might cover a more unusual type of loss due to special circumstances which were known or should have been known to the parties at the date of the contract.

The aim of contractual damages is to put the buyer in the position it would have been in if the contract had not been breached, subject to the duty to mitigate. This measure of damages allows recovery for loss of bargain.

5.4.2   Application of general principles

How are these general principles applied to breach of warranty on a share acquisition?

The buyer's loss in these circumstances is the difference between the value of shares if the warranty had been true and their actual value, ie the difference in the value of the shares with and without the breach. The basis used for valuing the shares will therefore be relevant in assessing the loss.

For example, the shares may have been valued on an earnings basis, perhaps by applying a multiplier to a warranted level of profit. If this profit has been overstated, the buyer's loss should be calculated by applying the same multiplier to the deficiency. On the other hand, where there is a breach of warranty which results in the assets of the target being less than expected, this may not have a direct effect on the value of the shares, unless they were valued on an assets-related basis.

5.4.3   Pre-estimate of damages

The parties will often seek to reduce the uncertainty involved in assessing loss in this way by specifying in the agreement how the loss should be quantified if certain warranties are broken. For example, where profit levels have been warranted, the parties may agree a formula which specifies an appropriate multiplier to apply to any shortfall. It is also quite common for a clause to be included which obliges the seller to pay for any deficiency in assets or any undisclosed liability arising from a breach of warranty, thus avoiding the need to prove an equivalent diminution in the value of the shares (the seller may resist what is essentially an indemnity basis for breach of warranty).

Is there any restriction on the parties' freedom to agree the measure of damages in advance in this way? The parties to a contract are free to agree in advance a sum payable in damages in the event of a breach of contract, provided it is a genuine pre-estimate of the actual loss which would be suffered by the innocent party ('liquidated damages') as opposed to a fine or penalty in the nature of a threat held over the other party (a 'penalty'). The distinction depends on the intentions of the parties, which are to be gathered from the whole of the contract.

5.5   Representations

Typically, the signing of the acquisition agreement will be the culmination of extensive contact and correspondence between the parties and their advisers. The buyer and its advisers will have sought replies to a whole range of questions affecting the target and its business. If any statements which have been made by or on behalf of the seller prove to be untrue, will the buyer have a claim for misrepresentation? How does this tie in with the buyer's express protections included in the acquisition agreement?

5.5.1   General principles

A misrepresentation is a false statement of fact made by one party to the contract to the other, which induces the other party to enter into the contract. Accordingly, where a buyer has relied on a representation of past or existing fact about the target which turns out to be untrue, it will, prima facie, have a claim for misrepresentation, the remedies for which are rescission or damages.

5.5.1.1   Rescission

Whether the misrepresentation is fraudulent, negligent or innocent, the buyer has the right to rescind the acquisition agreement. Rescission is a remedy aimed at putting the parties back into the pre-contract position. However, the right to rescind is subject to two important qualifications.

First, s 2(2) of the Misrepresentation Act 1967 enables the court to award damages instead of rescission for 'innocent misrepresentation', that is, a representation which is neither fraudulent nor negligent. The court may exercise this discretion if it feels that rescission is too drastic a remedy in the circumstances (see **5.5.1.2** below for further discussion of the discretion to award damages under s 2(2)).

Secondly, rescission is an equitable remedy and will not be available if, for example:

(a)   it is impossible to restore the parties to their pre-contract position; or

(b)   bona fide third party rights have been acquired; or

(c)   the innocent party, knowing of the misrepresentation, takes some action affirming the agreement; or

(d)   there is undue delay in seeking relief.

These 'bars' to rescission may mean that the remedy will not be available once a share or business acquisition has been completed, because of the difficulties in restoring the parties to their pre-contract position. On the other hand, where exchange and completion are not contemporaneous, rescission should be available if a misrepresentation is discovered between exchange and completion.

5.5.1.2   Damages

If the misrepresentation is innocent, s 2(2) of the Misrepresentation Act 1967 provides that the court 'may award damages in lieu of rescission'. It should be noted that the court has a discretion to award damages; there is no right to damages. The question arises as to whether the court can still award damages in lieu of rescission if rescission itself has been lost due to one of the equitable bars. In *Government of Zanzibar v British Aerospace (Lancaster House) Ltd* [2000] 1 WLR 2333, it was held that, in order for the court to award damages in lieu of rescission, the right to rescind must not have, in fact, been lost. This conflicts with the earlier obiter statement by Jacob J in *Thomas Witter Ltd v TBP Industries Ltd* [1996] 2 All ER 573.

Where the misrepresentation is negligent, ie the maker is unable to show that he had reasonable grounds for believing, and did believe, that the statement was true, the innocent party is entitled to damages under s 2(1) of the 1967 Act.

Damages are also available in the tort of deceit for a fraudulent misrepresentation. However, for this, it is necessary to show that the maker had no genuine belief in the truth of the statement. Usually, there is little point trying to prove fraud as damages are assessed on a very similar basis to negligent misrepresentation. In both cases, damages are measured on the tortious basis, which aims to put the innocent party in the position it would have been in if the tort had not been committed. In the context of an acquisition, this involves restoring the innocent party to the position it would have been in if it had not entered into the acquisition agreement; in other words, the court must try to assess to what extent the innocent party has lost out by entering into the agreement.

5.5.2 Representations and warranties

The nature of an acquisition agreement renders it likely that any representations made by the seller in pre-contract discussions and negotiations, which induce the buyer to enter into the agreement, will be included as warranties in the agreement. It is rare, therefore, for a claim for misrepresentation to be founded on a matter which is not included in the contract. Indeed, it is common for the agreement to incorporate an acknowledgement by the buyer that it has not relied on any representations which are not contained in the contract (a 'non-reliance' provision), and that the contract sets out the entire agreement and understanding between the parties (known as an 'entire agreement clause'). Such a clause will usually attempt to exclude liability for misrepresentation, though the exclusions must be reasonable in order to be effective (Misrepresentation Act 1967, s 3, as substituted by the Unfair Contract Terms Act 1977 (UCTA 1977), s 8).

5.5.2.1 Entire agreement clause

An entire agreement clause was considered in the case of *Thomas Witter Ltd v TBP Industries Ltd* [1996] 2 All ER 573. Whilst doubting whether the wording of the clause was sufficiently explicit to exclude liability for misrepresentation, the judge ruled that it would, in any event, be unreasonable because it did not distinguish between different types of misrepresentation. He felt that it would never be reasonable to exclude liability for fraudulent misrepresentation. However, in *EA Grimstead & Son Ltd v McGarrigan* [1999] WL 852482, the Court of Appeal found an entire agreement clause to be reasonable even though it did not distinguish between liability for fraudulent and non-fraudulent misrepresentation. In spite of the discrepancy in judicial opinion, it is nevertheless considered good practice for the seller to ensure that the buyer expressly agrees to waive its right to damages or rescission only in relation to non-fraudulent misrepresentation arising from representations not included in the contract.

5.5.2.2 Non-reliance provision

In *Grimstead* (above), Chadwick LJ also considered the operation of the non-reliance provision, saying that the courts should be prepared to give effect to such a provision agreed between parties who have been professionally advised. This on the basis that the provision has been deliberately included to provide commercial certainty, and that it is reasonable to assume the contract price reflects the commercial risk accepted by the parties. The same judge clarified matters further in *Watford Electronics Ltd v Sanderson CFL Ltd* [2001] EWCA Civ 317, confirming that in order to rely on a non-reliance provision, the seller must prove that the provision itself is clear, that the buyer intended the provision to be acted upon, and that the seller believed the statement to be true (ie that the buyer was not, in fact, relying on any representations other than those expressly incorporated into the agreement). If the seller knows the statement to be untrue, it cannot rely on it as against the buyer.

5.5.2.3   Right of rescission

Even where an entire agreement clause is included in the agreement, this does not render misrepresentation redundant. Many of the representations which the seller makes to the buyer in the lead-up to the signing of the agreement will be included as express warranties in the agreement itself. If any of these warranties are broken, the buyer will be able to claim damages for breach of contract as explained at **5.5.1.2** above. Section 1 of the Misrepresentation Act 1967 makes it clear, however, that where a misrepresentation has become a term of the contract, this will not affect the innocent party's right to rescind (provided none of the equitable bars operates). In contrast, breach of warranty does not enable the buyer to discharge the contract. This may not be significant where the misrepresentation is discovered only after completion, if by then it is too late to rescind. However, it would be important if the buyer becomes aware of the falsity of the representation after exchange but before completion.

Where there is an interval between exchange and completion, the buyer will usually seek to negotiate a contractual right to withdraw from the contract if it becomes aware of any breach of warranty. This will often be backed up by obliging the seller to inform the buyer if the seller becomes aware of anything which is inconsistent with the warranties or makes them inaccurate.

Such a provision is of advantage to the buyer, as it will enable it to 'rescind' the agreement whether or not the breach of warranty is also a misrepresentation (avoiding argument as to whether the warranty repeated statements made pre-contract which the buyer relied upon, etc).

5.5.2.4   Measure of damages

Where the remedy sought is damages, the difference in the measure of damages for breach of contract and misrepresentation may also be significant. It has been seen that the contractual measure allows for loss of bargain and, on a share purchase, involves assessing the difference between the actual value of the shares and their value if the warranty had been true. On the other hand, the aim of tortious damages is to put the buyer in the position it would have been in if it had not entered into the agreement; this will involve calculating the difference between the price paid for the shares and their actual market value. The contractual measure will often lead to higher damages because of the ability to recover for loss of bargain. However, this will not always be the result, particularly where the bargain is not a good one (eg in a share acquisition, where a buyer has paid more than market value for the shares). In these circumstances, the buyer may be better off with the restitutionary approach.

5.6   Indemnities

The buyer may seek further contractual protection in the form of indemnities included in the acquisition agreement or, occasionally, incorporated in a separate deed.

5.6.1   What is the difference between a warranty and an indemnity?

A warranty is an undertaking by the seller that a particular state of affairs exists. On a breach of warranty, the buyer must establish its loss under normal contractual principles. For example, on a share sale, it will have to establish the reduction (if any) in the value of the shares (see **5.4.2**).

An indemnity, on the other hand, is essentially a promise to reimburse the buyer in respect of a designated type of liability which may arise in the future. On a share sale, there is no need to assess any reduction in the value of the shares; the recipient of the indemnity simply receives an amount equal to the actual liability (the indemnity clause will usually provide for costs and expenses relating to it to be recovered as well). For example, if the buyer is worried about an outstanding debt owed to the target, it could seek an indemnity against the possibility of the debt becoming bad. If this happens, the buyer will receive the amount of the outstanding debt and, possibly, incidental costs in seeking to recover it.

Another difference between a warranty and an indemnity is that, in the case of the latter, there is no duty to mitigate the loss; such a duty may, however, be incorporated in the contract.

5.6.2 Taxation indemnities

It is common for buyers of shares to seek protection from tax liabilities in the form of both warranties and indemnities. On an asset acquisition, extensive safeguards are unnecessary because almost all tax liabilities remain with the seller.

The warranties usually deal with the target's compliance with tax and VAT requirements, such as the proper submission of returns and the correct implementation of the pay as you earn (PAYE) system, etc, as well as other areas where the buyer is mainly concerned with prompting disclosures from the seller (eg whether there are any existing disputes with HMRC). The indemnities, on the other hand, will cover specific tax charges which may arise over and above those provided for in the accounts, and which are referable to the seller's period of ownership.

Dealing with most tax matters by way of indemnity has the advantage to the buyer that there is no need to prove the link between the unexpected tax liability and the value of the shares. However, warranties are often appropriate for many matters in respect of which buyers seek indemnities, and the seller should consider arguing this point.

5.7 Tax consequences of payments under warranties and indemnities

The following discussion applies to payments made by the seller under any warranty or indemnity brought by the buyer following completion of the acquisition, not merely to payments in respect of taxation warranties and indemnities.

5.7.1 Warranties

Warranties are always given in favour of the buyer.

On the sale of the assets of a business or shares, the seller may have made a chargeable capital gain on the disposal, based on the consideration received. Let us assume that the seller later has to make a payment to the buyer under a warranty contained in the sale and purchase agreement. What are the tax consequences for the seller and the buyer of such a payment?

Section 49 of the TCGA 1992 provides that no tax allowance will be made in the first instance for any contingent liability in respect of a warranty or representation. However, if the liability crystallises, an adjustment will be made to the price of the target for capital gains purposes. If, therefore, the seller makes a payment under a warranty to the buyer, the capital tax computation would be adjusted as follows:

(a)   The consideration which the seller is treated as having received on completion will be reduced by the amount paid out under the warranty claim, thus reducing any gain. If the seller has already paid the tax, it will be entitled to a refund.

(b)   The buyer's acquisition cost is reduced by the same amount: its potential gain on a subsequent disposal of the target is therefore increased because its acquisition cost has reduced.

5.7.2   Indemnities

The position is not as straightforward when it comes to payments under indemnities. Consider the example of a standard tax indemnity in a sale of shares. The buyer will be keen to ensure that the target company has accounted for all outstanding taxes and has no hidden tax liability. The sale agreement will contain an indemnity in the event of the target company being called upon to pay additional tax. It used to be the practice that indemnities were often given in favour of the target company itself, not the buyer, as it is the target company on which the tax liability would fall. The case of *Zim Properties Ltd v Procter (Inspector of Taxes); Procter (Inspector of Taxes) v Zim Properties Ltd* [1985] STC 90, however, threw considerable doubt on the tax efficiency of this practice.

In *Zim*, a firm of solicitors acting for a taxpayer in a conveyancing transaction was allegedly negligent, with the result that a sale of three properties owned by the taxpayer fell through. The action for negligence was settled, with the taxpayer receiving compensation of £69,000. Undoubtedly, this was a capital sum, but the question arose as to whether it derived from the disposal of a capital asset.

Warner J in *Zim* held that the right to sue the solicitors was an asset for CGT purposes (since it could be turned into a capital sum by negotiation of a compromise). Thus, the settlement of the action was the disposal of a chose in action (a personal right to property which can be claimed or enforced only through legal action) giving rise to CGT. Furthermore, the case also established that this chose in action would normally have a nil acquisition cost; accordingly, the amount received in settlement would be liable to tax in full.

It is considered that this principle could apply to an indemnity *in favour of the target company*. In order to indemnify the target fully, it would be necessary to gross up any sum paid to take account of this tax liability (the relevant indemnity clauses should contain a *grossing-up clause*).

Example

The buyers purchase from the sellers the entire share capital of Target Limited.

In the sale and purchase agreement the sellers give a tax indemnity in favour of Target Limited.

Target Limited is later required to pay £50,000 in unpaid tax and claims under the indemnity.

Assume that Target Limited receives from the sellers the sum of £50,000.

If the *Zim* principle applies to indemnities, Target Limited is treated as having disposed of a chargeable asset and will be liable to tax on the amount of consideration less the acquisition cost. There is a nil acquisition cost. Target Limited is treated as having made a chargeable gain of £50,000 upon which it has to pay corporation tax.

The indemnity should contain an appropriate grossing-up clause, so that Target Limited will receive from the sellers a sum, which, after tax, leaves Target Limited with £50,000 (eg assuming Target Ltd pays corporation tax at 28%, it would need to receive approximately £69,444).

Many sellers will be unwilling to agree to a grossing-up clause (perhaps for obvious reasons!). The Inland Revenue sought to clarify the position through the issue of an Extra Statutory Concession (ESC D33) on 19 December 1988 (see below).

5.7.3 Extra Statutory Concession (ESC D33)

In ESC D33, the Inland Revenue made it clear that it would not regard the principle in *Zim* as applicable where payments are made to the buyer under warranties. The Concession also states that indemnity payments 'by the vendor *to the purchaser*' (emphasis added) will be treated the same way as warranties, ie the seller's sale proceeds are adjusted and the buyer's cost of acquisition in the event of a further disposal is reduced by the sum received. The Concession does not deal with payments made to the target company itself. Therefore, the safe approach is that indemnities should be expressed to be *in favour of the buyer*, not in favour of the target company.

The practice of providing that payments under indemnities are made to the buyer has been widely adopted, and relevant provisions are now normally contained in the main acquisition agreement. Although they are not always described as indemnities (eg they may be described as 'taxation covenants'), they are invariably still drafted like indemnities, ie to compensate the buyer for an amount equal to the liability imposed on the target.

5.8 Who gives warranties and indemnities?

The sellers of the target and those giving the warranties and indemnities are not always one and the same. Some sellers may be unwilling to accept any liability, or at least may try to limit their share of liability. The buyer, on the other hand, will usually want all the sellers to give the warranties and indemnities, and to do so on the basis that they are jointly and severally liable for any breaches.

5.8.1 Joint and several liability

Where there is more than one warrantor the buyer will invariably insist that they accept joint and several liability; this will enable it to sue any one of the warrantors for the full amount of the liability. Although this will not be of concern to the buyer, s 1 of the Civil Liability (Contribution) Act 1978 gives the party called upon to discharge the liability the right to recover a contribution from the other warrantors who are liable in respect of the same damage.

In proceedings under s 1, the court determines the amount of the contribution recoverable from the others on the basis of what it considers just and equitable having regard to the extent of their responsibility for the particular damage (s 2). It is likely that these contributions would reflect the amount of the purchase price which each warrantor received, although there is nothing to prevent the court from also taking into account other factors connected with the acquisition. As a result of this uncertainty, it is common practice for the warrantors to agree how any liability should be borne between them. This is permitted by the 1978 Act, and will usually be on the basis that liability is shared in proportion to the allocation of the purchase consideration. Such an agreement may be in a separate document ('a deed of contribution'), or it may be incorporated in the main acquisition agreement. In the latter case, the clause allocating liability will usually be expressed to be 'as between the warrantors'. It is important to appreciate that the buyer will not be affected by an agreement in these terms and will still be able to sue any warrantor for the full amount. In other words, the risk of a warrantor being unable or unwilling to pay his share falls on his fellow warrantors and not on the buyer, whose concern is simply that it should be able to recover compensation from someone.

5.8.2 Who may be unwilling to give warranties?

On a share sale involving a large number of shareholders, the buyer will not always insist that all of them give the warranties and indemnities. This is particularly so in relation to minor shareholders who may, often justifiably, not wish to be exposed to the risk which joint and several liability entails.

Problems often arise where some of the shares of a company are held in trust. Trustees will wish to avoid personal liability and may refuse to give any warranties or undertakings, other than that they have unencumbered title to the shares. If the trust holds a significant number of shares, this puts both the buyer and the other shareholders in a dilemma; the buyer has less security in the event of a breach and the other shareholders may feel aggrieved at undertaking a contingent liability disproportionate to the benefit they are receiving.

A solution which may be acceptable to all concerned is for the buyer to acknowledge in the sale and purchase agreement that the trustees' liability is limited to the net value (ie after tax) for the time being of the capital of the trust. The danger to the buyer of the capital being distributed shortly after completion may be met by obliging the trustees to require any beneficiary receiving capital to give appropriate warranties to the buyer. However, the terms of the particular trust may preclude the trustees from committing themselves to doing this.

Lastly, even relatively substantial shareholders will sometimes try to avoid giving warranties and indemnities, on the grounds that they have had no involvement with the management of the target company and therefore cannot be expected to give promises in relation to matters about which they know nothing. It is true that one of the purposes of warranties is to extract information about the target and that this information will generally come from the target's management. Nevertheless, the other (and probably more important) role of warranties is to allocate risk between seller and buyer. The price will be negotiated on the assumption that the warranties are true, and this is the basis on which all the shareholders (whether executive directors or not) receive their share of the consideration. If a breach of warranty means that the shares are not as valuable as the parties envisaged when entering into the deal, then it seems reasonable that there is an adjustment to the amount received by each shareholder; otherwise those shareholders who are not also warrantors effectively receive a windfall benefit.

5.8.3 Seller's rights against the management of the target

On a share sale, where the shareholders of the target company are not also directors, it will be the latter who will provide much of the information about the business which is requested by the buyer. Where this information is inaccurate or incomplete, this may lead to the selling shareholders becoming liable to the buyer for breach of warranty or misrepresentation; they may in turn be inclined to shift responsibility to the directors of the target by bringing a claim against them.

The buyer will wish to avoid the sellers' responsibility for breach of warranty effectively being shifted back onto the directors of the target who may well still be employed by the target. This is usually achieved by the selling shareholders waiving any right they may have to bring a claim against the management or the target itself in these circumstances (except in the case of any directors of the target who are also sellers).

5.8.4 Assignment of warranties and indemnities

If the buyer decides to sell the target soon after acquiring it, will it be able to assign the benefit of the warranties and indemnities which it received from the seller to the 'new' buyer? It is generally considered that the benefit of warranties is personal to the buyer and cannot be assigned, at least without the consent of the warrantor. This is also likely to be true in relation to indemnities given to the buyer (this problem will not arise if the indemnity is in favour of a target company).

If the buyer foresees the possibility of selling the target, it may try to negotiate with the seller an express right to assign the benefit of the warranties and indemnities. Its own buyer will certainly want the benefit of the usual protections, and an assignment of the existing warranties is a more attractive proposition than providing these warranties itself.

Prior to the introduction of the Contracts (Rights of Third Parties) Act 1999, even where such provision had been made, there was some doubt as to whether the assignee could recover substantial damages, due to the rules of privity of contract (ie the rights assigned are those of the immediate buyer, but, on assignment, the immediate buyer is unlikely to have suffered loss). The third party assignee therefore would not gain any benefit.

Under the 1999 Act, however, a person who is not a party to a contract may, nevertheless, have a right to enforce a term of the contract. This would occur either where the contract expressly confers a right in favour of a third party, or where the terms of the contract purport to confer such a right. Being a statutory right, a buyer of shares should be advised to structure the sale and purchase agreement to take advantage of the 1999 Act, so that the seller expressly agrees to confer the benefit of the warranties directly on subsequent buyers. If the seller has agreed to this, an assignee should not encounter problems recovering loss from the seller.

However, a seller is likely to oppose such express provision, as it would have no control over the identity of the assignee of the warranties. This is particularly the case where a buyer is an individual. In the case of a corporate buyer, the seller may agree to the buyer assigning the benefit of the warranties to members of the buyer's group. If assignment is agreed, the seller should ensure that the agreement provides that the assignee will be bound by the procedural provisions set out in the agreement (eg notification of claims and limitation periods) in the same way that the immediate buyer would have been.

5.9 Buyer's security for breach

The potential liability of the seller in relation to the warranties and indemnities is usually substantial, and may not come to light until some time after completion. The buyer is in an exposed position in relation to contingent liabilities which are the subject of warranties and indemnities. It, or the target itself, may be directly liable to third parties, for example, but may be unable to recover the loss if the seller is in financial difficulties. The buyer should consider reducing the risk by insisting on some form of security from the seller.

5.9.1 Guarantees

Where the sellers of a business or shares are individuals, the buyer will want to be satisfied as to the sellers' financial status and ability to cover any claims, so may insist on taking a charge over their assets or receiving a guarantee from a third party.

Where the seller of a business or shares is a company which is part of a group, the seller's parent company may be prepared to guarantee the seller's obligations. However, where a company owned by individuals is selling its business, it is likely to be a mere shell after completion which may be wound up shortly afterwards as a way of remitting the proceeds to the shareholders. In these circumstances, the financial security of the seller is clearly in doubt, and the buyer should seek guarantees from its shareholders at the very least.

5.9.2 Retentions from the purchase price

Another method of securing the buyer's position is for the acquisition agreement to provide for the buyer to retain part of the purchase price of the target for a certain period after completion and for this sum to be used to pay any successful claims under the warranties or indemnities. Such provision may be made in the following terms:

(a) payment of the retention into a joint account in the names of the seller's and buyer's solicitors;

(b) the retention to be remitted to the seller on a certain date after completion (eg 12 months after completion) unless the buyer makes a claim under the warranties or indemnities before that date;

(c) where the buyer does make such a claim, only the balance of the retention, after deducting the amount of the claim, to be paid to the seller on the specified date;

(d) the buyer to be paid the amount of the claim within a short period (eg 14 days) of this being determined and any balance remitted to the seller;

(e) payment of accrued interest on the fund to the parties in the same proportion that they receive the retention;

(f) an obligation on the buyer to pursue any claims against the seller which may delay the remittance of the fund promptly and diligently.

The seller may also insist that any claim which delays payment of the retention must be made properly. For example, the buyer may be obliged to provide full details of the claim, perhaps backed up with an opinion of counsel.

The retention will not affect the capital tax position of the parties. Only if it is used to pay warranty claims will there be an adjustment to the consideration for capital tax purposes, as explained at **5.6.3.1**.

5.10 Restrictions on the seller

Whether it is a business acquisition or a share acquisition, the value of the buyer's investment could be reduced substantially by the post-completion activities of the seller, whose detailed knowledge of the target would enable the seller to cause it considerable harm. It is in the buyer's interests to protect its investment by making express provision in the acquisition agreement to curtail any such activities of the seller. This section deals with the position where no express agreement is made, the type of restrictions which the buyer may seek to impose and whether the validity of such provisions can be challenged.

5.10.1 What can the buyer do if there are no express restraints?

The case of *Trego v Hunt* [1896] AC 7 established that on the sale of the goodwill of a business, the courts will refuse to imply a covenant by the seller not to set up in competition. In the absence of express provision, very limited protections for the buyer of goodwill (the position of a buyer of shares was not considered) will be implied into the agreement. The only implied undertakings of the seller are as follows:

(a)   not to use or disclose confidential information relating to the business;

(b)   not to represent itself as successor to the business, or as carrying on the same business;

(c)   not to solicit customers of the business (ie those who were customers prior to the sale).

5.10.2 Express restrictions

The buyer of a business or shares will usually value the target on the assumption that its goodwill will be preserved. Indeed, on the acquisition of a business, a specific value will be attributed to goodwill. The buyer is, in effect, paying for the benefit of the good name of the target and the expectation that existing customers (and suppliers) will continue to deal with it (and, indeed, that new customers will be attracted to it).

As the seller is being paid for goodwill, the buyer is justified in seeking ways of preventing the seller from damaging it by, for example, taking away customers of the business. The buyer does not, however, have unlimited scope to restrain the activities of the seller after completion, since the law is reluctant, on public policy grounds, to restrict competition in general and a person's ability to earn his livelihood in particular. The buyer must go no further than is reasonably necessary to protect the goodwill of the target.

The buyer commonly seeks to include in the agreement some or all of the following undertakings by the seller:

(a)   a covenant not to be engaged or concerned in any competing business for a specified period after completion;

(b)   a covenant not to try to solicit or entice away from the target customers or suppliers who have recently dealt with the target for a specified period after completion;

(c)   a covenant not to try to solicit or entice away from the target employees of the target for a specified period after completion;

(d)   an undertaking not to use or disclose any confidential information about the target or its customers;

(e)   a covenant not to use the name of the target (where a business is acquired from a company, the selling company may be required to change its corporate name).

5.10.3 Will these restrictions be valid at common law?

All covenants in restraint of trade are prima facie void at common law. However, the court will not strike down restrictive covenants which it considers to be reasonable to protect a legitimate interest of the buyer. The preservation of goodwill, which is reflected in the value of the business or shares, and the protection of business secrets are the interests which the buyer is concerned to protect; the restraints must therefore go no further than is strictly necessary to achieve this. The factors which the court considers relevant are the same on a business sale as on a share sale. It should also be noted that the courts are not as strict in striking down clauses in acquisition contracts, which are freely negotiable, as they are in employment contracts. The following factors are relevant:

(a)   the duration of the restraint;

(b)   the geographical area of the restraint;

(c)   the activities restricted.

5.10.3.1 Duration

The buyer will usually seek to prevent the seller from competing and soliciting customers, etc for between one year and five years after completion (see **5.10.5**). Where the seller is prevented from using or disclosing confidential information, it will not generally be necessary to stipulate a time limit on this restriction.

5.10.3.2 Area

The geographical area in which a covenant preventing the seller from setting up a business of the same type is intended to operate must be closely related to the area in which the target operates. What is permissible, therefore, varies considerably and depends on whether the business is based locally or nationally. If the covenant is appropriately worded, it may not be necessary to stipulate a geographical limit. For example, if the clause disallows the seller from setting up a 'competing business', this has the effect of limiting the restraint to the area in which the target carries on business (otherwise it would not be competing for the same clientele). If, on the other hand, the clause restricts the seller from carrying on a defined business, it will be necessary to specify a reasonable area of restriction to prevent it from being considered too wide.

5.10.3.3 Activities

Any attempt to extend the restrictions to activities which are not carried on by the target itself will fail, on the grounds that they are excessive in order to protect the goodwill of the target. Accordingly, the buyer will not be able to prevent the seller from competing with other businesses that the buyer owns or intends to acquire in the future. Indeed, in *Ronbar Enterprises Ltd v Green* [1954] 2 All ER 266, the court considered a clause preventing the seller carrying on a business 'similar to' that of the target to be too wide.

Another relevant factor is the extent to which the parties being asked to give the covenants have been actively involved in the business. It may be difficult, for example, to enforce a non-competition covenant against a minority shareholder who has taken no part in managing a target company and has never been involved in the same industry.

A non-solicitation clause should not be so wide as to include those who have had no recent dealings with the target prior to completion. It may, for example, be unreasonable to restrict the seller from contacting 'customers' or 'suppliers' who have not dealt with the target for more than one year before completion.

5.10.4 Enforcement

If the restrictive covenants are reasonable, the buyer will be able to claim damages for breach of contract and may be granted an injunction. But what if only some of the restrictions are reasonable?

If each restraint is contained in a different clause or sub-clause, and they are expressed to be separate and independent restrictions, even if the court considers one restraint to be too wide, the others will remain enforceable. Also, the court will not always strike out the whole of a clause or sub-clause. It is sometimes prepared to 'blue pencil' certain parts of a clause (ie to draw a line through certain words), leaving the remaining parts enforceable, but will not rewrite a clause to make it reasonable. It is quite common to find a clause in the acquisition agreement where the parties agree that, if any of the restrictions is found to be invalid, but would be valid if, for example, the period or area of the restriction were reduced, such restriction shall apply with such amendments as are required to make it valid. Such a clause is unlikely to be effective.

5.10.5 The Competition Act 1998

The Competition Act 1998 introduced provisions into UK law which are very similar to the regime which applies under Arts 81 and 82 of the EC Treaty. Section 60 sets out the governing principle, directing that questions relating to competition are to be:

> So far as is possible ... dealt with in a manner which is consistent with the treatment of corresponding questions arising in Community law in relation to competition within the Community.

There is therefore a general prohibition of anti-competitive agreements and a prohibition of abuse of a dominant position.

The Competition Act 1998 repealed the Restrictive Trade Practices Act 1976, the Resale Prices Act 1976 and the provisions of the Competition Act 1980 relating to anti-competitive practices.

If an agreement is found to breach s 2 or s 18 of the Competition Act 1998 (see **5.10.5.1** and **5.10.5.2**), the agreement or (subject to severance) the anti-competitive terms will be unenforceable.

The impact of the Competition Act 1998 on acquisition agreements is not clear. However, legal advisers are wise to consider its possible effect and to take action where appropriate. This may result in renegotiation of the agreement, or notification to the Competition Commission either for guidance or a decision.

5.10.5.1 Anti-competitive agreements

The wording of s 2 of the 1998 Act follows closely that of Art 81 of the EC Treaty. There is a prohibition on agreements and other business arrangements between two or more undertakings which may affect trade in the UK and which have as their object or effect the prevention, restriction or distortion of competition within the UK. Section 2(2) provides a non-exhaustive list of agreements which infringe the prohibition, similar to that found in Art 81(2) of the EC Treaty.

As with Art 81, there are block and general exemptions. The exemptions cover similar ground to that covered by the Art 81 exemptions, with block exemptions dealing with common agreements such as exclusive distribution agreements, franchise agreements and distribution agreements. In any event, parallel exemptions apply to agreements which are covered by a European Commission exemption under Art 81(3), or would be covered if the agreement had an effect on trade between Member States. There are also *de minimis* provisions similar to those contained in the Notice on Agreements of Minor Importance. Significantly, any agreement which is exempt under EC law will also be exempt under UK legislation.

5.10.5.2 Abuse of a dominant position

The wording of s 18 of the 1998 Act concerning abuse of a dominant position is similar to that of Art 82 of the EC Treaty. There is a prohibition on the activities of one or more undertakings which amount to the abuse of a dominant position within the UK or a substantial part of it.

In the context of an acquisition agreement, a buyer should be aware that, in particular, restrictive covenants could fall foul of UK competition law.

5.10.5.3 Consequences of infringement

Restrictions in breach of the 1998 Act will be void. The OFT is empowered to impose fines of up to 10% of an undertaking's turnover. The parties may be ordered to cease or modify the agreement. As with EC law, notification of an agreement will bring an exemption from fines until the OFT makes a decision. The OFT has substantial investigative powers, including the right to raid premises unannounced (the so-called 'dawn raid'), provided a search warrant has been obtained from a High Court judge. There is the possibility of an appeal from the decisions of the OFT to the Competition Commission.

5.10.6 EC v UK competition law

Restrictive covenants in acquisition agreements may breach Arts 81 and 82 of the EC Treaty (particularly Art 81). These Articles are considered in *Business Law and Practice*. Trade between Member States must be affected for either Article to apply. If Art 81 applies, the acquisition agreement may come within the scope of the Notice on Agreements of Minor Importance.

In relation to restrictive covenants, useful guidance is provided by the EC Commission's Notice of August 2004 (OJ C56/24) on restrictions directly related and necessary to concentrations. In issuing the Notice, the Commission recognises that certain restrictions are necessary to guarantee the stated value of the shares transferred to the buyer. Restrictions falling within this Notice are automatically covered by any EC merger clearance decision. The Notice confirms that, on a transfer of goodwill, a non-compete period of up to two years will be appropriate, whereas a period of three years is justified where the buyer acquires know-how and goodwill. Non-solicitation clauses should be considered in the same way as non-compete provisions.

If there is a Community dimension, compliance with EC competition law will also satisfy UK competition law.

The Competition Act 1998 is considered in more detail in *Commercial Law and Practice*.

Chapter 6

Allocation of Risk: Seller's Limitations

6.1 Limiting the scope of warranties, representations and indemnities

As seen in **Chapter 5**, the buyer will seek to include warranties and indemnities in the sale and purchase agreement to provide contractual reassurances about what is being acquired. For its part, the seller will seek to limit its potential exposure to liability by negotiating specific provisions in the sale and purchase agreement, and by making appropriate disclosures in the disclosure letter.

The first draft of the sale and purchase agreement prepared by the buyer will invariably include extensive warranties and indemnities with no specific limitations on the seller's liability. In most cases, there is considerable scope for negotiating the agreement, and it is the warranties and indemnities which usually take up most of the time and energies of the parties' solicitors. Indeed, the final agreed version often bears little resemblance to the original draft.

The seller may be able to limit its liability by arguing successfully for the deletion of certain of the warranties and indemnities. Even if it is unable to achieve this, negotiating changes to the wording of a clause which effectively 'water it down' may make a significant difference to the seller's exposure. There is considerable merit in analysing carefully the wording of each warranty and indemnity. For example, the initial draft of a warranty may state: 'No customer of the company will cease to deal with it as a result of the acquisition.' The seller's solicitor may try to amend this by requiring knowledge of the seller and restricting the warranty to substantial customers; thus the agreed version may read: 'The seller has no knowledge, information or belief that any substantial customer of the company will cease to deal with it as a result of the acquisition.' Similarly, the seller may be asked to warrant that the company is not in breach of a particular agreement. The seller's solicitor may be able to limit the scope of the warranty by again requiring knowledge of the seller and by restricting it to breach of 'material terms' of the agreement.

Where warranties are given by reference to the 'knowledge, information or belief' of the seller in this way, the buyer may insist on the seller acknowledging that in giving the warranties it has made all due enquiries and taken all reasonable steps to ensure their accuracy.

6.2 Limitations on claims

In addition to negotiating the terms of each warranty, the seller will also seek to restrict its liability in relation to the warranties and indemnities generally by including a set of standard limitation clauses in the agreement. Such limitations on the seller's liability for breach of warranty contained in a share sale agreement are not controlled by the Unfair Contract Terms Act 1977 (UCTA 1977) (Sch 1, para

1(e) precludes the operation of its relevant provisions to any contract so far as it relates to the 'creation or transfer of securities or of any right or interest in securities'). Asset sale agreements are not the subject of a similar specific exclusion. However, s 3 of UCTA 1977, which invalidates attempts to exclude liability unless they satisfy the requirement of reasonableness, applies only where one party deals on the other's written standard terms of business or 'as a consumer' (ie it neither makes the contract in the course of a business nor holds itself out as doing so and the other party does make the contract in the course of a business: s 12). In any event, freely negotiated warranty limitations contained in an acquisition agreement are unlikely to be the subject of a successful challenge.

6.2.1   Limits on the amount of claims

The concept of joint and several liability and attempts by sellers to limit their share of liability have already been discussed (see **5.8.1**). In addition, it is usual to include maximum and minimum limitations.

6.2.1.1   Maximum limits

The seller will negotiate for a maximum liability under the warranties and indemnities. The limit which is often agreed upon is the price which the buyer paid for the target. It is possible, particularly on a share sale, that the buyer's loss, recoverable under the rules of *Hadley v Baxendale* (see **5.4.1**), may exceed the amount paid for the target. Few sellers, however, are prepared to risk being sued for more than they receive for the shares or assets, and most buyers will accept this limitation. The buyer must take care in agreeing to such a clause, however, if the actual purchase price is relatively low but it is obliged as part of the deal to inject money into the target to discharge certain liabilities, such as outstanding loans owed by the target to the sellers. The amount of such liabilities should be treated as part of the consideration for this purpose.

6.2.1.2   Minimum limits

The parties will often agree a minimum threshold for claims. This will typically be about 1% of the consideration. In other words, the buyer is prevented from making any claim unless the aggregate of all claims exceeds the threshold. This is really on the basis that it is virtually impossible to gauge precisely the value of a business or a company and the parties accept that there is margin for error. The effect of warranty claims is to adjust retrospectively the purchase price, and it seems reasonable for the parties to take the view that relatively minor adjustments do not justify the expense and inconvenience involved in pursuing warranty claims. The buyer is, however, wise to insist that once the threshold is exceeded, it can recover the full amount, rather than just the amount by which the threshold is exceeded. So, for example, on a £5 million sale, where the threshold is £50,000 and the loss suffered is £60,000, the buyer will be entitled to recover £60,000 rather than £10,000.

The seller may also seek to set a *de minimis* limit on individual claims, to apply even where the aggregate threshold has been exceeded. For example, the buyer may be prevented from bringing any claim worth less than £5,000. Difficulties can arise, however, in respect of continuing breaches and claims which are similar in nature or arise from the same default. Where, for example, the seller has warranted that all book debts will be fully recoverable, claims relating to debts from different sources should not be treated as separate for this purpose. As so often with acquisition documentation, careful attention to detail in drafting such a clause is necessary.

6.2.2 Time limits

The limitation period for bringing a claim for breach of contract is normally six years from the date of the contract. Where the share or asset sale is by deed, the limitation period is 12 years (or if there is a separate deed of tax indemnity, the period will be 12 years in relation to the tax matters covered).

Most sellers will wish to be 'off the hook' well before the limitation periods expire. It is common to restrict the period in which the buyer can make claims relating to tax matters to six years from the date of the contract. This is related to HMRC's time limit for making an assessment to tax (six years from the end of the relevant tax year except to recover tax lost through fraudulent or negligent conduct). To be safe, the buyer may insist on the period being seven years.

For non-tax matters, the period negotiated is usually much shorter and, on a share sale, tends to be linked to the target company's audit (on the basis that the audit may 'flush out' breaches of warranty). A period allowing for two full audits to be carried out and their results digested is commonly agreed.

The agreement may allow the buyer to bring claims outside these time limits provided it has notified the details to the seller (ie sufficient information to identify the nature and substance of the claim). In these circumstances, there should be a long-stop time limit for instituting proceedings, so that the buyer is not able to extend the limitation period 'by the back door'!

6.2.3 Insurance cover

The seller will invariably seek to prevent the buyer from bringing a claim where the loss is covered by insurance taken out in relation to the target. The main argument between the parties often centres around whether this should extend to insurance cover that the buyer could reasonably be expected to take out (perhaps related to the level of cover in place before the acquisition).

6.2.4 Recovery from third parties

The buyer may also be required to give credit for any sums received from third parties in relation to the subject matter of the claim. This will usually be expressed widely enough to cover tax reductions (eg an undisclosed liability may be a deductible expense for tax purposes, resulting in a saving of tax).

6.2.5 Assets understated in the accounts

The seller may want to include a provision that any claim will be reduced by the amount by which the seller can show that the net assets of the target were understated in the accounts drawn up before completion, for example, by demonstrating either of the following:

(a)   that assets have been realised for more than their value in the accounts; or

(b)   that liabilities have been satisfied for less than is specified in the accounts.

The buyer should be wary of accepting this, particularly where the valuation of the target was not assets-based.

6.2.6 Conduct of claims

Claims made by third parties against the target may result in the seller becoming liable to the buyer under a warranty. The seller may, for example, have warranted that the target company has not manufactured any products which are faulty in any material respect. A successful action against the target under the Consumer

Protection Act 1987 in respect of damage caused by a defect in a product manufactured by the target prior to completion would amount to a breach of this warranty. The buyer will seek to reclaim the amount of any judgment entered against the target and costs incurred in connection with the claim.

The seller may argue that since it will ultimately bear the liability, it should have the right to have conduct of the claim. It may be worried that if the buyer has control over the dispute, the buyer may be less than vigorous in defending a claim when it knows that it will be able to sue under a warranty if it succeeds. The buyer is under a duty to mitigate its loss, but it may be difficult for the seller to prove a failure to mitigate in these circumstances.

The buyer, on the other hand, may have reservations about allowing the seller to have control, on the basis of the possible damage to the reputation and goodwill of the target which may ensue as a consequence. For example, it may feel that the seller's main concern will be to protract the matter rather than come to a settlement which leaves the target's reputation intact.

Whichever party it is decided should have control of claims, the agreement will often provide for the other party to have some influence over its conduct (eg requiring consent to settle the claim). If the seller is given control, the buyer may reserve the right to require the provision of security and/or an indemnity in respect of costs and expenses which the target or buyer may incur in relation to the claim. The buyer, for its part, will be obliged to notify the seller promptly of any circumstances which may give rise to a claim.

6.3 Disclosure

6.3.1 Nature and purpose of the disclosure letter

One of the aims of including a long list of warranties in the sale and purchase agreement is to elicit information about the target from the seller. Warranties can be seen as providing a checklist for the buyer of all the matters which may be of concern to it in relation to the acquisition. Much of the information requested by the buyer is produced in the form of disclosures by the seller, which have the effect of qualifying the warranties. The incentive for the seller in making disclosures is that they avoid it being in breach of warranty in relation to those matters disclosed. This can be illustrated by considering a few examples in the context of some standard warranties.

Example 1

The agreement includes a warranty that the target is not engaged in any litigation as claimant or defendant. The target is, however, being sued for breach of copyright.

The seller can avoid liability for breach of warranty by disclosing full details of the copyright action. This is easier than negotiating an alteration to the terms of the warranty to exclude the copyright action from its scope (the buyer would not agree to the deletion of the warranty as it would be left without any protection against undisclosed claims). The buyer must take a view on the significance of the disclosure to the deal which has been negotiated. It may prompt it to withdraw from the acquisition, renegotiate the price, or ask the seller for an indemnity for any damages awarded against the target and any costs incurred in relation to the claim.

Example 2

The agreement includes a warranty that the target company is not party to any contract or agreement which cannot be terminated by the company on three months' notice or less. The company is, however, party to a distribution agreement which either party can bring to an end by giving 12 months' notice, and two of the directors have nine months of their fixed-term service contracts to run.

Once again, the simplest way for the seller to avoid liability is to disclose the existence and main terms of the three agreements, and attach copies to the disclosure letter.

Example 3

The agreement includes a warranty that the disclosure letter contains full particulars of the pension scheme for the target's employees.

This is a different type of warranty which obliges the seller to give full and accurate details of the pension scheme (the seller will normally provide copies of the trust deed and rules).

The disclosure letter has such an important role in determining the potential liability of the seller and, correspondingly, the risk undertaken by the buyer, that it will be the subject of the same careful scrutiny by the parties as the sale and purchase agreement itself. Several drafts will pass between the parties, and the buyer may ask for further information on any issues included within the disclosure letter so as to perfect its knowledge of the target well ahead of the completion date. The seller is advised to make full and early disclosure of potential issues – late disclosures carry the risk that the buyer will either refuse to accept the disclosure as fully limiting the seller's liability in the relevant area, or even that the buyer will withdraw from the deal at a stage when significant professional costs have been incurred.

6.3.2   Format of the disclosure letter

The disclosure letter will be in the form of a letter from the seller to the buyer. A bundle of documents (referred to as the disclosure bundle) will be attached to the letter, comprising all the documents referred to in the letter as providing information which qualifies the warranties (such as the distribution agreement referred to in Example 2 and the pension details in Example 3 in **6.3.1** above).

The parties' legal advisers will negotiate the disclosure letter and bundle until it is in an agreed final form ready for completion of the acquisition. Disclosure is a means by which the seller can negate its liability under a warranty, and therefore it is in the seller's interests to disclose as much information as possible. However, the buyer must consider whether it is prepared to accept every disclosure without further information or contractual protection. If the disclosure relates to a matter of significance to the buyer, it may decide to require an indemnity from the seller to cover any identified potential liability, to reduce the purchase price it is prepared to pay or, if the matter is very significant, to withdraw from the purchase.

On exchange of contracts, two copies of the agreed form of disclosure letter and bundle will be available; one to be given to the buyer and one to be retained by the seller. The letters and associated bundles will be initialled by the parties as evidence that they are identical. Thus in the event of claim that there may have been a breach or warranty, each party will be able to refer to the agreed disclosure documentation.

The disclosure letter itself will generally be divided into two sections. First, general matters of which the buyer will be deemed to be aware, and secondly, details of specific disclosures.

6.3.2.1   Deemed disclosures

The disclosure letter will state that a number of matters are deemed to have been disclosed to the buyer. These deemed disclosures are often referred to as 'general disclosures'. These general disclosures relate to publicly available information which the buyer can be expected to find out for itself and, occasionally, to information that has been made available to the buyer during the due diligence investigation. The effect of deemed or general disclosure is to pass to the buyer the risk that elements of this information will qualify the warranties and therefore limit the seller's liability post-acquisition. The deemed disclosures will usually include the following types of information:

(a)   information on a target company's file at the Companies Registry;

(b)   matters apparent from the deeds of properties owned or occupied by the target and any information available from Land Registry or the Land Charges Department, or which would be revealed by appropriate searches and enquiries of local authorities. This extensive disclosure is likely to qualify a number of property warranties (eg that the target has good title to the properties, that they are free from mortgages and charges, and that the use of each property is a permitted use for planning purposes);

(c)   matters which would be disclosed by physical inspection of each property. The buyer should be prepared to accept this only if it has commissioned a survey of all the target's properties (time constraints will often prevent this);

(d)   matters which are in the public domain. This is very wide-ranging and the buyer may try to restrict its scope to matters of which the buyer could reasonably be expected to be aware as affecting the target;

(e)   matters disclosed or referred to in the audited accounts of the target company (eg for the last three years);

(f)   matters included or referred to in the accountants' report prepared on behalf of the buyer. The nature and purpose of the accountants' report is discussed in **Chapter 3**. There is often considerable disagreement between the parties as to how the report should be treated for this purpose. Reports are often very comprehensive, covering a great deal of ground; accordingly, a disclosure in these terms may reduce considerably the buyer's scope for suing for breach of warranty (eg where the inaccuracy of certain warranties could have been ascertained from the contents of the report). The buyer may, however, be prepared to accept this deemed disclosure in return for the seller warranting the accuracy of the report.

(g)   matters disclosed or referred to in the replies to the preliminary enquiries and the documents enclosed within those replies (or supplied in a data room). There is often some dispute between the parties as to whether these replies to enquiries should be deemed to be disclosed. The buyer will argue that this information is provided to assist in its assessment of the proposed acquisition and should not be used by the seller as a means of limiting its potential liability under the warranties. The relative bargaining strengths of the parties will determine whether this general disclosure is included in the final form disclosure letter.

6.3.2.2 Specific disclosure

Specific disclosures draw to the buyer's attention specific information about the target which is inconsistent with one or more warranties given by the seller. For ease of reference, the disclosures made will usually refer to specific warranty statements in the sale and purchase agreement. However, there is often a significant degree of overlap between the warranties, and so the disclosure letter invariably provides that each disclosure is deemed to be in respect of all the warranties and not merely the warranty referred to in it.

6.3.3 Standard of disclosure

It is in the interests of the buyer and the seller that all disclosures are fairly made. The buyer will want as accurate a picture as possible of the target at a time when the terms of the acquisition are still in the course of negotiations, and the seller will want to negate the possibility of any later warranty claim.

The sale and purchase agreement will usually specify the standard of disclosure required for a disclosure effectively to negate a liability under the warranties. This standard will usually apply to both deemed disclosures and specific disclosures. However, in relation to deemed disclosures, the agreement will often require that the disclosure will be effective only if it could reasonably be expected that the buyer would become aware of the relevant breach of warranty from an examination of the documents (see **6.3.3.2**).

6.3.3.1 Full disclosure

The sale and purchase agreement will provide that the warranties are given subject to matters disclosed in the disclosure letter. The buyer may insist that the disclosures are properly made, ie that they are accurate and fully disclose the matters to which they relate. It is understandable that the buyer will not want to accept limitations on the seller's potential liability under the warranties unless it has full details of the relevant circumstances. From the seller's point of view it will also be advisable to make any disclosures to the buyer as specific as possible. Following the case of *Levison v Farin* [1978] 2 All ER 1149, it is clear that in order for a disclosure to be effective the buyer must be given specific notice of the particular issue qualifying the warranty. In this case, the buyers were generally aware of the run-down condition of the business, but this did not preclude them from successfully claiming for breach of a warranty which said that 'there will have been no material adverse change in the overall value of the net assets of the Company'. It was held that the disclosure about the drop in business was only disclosing a 'possible cause of loss, not an actual drop in net asset value'. Merely putting the buyer on enquiry or making the buyer aware of certain facts did not constitute adequate disclosure in the context of this particular warranty.

6.3.3.2 Are warranties limited only by disclosure letter?

The seller (or its advisers) will normally have passed a great deal of information to the buyer in the pre-contract period and may wish the buyer to acknowledge that the disclosure letter is deemed to include all this information. The buyer will usually prefer that copies of all information and documentation which it or its advisers have received in this way and which are to be taken to be disclosed are attached to the disclosure letter. Although the buyer's solicitor will have the task of working through the attached bundle of documents, there is less chance of the buyer inadvertently accepting disclosures. Indeed, the buyer will usually insist on limiting disclosure specifically to matters revealed in the disclosure letter and bundle, and there will be a clause in the sale and purchase agreement saying that the warranties are only qualified by matters contained in these documents and not by the buyer's own knowledge. The buyer should, however, be aware of the fact that it may not be able to rely on such a clause. In the case of *Eurocopy plc v Teesdale* [1992] BCLC 1067, the general rule that the buyer's own knowledge will not provide a defence to breach of warranty was brought into question. In this case, the sellers had warranted that all material facts had been disclosed to the buyers. The buyers brought a breach of warranty claim on the grounds that the sellers had failed to disclose certain material facts (relating to maintenance contracts for photocopiers). The sellers claimed that the buyers had actual knowledge of those facts from their due diligence. The buyers moved to strike out this aspect of the defence, on the basis that the agreement stated that the warranties were subject only to the disclosure letter and that no other information relevant to the target of which the buyers had knowledge affected any warranty claims. The Court of Appeal refused to strike out this aspect of the defence, partly on the basis that the price they paid 'must have been influenced by their knowledge of material facts and circumstances'.

Whilst it is accepted that this case was only an interlocutory application, it must still be borne in mind when advising a buyer who has information on the target which may lead to a warranty claim.

6.3.3.3 Case guidance on disclosure

The situation where the buyer's agent has information which could lead to a warranty claim was considered further in the case of *Infiniteland Ltd v Artisan Contracting Ltd* [2005] All ER (D) 236, which concerned the acquisition by share purchase of a group of companies. The seller warranted that, save as disclosed, the accounts gave a true and fair view of the group's financial position. Specific disclosures against each warranty were not sought by the buyer, but there was deemed disclosure of all matters contained in documents provided to the buyer's accountants. The agreement contained a provision stating that the buyer's right to claim a breach of warranty would not be affected by its investigation save in so far as it gave the buyer actual knowledge. An exceptional item in the accounts of one group company was revealed post-completion – an issue that had been disclosed to the buyer's accountants but of which the buyer had no actual knowledge on completion. The buyer sued for breach of warranty.

In deciding the case, the Court of Appeal gave general consideration to the standard of disclosure required to defeat a breach of warranty claim, and also examined the effect of a *Eurocopy* clause (see **6.3.3.2**) and whether knowledge of the buyer's agents could be imputed to the buyer. The judgment therefore contains a number of useful indicators for acquisitions lawyers.

Standard of disclosure

In relation to disclosure, the Court held that there is no universal test that should be applied, and the sufficiency of disclosure must therefore be measured by reference to the agreed contractual provisions. The disclosure that is made must match this agreed standard in order to negate a warranty claim. If the parties agree on specific disclosure, only such disclosure will rule out a warranty claim. Where general disclosure of documentation is accepted by the buyer, the sale and purchase agreement will usually provide that any matter contained within that documentation will be deemed as disclosed only if it could fairly be expected that the buyer would become aware of the relevant breach from examination of the documents in the ordinary course of due diligence. A buyer should therefore be wary of accepting general disclosures, although it is some comfort that in *MAN Nutzfahrzeuge AG v Freightliner Ltd* [2005] EWHC 2347, the judge considered (obiter) that matters deemed to be disclosed in connection with a general disclosure would not extend so far as to include inferences which might be drawn from the documents inspected.

Effect of buyer's knowledge on damages

In *Infiniteland* at first instance, the judge said that the buyer's knowledge of a breach at completion would not bar a claim as a matter of law (so a *Eurocopy* clause may be effective). However, the Court of Appeal made it clear that a buyer who completes with actual knowledge of a breach may not be welcomed by the courts if it subsequently sues on that breach – the court may suspect fraud and, even if the claim is successful, the buyer may be penalised on the measure of damages. It will therefore always be preferable for a buyer to acknowledge full disclosure of a breach and seek an indemnity or reduction in the purchase price before completion.

The Court further confirmed that it will give effect to an express provision in the sale agreement prohibiting warranty claims of which the buyer is aware at completion, but knowledge of the buyer's agents will not generally be imputed to the buyer unless the contract provides for this. A reference to 'actual knowledge' means the buyer's own knowledge, and 'constructive knowledge' covers those matters of which the buyer should have been aware.

Pre-contractual statements

A further disclosure issue for the parties (and in particular the seller) to consider is the impact of statements made by employees or agents of the seller or the target company during negotiations or the due diligence process. In *MAN v Freightliner* (above), Moore-Bick LJ held the seller to be vicariously liable for the fraudulent pre-contractual statements of its agent, who had been put forward as having authority to speak on its behalf. Although the seller in this case has been granted leave to appeal to the Court of Appeal, a prudent seller should exercise some caution when putting together its negotiating team and, to a lesser extent, when allowing employees of the target company to provide information during the transaction. (There is less risk that the seller would be vicariously liable for statements made by target employees during due diligence, but care should be taken if target employees are to be involved in the negotiation of terms.)

6.3.4 Deliberate non-disclosure

A practical problem can arise where the seller deliberately fails to disclose the existence of particular facts, such as a pending dispute, which may later lead to a warranty claim. The seller may prefer to compensate the buyer in due course after completion rather than raise the issue during negotiations, for fear that the buyer may withdraw from the purchase. However, in these circumstances the buyer will have been induced to enter into the sale and purchase agreement by way of a deliberate concealment and this would constitute fraud.

In addition, in the context of a share acquisition, s 397(1) and (2) of the FSMA 2000 make it a criminal offence for a person knowingly or recklessly to make a statement, promise or forecast which is misleading, false or deceptive. It is also an offence under the section for a person with the requisite intent to conceal dishonestly any material facts. The person will be guilty of the offence if he makes the statement, etc or conceals the facts for the purpose of inducing, or is reckless as to whether it may induce, another person, inter alia, to enter into an investment agreement (which includes a share sale agreement, though not an asset sale agreement). A person guilty of an offence is liable to a fine, or imprisonment for a maximum term of seven years for conviction on indictment, or to both.

6.4 Insuring against liability

Increasingly, buyers and/or sellers are seeking to cover the risk of potential warranty claims by taking out warranty and indemnity insurance. The price of securing the seller's peace of mind in this way can be high (premiums being between 1% and 5% of the limit of liability) and will often involve the insurers in picking through the acquisition documentation (usually via their own solicitors and at the seller's expense). The insurers will not agree cover until they have analysed the scope of each warranty, the effect of the disclosures and the extent of the general limitations on the seller's liability. Any policy is likely to contain a number of general exclusions (eg excluding liability in respect of matters within the knowledge of the seller at the date of the contract).

The sale and purchase agreement should incorporate a clause which obliges the buyer to claim from an insurer before commencing an action against the seller.

Chapter 7

Completing the Acquisition

The sale and purchase agreement is a contractual agreement which sets out the terms on which the acquisition will take place. On the exchange of the duly executed sale and purchase agreement, the parties undertake to perform the agreed steps required to transfer the legal interest in the shares or assets to the buyer. This is known as completion. In most acquisition transactions, the actual transfer of the assets or shares occurs as soon as the parties have become contractually bound to do so, ie exchange and completion are simultaneous. However, it is not always possible to achieve this. In this chapter, the reasons why a sale and purchase agreement may be entered into on a conditional basis are discussed. Provisions dealing with the possible risks that may arise while the conditions are being fulfilled, and the mechanics of completing the transfer of the shares or the assets of the business are also considered.

7.1 Reasons for conditionality

Before completing an acquisition various approvals, consents and clearances may be required, and ideally should be obtained before the sale and purchase agreement is signed. However, obtaining the necessary consents and approvals can take some time, and the parties may prefer not to delay exchange of contracts until all such matters have been resolved.

The sale and purchase agreement may, therefore, be made conditional on one or more matters, for example:

(a) HMRC issuing a clearance, say, on a share acquisition in relation to roll-over relief from capital tax on a securities exchange (see **9.4.2.3**);

(b) the OFT notifying the buyer that it does not intend to refer the acquisition to the Competition Commission (see **2.2.1**);

(c) the provision or transfer of a regulatory licence for the particular industry, for example environmental licences for regulated industrial processes;

(d) a substantial customer or landlord providing its consent to an assignment, or confirming that it will not exercise a contractual right to terminate an agreement with the target company on the change in control of the target company;

(e) the shareholders of a corporate buyer passing a resolution, for example for the issue of shares to the seller in consideration for the target and, if required, making arrangements for such shares to be listed on a market.

In some of these situations, the parties will not want to make the required applications, so making the proposed acquisition public knowledge, until both parties are contractually committed to the acquisition. In other circumstances, the conditions may simply be those required to complete the agreed terms of the purchase. Whatever the reason for the conditional exchange of contracts, both parties will be concerned to agree terms covering satisfaction of the conditions, how and when completion will finally take place, and how the target business will be conducted during the period between signing the sale and purchase agreement and completing the acquisition.

7.2   Risk allocation on conditional contracts

If completion of the sale and purchase agreement is to be made conditional, the agreement must clearly state each party's obligations in respect of each condition, the date by which each condition must be met, and any right to terminate the agreement prior to completion. Express provisions will also be included to try to provide for unexpected events that may occur between signing the contract and completion of the acquisition.

The buyer will usually seek to include a contractual right to withdraw from the purchase if a major problem occurs prior to completion. However, the amount of protection given to the buyer often depends on the original reason for imposing the condition. If the condition is a requirement of the buyer, such as the need for shareholder approval, then the seller may justifiably argue that the buyer should assume the risk of any delay.

7.2.1   Conditions precedent

The sale and purchase agreement will set out the conditions to be fulfilled and specific terms relating to their fulfilment.

It is usual to include the following provisions:

(a)   an obligation on one party to take all reasonable steps to try to procure the satisfaction of the condition as early as possible (or, where appropriate, an undertaking by both parties to co-operate in taking such steps);

(b)   a long-stop date by which the conditions have to be satisfied (or, possibly, waived by the party for whose benefit they were included) and, in default, provision for the agreement to terminate automatically without any liability attaching to either party; and

(c)   if the conditions are satisfied prior to the long-stop date, provision for completion to take place within a specified period of this happening.

The above provisions outline the basis on which the parties are bound to proceed if the conditions are fulfilled, and on which they will be released from the agreement if the conditions are not fulfilled within the required time.

7.2.2   Management restrictions

After exchange of a conditional sale and purchase agreement, the buyer is contractually committed to proceed with the acquisition but will not actually take control of the target business until completion occurs. The buyer runs the risk that the seller may neglect the business, knowing that the buyer must go ahead with the purchase. The buyer will therefore require undertakings from the seller about how the target company or business will be run in the period between signing the sale and purchase agreement and completion.

The buyer may insist that the seller supplies it with any information concerning the business and that it (or, in the case of a corporate buyer, an authorised representative) is allowed to attend all board meetings relating to the business or, on a share sale, the target company. The buyer may also seek undertakings from the seller in relation to the carrying on of the business, for example, that the seller will procure that the company does not do any of the following (unless the buyer gives prior consent):

(a) lend or borrow money except in relation to routine matters in the ordinary course of business, or grant any mortgage, charge or debenture over its assets;

(b) settle any claim or dispute;

(c) acquire or agree to acquire any property, commit itself to any capital expenditure, or enter into any hire-purchase or leasing arrangements;

(d) enter into any agreement, or dispose of all or part of its business or assets, except in relation to routine matters in the ordinary course of its business;

(e) alter the terms of employment of any employee or director;

(f) in the case of a share acquisition, appoint any additional directors of the target.

7.2.3 Repetition of warranties

A buyer often seeks to protect its position by requiring that the representations and warranties made in the sale and purchase agreement are repeated as at the date of completion.

A buyer in a strong bargaining position may seek to include this as an additional condition precedent, giving the buyer the right to withdraw from the purchase in the event that there is a breach. This provision should be strongly resisted by the seller; and if eventually accepted, the right should be limited to instances of material breach.

If the buyer is given a substantial degree of control over the target business in the period between signing and completion, the seller is unlikely also to agree to a right to withdraw for a breach of warranty (in particular where it may be argued that the breach arises as a result of the buyer's exercise of control).

Consideration should also be given to the effect of any disclosure against such repeated warranties. Generally, disclosure will negate liability under the warranties (see **6.3.1**). However, the buyer is at risk in relation to disclosures made between exchange of contracts and completion because, regardless of the breach disclosed, it is still bound to complete the purchase. To address this issue, the agreement usually provides an obligation to disclose which is subject to the buyer's right to claim damages or exercise any right to terminate for breaches occurring in the gap between exchange and completion.

7.2.4 Material adverse change

In addition to the repetition of warranties, a buyer in a strong negotiating position may also seek to include a right to terminate the agreement in the event of a material adverse change in the business, assets or profits of the target. This provision (known as a MAC clause) is intended to protect the buyer against the general risk of adverse events that may occur in the period between signing the agreement and completion of the acquisition. As with the repetition of warranties, it may be included as a further condition precedent. Such a condition should be strongly resisted by the seller on the basis that any general risk should pass to the buyer on the signing of the agreement. If the seller is forced to agree to such a term, it should limit the provision to specified events such as the loss of a particular customer.

7.3 Completing an acquisition

Successful completion of an acquisition requires a great deal of organisation and project management, usually co-ordinated by the solicitors of both the buyer and seller. The lawyers need to determine who should be present at the completion meeting, whether any authorisations are required, what documents must be produced and by whom. Much of this process is managed through the use of an agreed checklist known as the 'completion agenda'. The completion agenda sets out the steps and documentation required, and who is responsible for them at completion. It will be circulated and regularly updated to ensure that completion of the transaction runs as smoothly as possible.

If there is to be a delay between signing the sale and purchase agreement and completing the acquisition, the completion agenda will be an agreed document referred to in the sale and purchase agreement or set out in a schedule to it. Where exchange and completion are simultaneous, the completion agenda will also detail the documentation required to enter into the sale and purchase agreement. This will include the appropriate number of copies of the sale and purchase agreement and the disclosure letter, in the agreed form, together with any separate indemnities to be provided.

7.3.1 Preparing for completion

One of the first steps in organising a completion meeting is making sure that the appropriate personnel are available and that the correct authorities have been given to enable the execution of any required documentation.

If an individual is unable to attend the completion meeting in person, he may execute a power of attorney giving another person the power to sign the completion documents on his behalf. The terms of the power of attorney will usually be agreed between the parties, and will often be drafted in very broad terms to include a power to sign any additional documentation that may be required to effect completion.

7.3.1.1 Seller's preparations

If there is a corporate seller, a board meeting of the seller company should be held to approve the terms of the draft sale and purchase agreement, and to appoint an authorised signatory to execute it. The board may appoint a single director or a committee to attend to completion arrangements on behalf of the company. A certified copy of the minutes of this meeting must be given to the buyer on completion as evidence of the seller's representatives' authority to act (and sign documents) on its behalf. As a third party acting in good faith, the buyer will be able to rely on this certified copy of the board meeting minute as evidence of the corporate seller's authority. However, the parties' solicitors will nonetheless check the seller's articles of association together with any relevant banking security documentation to ensure that all appropriate steps have been taken to authorise the sale.

Approvals may also be required under company law – the legal advisers should confirm that the sale is in accordance with the directors' duties and, if the sale is to a director or person connected to a director of the target company or its holding company, approval of the shareholders (as substantial property transaction (CA 2006, s 190)) may be required.

On a share sale, the buyer will also require that a board meeting of the target company is held at completion in order to approve registration of the transfer of the shares (see **7.3.3**). The seller must ensure that the completion board meeting of the target company is quorate and that there is a sufficient majority present to pass the requisite resolutions. If provided for in the target's articles, any director of the target company who is unable to be present at this meeting may appoint an alternate director to attend and vote on his behalf.

7.3.1.2 Buyer's preparations

A corporate buyer must also hold a meeting to approve the terms of the draft sale and purchase agreement, and to authorise the signing and completion of it. The board may appoint a single director or a committee to attend to completion arrangements on behalf of the company. A certified copy of the minutes of this meeting will be handed to the seller on completion as evidence of the authority of the buyer's representatives to act (and sign documents) on its behalf.

If the consideration for the acquisition includes shares in the buyer company, shareholders' resolutions may be necessary to authorise the issue of those consideration shares. On the other hand, where the consideration is to be raised by borrowing, the buyer's solicitor must confirm that the requirements necessary for the provision of the finance have been complied with and that the funds will therefore be available at completion.

As a last-minute check before completion, the buyer usually repeats some of the searches made in the early, information-gathering stages of the transaction. In particular, it should repeat searches at the Companies Registry against a corporate seller, and bankruptcy searches against individual sellers. On a share acquisition, searches should also be made against the target company itself (and any of its subsidiaries). If intellectual property rights are an important aspect of the acquisition, the buyer is well-advised to repeat patent and trademark searches.

On a share purchase, the buyer may also wish to make an appointment with the seller to inspect the statutory books of the target company prior to completion.

7.3.2 Completion of asset acquisition

Although the general preparations and mechanics of the completion process are the same for all acquisitions, the assets being transferred do, of course, vary. On an asset purchase, all the assets of the business must be transferred individually as discussed below. The sale and purchase agreement will usually provide that such transfers take place simultaneously, so the seller's solicitor must make all necessary preparations to ensure that this happens.

7.3.2.1 Transferring title

The following formalities are required to transfer the legal interest in the assets of a business to the buyer:

(a)   conveyances, transfers or assignments of land and premises;

(b)   assignments of goodwill, certain intellectual property rights (including copyrights, patents and trade marks) and the benefit of contracts.

Stock and movable assets, such as loose plant and machinery, are transferable by delivery; it is sufficient if the sale and purchase agreement requires delivery to be given on completion.

7.3.2.2   Documents to be handed over at completion

As indicated above, the parties will agree a detailed completion agenda, setting out the responsibilities of the respective parties with regard to matters to be dealt with and documents to be handed over at completion.

The detail of the completion agenda will vary with the terms of each transaction, but in general, whilst the buyer will make the sale and purchase agreement available, the seller is usually required to hand over or make the following available to the buyer on completion of an asset acquisition:

(a)   where there is no delay between exchange and completion, the agreed form of disclosure letter;

(b)   documents transferring title to the assets (drafts should have been agreed by the parties prior to completion, and the agreed form may be annexed to the sale and purchase agreement);

(c)   deeds and documents of title to the assets, including freehold and leasehold properties (or confirmation of title from the bank if the properties remain subject to a charge);

(d)   duly executed releases of charges over the assets and confirmation of non-crystallisation of floating charges;

(e)   financial records and books of account, customer lists, computer programs, designs, drawings, plans, sales and promotional materials, National Insurance, PAYE and VAT records, employee records, and other documents required by the buyer to run the business. The seller is advised to reserve the right for a certain period after completion to inspect and take copies of the records, etc which are handed to the buyer, in case these are needed in relation to the seller's affairs (eg by the tax authorities);

(f)   originals, counterparts or certified copies as appropriate of licences to assign leasehold property, novation agreements and consents from third parties to assignment of contracts, etc;

(g)   a certified copy of a special resolution of the selling company resolving to change its name if it has been agreed that the buyer will acquire the right to use the seller's corporate name (see **5.10.2**);

(h)   where the seller is a company, a board resolution authorising a representative to sign the documentation.

The buyer will be required to pay the amount of the purchase price due on completion, usually by banker's draft or telegraphic transfer to the seller's bank account. A corporate buyer will also be required to produce a board resolution authorising a representative to sign the transaction documentation.

7.3.3   Completion of share acquisition

As with an asset acquisition, the parties will agree a completion agenda, setting out steps to be taken and documents to be provided to complete the acquisition. However, on a share acquisition only one asset, the shares, will be transferred, and the remaining documentation will deal with steps required to transfer control of the target company effectively.

7.3.3.1   Transferring shares

The following documents are required to transfer the legal interest in the shares:

(a)   stock transfer form; and

(b)   share certificate.

Although a duly executed stock transfer form will transfer the shares, the buyer is not entitled to exercise its shareholders' rights (including voting at general meeting) until the transfer is registered by the target company. The buyer will therefore require the seller to procure registration of the transferred shares, usually (in a private company) by procuring a board meeting of the target company to consider the transferred shares for registration. The existing shareholders may also be required to waive any rights of pre-emption on the transfer of shares that may exist under the constitution of the company.

7.3.3.2 Completion board meeting

As part of the completion process on a share acquisition, the seller will be required to procure a board meeting of the target company to implement any decisions that the buyer requires in order to take immediate control of the target. To ensure the meeting takes place in accordance with the buyer's wishes, the minutes of this required meeting will be prepared in advance by the buyer's solicitors and circulated for approval.

The matters to be covered in a completion board meeting of the target company will depend on the extent to which the buyer wishes to make immediate changes to the way the target company is run.

The matters a buyer will usually require to be dealt with at a completion board meeting of the target are set out below:

(a) approval of the transfer of shares (subject to payment of stamp duty);

(b) appointment of new directors and company secretary (including obtaining consents to act, any required disclosure of interests, and approval and authorisation of service contracts);

(c) acceptance of resignations of directors and company secretary (including agreeing any severance payments);

(d) acceptance of the resignation of the company's auditors and appointment of new auditors;

(e) change of accounting reference date;

(f) change of registered office;

(g) alteration of existing bank mandates and the completion of new finance arrangements.

If the target company also has subsidiaries, the buyer will usually require each subsidiary company to hold a board meeting implementing any required changes to personnel, finance arrangements and administrative matters.

7.3.3.3 Completion general meeting

The buyer may also require a completion shareholders' meeting to grant any necessary approvals or make any required changes to the constitution of the company.

Matters that may require shareholder approval include:

(a) giving consent to a substantial property transaction under s190 of the CA 200, if the sale of the shares is to a director or a person connected to a director of the target company or its holding company;

(b) consenting to a term in a director's service contract whereby the employment is for a term in excess of two years (CA 2006, s 188);

(c)   altering the articles of association of the target company. A corporate buyer may, for example, want to amend the articles so that they are suitable for a wholly-owned subsidiary, or so that they conform with those of other companies within its group.

In practice, changes or approvals to be effected by the shareholders will usually be dealt with by written resolution presented at the completion board meeting of the target company. The buyer does not become a member of the target company until its name is entered into the register of members (CA 2006, s 112). As registration cannot take place until the stock transfer form has been properly stamped, the buyer will not be able to exercise its voting rights until after completion of the acquisition. Consequently, the written resolution (drafted by the buyer's solicitor) must be passed by the sellers as the registered holders of the shares.

7.3.3.4   Documents to be handed over at completion

As with an asset acquisition, the parties will agree a detailed completion agenda, setting out the responsibilities of the respective parties with regard to matters to be dealt with and documents to be provided at completion.

Although the detail of the completion agenda will, again, vary from transaction to transaction, whilst the buyer will take responsibility for producing the final form sale and purchase agreement, the seller is usually required to hand over the following documents or procure the following events on completion of a share acquisition:

(a)   where there is no delay between exchange and completion, the agreed form of disclosure letter;

(b)   if the seller is a company, a board resolution authorising its representative to sign the documentation;

(c)   a stock transfer form duly executed and delivered by each seller together with the relative share certificates;

(d)   a completion board meeting of the target company to implement any specified board decisions (see **7.3.3.2**);

(e)   any written resolutions that may be required, duly executed by the sellers as the registered holders of the shares (see **7.3.3.3**);

(f)   the discharge of outstanding loans made by the seller(s) to the company or vice versa (existing banking arrangements may also be replaced with the buyer's arrangements);

(g)   the delivery by the seller's solicitor of the statutory books of the target company, the title deeds to its properties (or confirmation of title from the bank for properties remaining subject to a charge), any certificates of title given by the seller's solicitor, documents of title relating to other assets, financial records, agreements to which the target is a party and insurance policies.

The buyer will be required to pay the amount of the purchase price due on completion, usually by banker's draft or telegraphic transfer to the seller's bank account. A corporate buyer will also be required to produce a board resolution authorising a representative to sign the transaction documentation.

7.4 Post-completion matters

After completion of the acquisition there are still a number of tasks to be undertaken by the solicitors for both the buyer and the seller.

7.4.1 Stamp duty and filing

On a share purchase, the buyer's solicitor must ensure that the duly executed stock transfer forms are delivered to the HMRC Stamp Office within 30 days together with the requisite transfer duty. In practice this is usually undertaken immediately, as the buyer will want to be entered in the register of members as soon as possible and this can only be done after any stamp duty has been paid.

In addition, on a share purchase the buyer's solicitor must also file the following at the Companies Registry in relation to the target company and any of its subsidiaries:

(a)   forms notifying any change of registered office (CA 2006, s 87), changes of directors and secretary, and change of accounting reference period;

(b)   a copy of the letter of resignation of the auditors (CA 2006, s 517);

(c)   a copy of any special resolution of the company;

(d)   a print of any new articles of association of the company.

Where a company has issued shares as consideration, the buyer's solicitor may also need to file the following:

(a)   a copy of a special resolution suspending any applicable pre-emption rights;

(b)   a return of allotments (CA 2006, s 555) and a copy of the sale and purchase agreement.

In addition, the buyer's solicitor should complete the statutory books of the target company, including the registers of members (after the stock transfer forms have been stamped), directors and secretary, and minutes.

7.4.2 Matters outstanding on completion

There are often matters that may have been left outstanding on completion of a transaction. The parties may have agreed that part of the purchase price will be determined by accounts prepared after completion, or a particular release or transfer may have been left outstanding. The parties will have agreed timetables for dealing with these additional matters and will often have indemnities in place in relation to any costs that may be incurred. The buyer will also take practical steps after completion to implement any changes required to incorporate the target into its existing business, such as informing customers and suppliers of the acquisition.

7.4.3 'Bibles'

The parties' solicitors will often compile so-called 'bibles' after completion, containing copies of the complete set of documents used in the acquisition, which can be used as a source of reference should any problems crop up in the future (eg in relation to warranties).

Part III
VARIATIONS

Chapter 8

Asset Acquisitions

8.1 Agreeing what to transfer

The fundamental nature of an asset acquisition is that the buyer agrees to purchase a collection of assets, the make-up of that collection being dependent upon the negotiations between the buyer and seller, and on their respective commercial objectives. In this book, an asset acquisition is considered where the buyer's objective is to continue to run the target business after its acquisition, either as a stand-alone business or by incorporation of the acquired assets into the buyer's existing business operations. To achieve this objective, the buyer must ensure that it will acquire all the necessary assets, and that crucial trading arrangements will remain in place after completion of the purchase.

The terms of the acquisition will be set out in the sale and purchase agreement, with further detail in the schedules to that agreement (see **4.4**) of the assets and liabilities (if any) that are to be included in the sale. Although ideally the parties should try to specify exactly which assets are to transfer, it is not always possible to identify every asset separately, so sometimes the buyer will seek to include more general provisions to encompass all assets used in the target business. It is therefore usual to include a definition of the 'business' of the target, together with provisions dealing with the transfer of goodwill (see **8.2.8**).

In addition to detailing the assets and liabilities included in the sale, the parties will often include a list of assets which are specifically excluded. For example, the seller may wish to retain certain assets for which it will continue to have use after completion, and some assets may simply be surplus to the buyer's requirements. Further, there is usually little point in including cash in hand or on deposit in the sale, since this would just involve the buyer paying an equivalent sum as part of the purchase price, and debtors and creditors are also commonly left with the seller (see **8.2.7**).

The sale and purchase agreement should also address the issue of the timing of the completion of the acquisition, and will usually specify that the transfer of all the required assets will take place simultaneously at completion. However, sometimes a formal transfer of an asset is not possible at completion, for example if consent to the transfer is required. In these circumstances, the sale and purchase agreement will usually provide that the buyer will hold the asset on trust pending the formal transfer, so effectively enabling the entire operation of the target business to transfer at a given moment in time. In larger transactions, where it may be important to ascertain the exact moment that the business operation transfers from the seller to the buyer, the sale and purchase agreement will specify an 'effective time' (usually close of trade on the day of completion of the acquisition). Any trade undertaken or costs incurred by the seller prior to the effective time will be allocated to the seller, and trade undertaken or costs incurred after this time will be apportioned to the buyer (see **8.2**).

8.2 Transfer of assets

In this section, consideration is given to the particular factors relevant on the transfer of each type of asset, including the nature of the warranties generally sought by the buyer (see **Chapter 5**).

8.2.1 Land and premises

8.2.1.1 General considerations

Any freehold and leasehold premises which are to be transferred will normally be listed in a schedule to the sale and purchase agreement. The buyer will assume risk on the premises as from exchange of the agreement and should take out insurance from this date, or, in the case of leasehold property where the lease obliges the landlord to insure, have its interest noted on the landlord's policy. On completion of the acquisition, suitable conveyancing arrangements will be put in place for the formal transfer of the premises to the buyer.

8.2.1.2 Licence to assign

Requesting consent

Where the terms of a lease require the consent of the landlord to assignment, there is often considerable delay in obtaining a formal licence to assign. The seller should therefore request consent from the landlord as early as possible, in the hope that the licence will be available in good time for exchange of contracts. The buyer is also advised to give the seller details of referees so that these can be passed on to the landlord immediately (the provision and taking up of references is commonly a chief cause of delay).

The seller, as the existing tenant, does have some redress if the landlord acts unreasonably. Section 19 of the Landlord and Tenant Act 1927 provides that, where the lease contains a covenant not to assign without the landlord's consent (such qualified covenants against assignment are standard in commercial leases), the landlord cannot unreasonably withhold its consent. The landlord is also under a duty to give its decision within a reasonable time and to give reasons for a refusal (Landlord and Tenant Act 1988, which entitles tenants to damages if the landlord unreasonably refuses or delays the granting of a licence to assign).

For leases granted on or after 1 January 1996, landlords are able to exercise greater control by stipulating in the lease any conditions which they will require the tenant to fulfil in order to assign the lease, or any circumstances in which a refusal of consent to assign will be deemed to be reasonable.

Guarantees

A landlord will often require that obligations under the lease are guaranteed by third party guarantors. The landlord will not normally be willing to grant a licence to assign and to release guarantors of the seller's obligations under the lease unless he is provided with equivalent guarantees of the buyer's obligations (eg from the directors of a corporate buyer). Indeed, the lease may stipulate that the landlord is not obliged to consent to the assignment unless this is done.

Conditional contract

If the licence to assign is not ready by the time the parties are in a position to sign the acquisition agreement, they may decide to make the agreement conditional on the consent of the landlord to the assignment and incorporate a right for the parties to rescind if this is not obtained within a specified time limit (conditional contracts are discussed further in **Chapter 7**).

Costs of licence

The terms of the licence to assign will oblige the tenant to pay the costs of the landlord's solicitor in dealing with the matter. It is rare for the seller in an asset sale of a business to pass this cost to the buyer (although it is common practice for the assignee to bear these costs on the assignment of a lease by itself).

Warranties

The buyer will seek to include warranties covering the state of the premises to be acquired and any relevant environmental matters (see **3.5.6** and **3.5.7**).

8.2.2 Plant and machinery

8.2.2.1 General considerations

A schedule of the items of plant and machinery (including vehicles) which are part of the sale should be attached to the sale and purchase agreement. A buyer who wishes to purchase all of these assets of the business may seek to safeguard itself by providing that plant and machinery 'used in the business' are to be transferred, including those items listed in the schedule. Thus items omitted from the schedule by mistake (it may be difficult for the buyer to check the accuracy of the schedule) will, nevertheless, be included in the sale. No particular formalities are required for the transfer of plant and machinery which will pass on delivery at completion.

8.2.2.2 Warranties

The buyer will often seek to include the following warranties as to the state of the items of plant and machinery listed in the schedule:

(a)   they are in a proper state of repair and condition and in satisfactory working order;

(b)   they are not dangerous, obsolete or in need of replacement;

(c)   they have been properly and regularly maintained;

(d)   they are adequate for (and not surplus to) the needs of the business.

The seller should think twice before accepting these warranties and consider trying to restrict any liability to major defects. Also, in relation to (d), as it will have no control over how the buyer carries on the business after completion, it may wish to add the words 'as carried on by the seller prior to the agreement'.

8.2.3 Intellectual property

Ideally, all trademarks, service marks, registered designs, copyrights and patents which are to be included in the transfer should be listed in a schedule or an appendix to the sale and purchase agreement. Appropriate assignments of any licences and other intellectual property rights will be required to transfer title at completion.

The buyer may seek warranties in relation to the following matters:

(a)   that the seller is the beneficial owner or registered proprietor of the intellectual property rights (as defined in the interpretation clause);

(b)   that to the best of the seller's knowledge and belief those rights are valid and enforceable;

(c)   that the seller has not granted any person a right to do anything which would otherwise be an infringement of those rights;

(d)   that no licences for the use of intellectual property have been granted to the seller or are required to run the business;

(e)   that the operation of the business does not infringe the intellectual property rights of any other person.

The buyer may also insist on a warranty that the seller has not disclosed trade secrets, know-how or confidential information (eg customer price lists) except in the normal course of business.

8.2.4   Leasing, hire-purchase and other finance contracts

Equipment employed by the seller in the business which is subject to hire-purchase, contract hire or leasing arrangements does not belong to the seller and cannot, therefore, be included in the transfer without the consent of the true owner. The owner may be prepared to consent to the assignment or novation of the agreement to the buyer, or may prefer to enter into a fresh agreement with it.

If these arrangements are not in place at completion the buyer may nonetheless be able to use the equipment from the completion date on the basis that it undertakes to discharge obligations under the contract (including payments due) on behalf of the seller until novation, or until a fresh agreement is entered into between the buyer and the third party .

8.2.5   Stock and work in progress

Stock will usually be defined as including raw materials, work in progress and finished goods. Since it is impossible to determine the level of completion stock in advance, it is unusual for the parties to agree a value for the stock prior to completion. They will often provide in the agreement for the stock to be valued at or shortly after completion, and for the price of the stock to be left outstanding until they have agreed the valuation.

Stock and work in progress will often be a significant element in the overall consideration for the target business, and the agreement should therefore specify who is to carry out the valuation, the basis on which the stock is to be valued, and the procedure to be followed if the parties dispute the valuation.

The parties may agree to carry out a joint stock-take, with the actual valuation to be prepared by the seller, or may provide for specified professional valuers to undertake the valuation.

The agreement may provide for the stock to be valued on the same basis as in the audited accounts (eg this will often be on the basis of the lower of cost or net realisable value); on some other general basis, such as market value; or in accordance with a detailed formula which, for example, takes account of slow-moving or obsolete stock.

Where the seller prepares the valuation, provision will usually be made for any dispute to be referred to an independent expert. The buyer may be obliged to pay a percentage of the valuation (eg 50%) immediately, with any balance payable within a specified time limit of its final determination – this should avoid the procedure being employed by the buyer simply as a method of delaying payment.

The buyer may wish to set a limit on the amount of stock it is obliged to purchase on completion and, in order to guard against the seller reducing stock to a level which will make it difficult for the buyer to meet orders, may also stipulate a minimum amount of stock. The buyer may also seek warranties that the stocks are of satisfactory quality and that none of the items is obsolete or unmarketable.

8.2.6   Contracts

8.2.6.1   Passing the benefit and burden

The buyer should ensure that it receives the benefit of all contracts entered into between the seller and third parties which are important to enable the business to continue trading after completion of the acquisition, such as agency or distribution agreements, contracts with suppliers or customers, and licensing agreements. One way to achieve this is to assign the benefit of the contract; if legal assignment is required, notice must be given to the other contracting party under s 136 of the Law of Property Act 1925. The buyer should, however, check whether or not the terms of the contract prohibit assignment or require the consent of the other party. It is important to remember that this method will transfer only the benefit of the contract and that the seller will still be liable to the third party to fulfil any outstanding obligations. For example, in an exclusive distribution agreement, if the seller is the distributor, the benefit under the agreement is the receipt of goods for resale in a given territory; the burden is payment for the goods. The right to receive the goods can be legally assigned by giving notice under s 136 of the Law of Property Act 1925 (unless the contract says consent is required), but the obligation to pay for the goods remains with the seller.

To get around this, the existing contract may be novated. This involves the other party to the contract agreeing to release the seller from the contract, allowing the buyer to take over the benefit and burden of the contract. Alternatively, the other contracting party may agree to enter into a fresh agreement with the buyer. This gives the buyer scope to negotiate new terms and conditions if the existing ones are commercially unacceptable in their present form.

As the co-operation of the other party to a contract is usually required, it is a time-consuming process to put all the necessary arrangements in place, and this may not coincide with the timetable the parties have agreed for the acquisition.

8.2.6.2   What if consents, etc are delayed?

Routine contracts

With some agreements (eg small or routine contracts) the parties will often be happy to proceed to completion without having obtained the required consents. They may agree between themselves that the buyer will take over the contracts on completion and that each will use its best endeavours to obtain the consents of third parties to assign or novate existing contracts or to enter into new contracts. The seller will, of course, remain liable on such contracts unless and until specifically released by the third parties. The buyer will therefore normally undertake to perform the contracts on behalf of the seller and to indemnify the seller against any liability arising under them.

Fundamental contracts

In relation to contracts which the buyer considers fundamental to the business, ideally the buyer should defer entering into the sale and purchase agreement until all necessary consents have been obtained. Alternatively, the parties may agree to the agreement being made conditional on the assignment or novation of specified contracts. The buyer should, in these circumstances, seek an undertaking from the seller not to vary the terms of the contracts during the period between exchange and completion without its consent.

8.2.6.3   Warranties on contracts

In relation to the contracts which it is taking over, the buyer may require the following warranties:

(a)   that none of the contracts is of an unusual or onerous nature, or was entered into otherwise than in the ordinary course of business;

(c)   that the seller is not in breach of any of the terms of the contracts and has not waived any rights under the contracts;

(c)   that no event has occurred which entitles the other party to the contract to terminate or rescind the contract;

(d)   that the seller has not sold or manufactured products which, in any material respect, are defective or do not comply with warranties or representations made by the seller.

8.2.7   Debtors and creditors

Sums owed to the seller by third parties (debtors) are an asset of the business; sums owed by the seller to third parties (creditors) are a liability of the business. There are a number of ways in which trade debtors and creditors can be dealt with in the agreement.

8.2.7.1   Transfer to buyer

The debtors and creditors may be transferred to the buyer. In this case, full details should be included in a schedule or an appendix to the sale and purchase agreement. In order for the assignment of debts to be a legal assignment (as opposed to an equitable one), s 136 of the Law of Property Act 1925 requires, inter alia, written notice of the assignment to be given to each debtor. The seller will remain liable to its creditors after completion, however, unless they agree to release it. Accordingly, where the parties have agreed to transfer the creditors, the seller should seek an indemnity from the buyer against such liability.

There are, nevertheless, several drawbacks to transferring debtors and creditors to the buyer. Apart from the complication of defining accurately the debts and liabilities involved, and of giving notice to all debtors, there is the difficulty of valuing the book debts. If these are transferred at their face value, the buyer will not only suffer a cash flow disadvantage but will also bear the risk of some of the debts proving irrecoverable. The amount of any discount on book value to reflect these uncertainties is likely to be the subject of much negotiation between the parties. Alternatively, the seller may be prepared to warrant that the debts are fully recoverable. The buyer should, however, be wary of any *de minimis* limit which applies to the warranties generally (see **6.2.1.2**).

8.2.7.2   Retention by seller

It is common for debtors and creditors to remain with the seller, although this can also give rise to a number of difficulties. The buyer will, for example, be keen to preserve the goodwill of the on-going business by maintaining good relations with suppliers and creditors of the business, and will, therefore, wish to ensure that the seller pays off its creditors promptly and is not too exuberant in chasing its debtors. The buyer may therefore insist on a retention from the purchase price which is to be released only once the creditors have been paid. It should also consider extracting an undertaking from the seller not to issue proceedings to recover debts for a specified period after completion, and to give the buyer the option to buy the debts from the seller at the end of this period (at least in relation to those debtors who continue to be customers of the business after the change in ownership).

A difficulty of this arrangement from the seller's point of view is that it may no longer have the means to collect the debts after completion, particularly where those employees responsible for debt collection have been transferred to the buyer. A solution to this problem, which often suits both parties, is for the buyer to agree to collect the debts as agent for the seller. The buyer will often be happy to assume this responsibility (usually on payment of a collection fee) as there will be less danger of the goodwill of the business being damaged if the process of collection of debts is undertaken by the buyer. The buyer will usually be required to use its best endeavours to collect the debts but without being obliged to commence legal proceedings. As an incentive to the buyer, the collection fee may be based on a percentage of debts successfully recovered.

A complication which arises where debtors continue to deal with the business after its change in ownership is the application of sums received by the buyer after completion. For example, should such sums received reduce the debtor's original liability to the seller, or any liability of the debtor to the buyer incurred since completion? The sale and purchase agreement should specify the order in which the buyer should apply sums which it receives in these circumstances.

8.2.7.3   Who takes responsibility for on-going service and repair obligations?

Depending on the type of business, the seller may have entered into commitments to customers to provide an after-sales service in relation to products or services supplied prior to completion. It is in the interests of the buyer that these obligations are met in full, since a failure to do so may have a detrimental effect on goodwill and may reflect badly on the buyer. However, once it has disposed of the assets of the business, the seller is unlikely to be in a position to carry out repairs or provide an after-sales service. A solution to this problem is for the buyer to agree to perform the seller's obligations and to be reimbursed the cost of doing so by the seller (the buyer may also be able to negotiate a mark-up on the direct costs which it incurs).

8.2.7.4   Apportionment of outgoings and payments

The seller will have incurred various liabilities to, for example, utility companies for the use of gas, electricity, telephones, etc which have not been billed at the date of completion. Similarly, the seller may have made payments in advance which relate to periods after completion, for example rental payments or payments due under continuing contracts. Whichever method the parties choose to deal with the creditors and debtors, it will be necessary to apportion the outgoings and payments to the date of completion (or such other date agreed upon by the parties). The seller will usually be responsible for making the apportionments and providing full details with supporting documentation. As with the valuation of stock, the agreement may incorporate a system for resolving disputes between the parties. In any event, it is normally impractical for the apportionments to be made and agreed by completion, and consequently provision is usually made for the buyer to draw up a completion statement after completion and for adjustments to be made to the consideration when the parties have agreed the statement.

8.2.8   Goodwill, name and restrictions on the seller

8.2.8.1   Goodwill

Goodwill is an intangible asset of the business which is as difficult to define as it is to value. Where a business is sold as a going concern, a value is usually placed on the good name and reputation of the business and the likelihood that customers and suppliers will continue to deal with it in the future. In other words, the value of goodwill reflects the fact that the business is 'up and running', has traded successfully in the past and should continue to do so in the future.

A crude method of valuing goodwill is to apply a multiplier (usually between one and three) to the net profits of the business. In the case of a partnership, the net profit figure before any salaries or interest on capital payable to partners are deducted should be used for the calculation, as these items are merely allocations of the profit. However, the amount attributable to goodwill is extremely variable and, to a large extent, depends on the buyer's assessment of the potential of the business; the buyer may, for example, be prepared to pay a sum for the business which is well above its net asset value because it feels that it will fit in well with its existing businesses. Also, goodwill tends to be more of a factor in 'employee-orientated' businesses, ie those that rely on the flair and imagination of the employees, than in 'asset-orientated' businesses, such as property investment businesses, for example.

The buyer may try to negotiate the inclusion of a warranty that the seller is not aware of any matter arising since the date of the latest accounts which might adversely affect the trading prospects of the business and that the seller has not done anything (or omitted to do anything) which might adversely affect goodwill (see **8.2.8.3**).

8.2.8.2   Name

The goodwill to be acquired by the buyer will usually be defined to include the exclusive right of the buyer (or any assignee) to represent itself as carrying on the business in succession to the seller and to use the name of the business and all trade names associated with it. The seller will normally be required to undertake that it will not use the name, or any other name intended or likely to be confused with it, or hold itself out as being connected with the business, at any time after completion. The seller may even agree to covenant that it will endeavour to ensure that the buyer obtains full benefit of the goodwill and that customers, etc deal with the buyer instead of the seller.

On the acquisition from a company of its entire business, the agreement should provide that the seller changes its registered name to one that is acceptable to the buyer and does not suggest any connection with the business as transferred through the asset acquisition. As part of the completion arrangements, the buyer may require the seller to hand over the special resolution changing the name (and appropriate fee) and agree with the seller to file this at the Companies Registry.

8.2.8.3   Warranties on goodwill

A buyer acquiring the goodwill of the business has a legitimate interest in the way that the seller has conducted the business prior to completion. It will therefore require warranties from the seller that it has not conducted the business in any way that would damage its reputation or diminish the value of the goodwill (see **8.2.9.3**).

8.2.8.4   Restrictive covenants

The buyer will seek to protect the goodwill of the business by restricting the activities of the seller after completion, thereby preventing it from damaging goodwill. The seller will be prevented from competing with the business, soliciting customers, suppliers and employees of the business, and disclosing confidential information. The nature, extent and validity of such restrictions on the seller are dealt with in **5.10**.

8.2.9   General warranties

In addition to specific warranties about the assets to be acquired, the buyer will also require some general warranties about the assets and, where the goodwill of the business is also being acquired, about the conduct of the business prior to completion.

8.2.9.1   Ownership of assets

The buyer will seek warranties that the seller owns the assets absolutely; that they are not subject to any charge, encumbrances, lien, option or retention of title provision; and that the seller has not agreed to dispose of them or grant security or any other encumbrance in respect of them.

8.2.9.2   Condition and adequacy

As mentioned above, whether the seller should give warranties as to the condition of, for example, fixed assets and stock, and as to the adequacy of the assets for the requirements of the business, will usually be a matter of much negotiation between the parties.

8.2.9.3   Trading and conduct of the business

The buyer will seek the following warranties:

(a)   that the business has been carried on in the ordinary course since the date of the last accounts, and that its turnover, financial or trading position has not deteriorated;

(b)   that the seller has obtained all licences and consents required to carry on the business properly and is not in breach of their terms;

(c)   that the seller is not aware of any suppliers or customers who will cease to deal with the business (or substantially alter their trading relationship with it) after completion;

(d)   that the seller has not been a party to any agreement, practice or arrangement relating to the business which contravenes, for example, the Trade Descriptions Acts 1968 and 1972, the Competition Act 1998, the Consumer Credit Act 1974, or the European Community Treaty 1957;

(e)   that the seller is not a party to any litigation proceedings in relation to the business and no such proceedings are pending, threatened or, to the seller's knowledge, likely to arise.

8.2.9.4   Accounts

The buyer may have used the accounts as a basis for agreeing a valuation of the target business, in which case it will normally seek a warranty that the latest accounts (including, possibly, management accounts) give a true and fair view of the financial position of the business and are not affected by extraordinary or non-recurring items. The buyer will also wish to ensure that the financial books and records which the seller is obliged to deliver to the buyer on completion are complete and accurate in all material respects.

8.3   Protection of employees

The parties must consider the impact of an asset acquisition on the employees working in the target business. How does the transfer affect their contracts of employment? Can the buyer choose not to take on employees who are surplus to its requirements? What are the implications if the buyer wishes to integrate the terms and conditions of the target's employees with those of its existing workforce? What claims can employees bring against the seller or buyer if they are dismissed before or after the transfer? Can the employees object to working for the buyer? The buyer will often have a clear idea of which employees it wishes to retain and how it intends to integrate them with its current workforce. However, the employment consequences of the transfer do not always coincide with the expectations of the parties; this is an area which may impact significantly on the purchase price.

The main obligations which an employer owes to its employees are dealt with in *Business Law and Practice*, including the duty imposed by s 1 of the Employment Rights Act 1996 (ERA 1996) to provide a written statement of the terms of employment, and the requirements for contractual claims for wrongful dismissal as well as employees' statutory protection with regard to unfair dismissal, redundancy and discrimination claims. In relation to an acquisition, the parties will generally seek the advice of employment law specialists. On a share acquisition, the buyer, in acquiring ownership of the target company, will indirectly acquire the target's liabilities to its employees, though the employer remains the same (ie the target company itself). On an asset acquisition, the parties must consider the impact of the Transfer of Undertakings (Protection of Employment) Regulations 2006 (SI 2006/246) (TUPE 2006).

8.3.1   TUPE 2006 (implementing the Acquired Rights Directive)

At common law the transfer of an undertaking from one employer to another automatically terminates the contracts of employment, which cannot be assigned as they are personal to the employer and employee. There is therefore a dismissal of the employees, and the seller of the undertaking may consequently be liable to the employees for contractual or statutory claims arising from that termination. In this situation, the reason for the dismissals would generally be redundancy (as the employer's requirement for employees to do work of a particular kind has ceased or diminished). However, the dismissed employees may also have claims for wrongful dismissal (if the correct notice was not given) and unfair dismissal by reason of redundancy (if the correct procedure was not followed or the employer acted unfairly) (see *Business Law and Practice*). If the buyer of the undertaking requires the employees' services, it may offer new contracts of employment on its own terms. However, the position is quite different where there is a 'relevant transfer' under TUPE 2006 (see **8.3.1.1**). In that situation, the employees' contracts will automatically transfer with the undertaking and continue as if originally made between the employees and the buyer. The transfer does not terminate the employees' contracts of employment and does not, therefore, operate as a 'dismissal'. In fact, TUPE 2006 also provide protection for employees who are dismissed, whether actually or constructively, before or after the transfer, if those dismissals are by reason of the transfer or a reason connected with it (see **8.3.1.5**).

The 2006 Regulations came into force for transfers taking place on or after 6 April 2006, replacing the Transfer of Undertakings (Protection of Employment) Regulations 1981 (SI 1981/1794) (TUPE 1981). Both sets of regulations were introduced to comply with EC Acquired Rights Directives and are intended to protect the rights of employees where an undertaking is transferred from one employer to another. The new legislation confirms and clarifies much of the old law, whilst also consolidating some of the existing case law in the area. Case law under the old Regulations will still be relevant in many circumstances.

8.3.1.1 A relevant transfer – reg 3

The TUPE 2006 will apply only to a 'relevant transfer', which under reg 3(1) is

> a transfer of an undertaking, business or part of an undertaking or business situated immediately before the transfer in the United Kingdom to another person where there is a transfer of an economic entity which retains its identity.

An 'economic entity' is defined in reg 3(2) as 'an organised grouping of resources which has the objective of pursuing an economic activity, whether or not that activity is central or ancillary'. This provision effectively incorporates relevant case law on the definition of a transfer of an undertaking which developed since the implementation of TUPE 1981. The two key cases in the area are *Spijkers v Gebroeders Benedik Abattoir CV* [1986] ECR 1119 and *Dr Sophie Redmond Stichting v Bartol* [1992] IRLR 366.

In ascertaining whether there has been a relevant transfer, it is necessary to determine whether what has been transferred is an economic entity which is still in existence, and this will be apparent from the fact that its operation, with the same economic or similar activities, is being continued or has been taken over by the new employer. Clearly, a transaction involving the break-up of a business, with various assets sold to different buyers and no one buyer able to continue the business in its original form, will not constitute a relevant transfer for TUPE 2006 purposes.

As well as being the transfer of an 'economic entity', to come within the definition in reg 3(1) the transfer must be from one person to another. This can include a transfer between two companies in the same corporate group. Subsidiaries within a group of companies are all separate legal entities, so when employees are moved from one company to another within the same group, TUPE 2006 apply in so far as there is a transfer of an economic entity which retains its identity (per the ECJ in Case C-234/98 *Allen v Amalgamated Construction Co Ltd* [2000] IRLR 19). This means that TUPE 2006 also apply on any hive-down of assets to a subsidiary company in preparation for an onward share sale (see **1.4.2**) (although TUPE 2006 do not apply where a buyer acquires a majority shareholding in a company, since there is no change in the identity of the employer (see *Brookes v Borough Care Services and CLS Care Services Ltd* [1998] IRLR 636)).

In addition to the main description of a 'relevant transfer', reg 3(1)(b) contains a second definition which makes it clear that TUPE 2006 also apply to a 'service provision change', that is, where there is a change of service provider, eg in a situation where services, such as cleaning, catering or maintenance, are contracted out. The 2006 Regulations will apply to a service provision change if reg 3(3) applies, that is:

(a)   immediately before the service provision change:

    (i)   there is an organised grouping of employees situated in Great Britain which has as its principal purpose the carrying out of the activities concerned on behalf of the client;

    (ii)   the client intends that the activities will, following the service provision change, be carried out by the transferee other than in connection with a single specific event or task of short-term duration; and

(b)   the activities concerned do not consist wholly or mainly of the supply of goods for the client's use.

Therefore, TUPE 2006 will clearly apply to most situations involving the contracting out of services, save where the service is for a single event, is of short-term duration, or concerns the supply of goods.

The parties cannot agree to exclude the operation of TUPE 2006 (reg 18). Whether a transfer is a 'relevant transfer' is a question of fact. The court or tribunal will look behind the label which the parties put on the transfer and will instead examine the substance of the transaction.

If it is not a relevant transfer, any rights which the employees have (eg to claim wrongful dismissal, redundancy, or unfair dismissal) must be enforced against the seller. If the seller is insolvent, certain claims, such as redundancy and the basic award for unfair dismissal, will be met by the Secretary of State for Employment (ERA 1996, s 182). However, the employees will be unable to recover the compensatory award for unfair dismissal in these circumstances. It should be noted that TUPE 2006 include provisions governing the transfer by an insolvent transferor (regs 8 and 9) which are beyond the scope of this book.

8.3.1.2   Effect of a relevant transfer – reg 4

It is necessary to consider the effect of a relevant transfer on the employment relationship.

Automatic transfer of contracts of employment

Regulation 4(1) protects the employees' employment in the event of a transfer, and reg 4(2) confirms that all the transferor's rights, powers and duties under the contracts of employment transfer to the transferee.

Regulation 4(1) provides that

> ... a relevant transfer shall not operate so as to terminate the contract of employment of any person employed by the transferor and assigned to the organised grouping of resources or employees that is subject to the relevant transfer, which would otherwise be terminated by the transfer, but any such contract shall have effect after the transfer as if originally made between the person so employed and the transferee.

In other words, an employee's contract of employment is not brought to an end by reason of the transfer but instead transfers from the old employer to the new.

Employees do have the right, however, to object to the transfer of their contracts in this way (see **8.3.1.3**).

Regulation 4(2) states that, on the completion of a relevant transfer:

(a)   all the transferor's rights, powers, duties and liabilities under or in connection with any such contract shall be transferred by virtue of this regulation to the transferee; and

(b)   any act or omission before the transfer is completed, of or in relation to the transferor in respect of that contract or a person assigned to that organised grouping of resources or employees, shall be deemed to have been an act or omission of or in relation to the transferee.

Therefore, the employees have the same rights against the transferee as they had against the transferor, and their continuity of employment is not affected by the transfer.

8.3.1.3   Who is covered by reg 4(1)?

Regulation 4(3) states that any reference

> ... to a person employed by the transferor and assigned to the organised grouping of resources or employees that is subject to a relevant transfer, is a reference to a person so employed immediately before the transfer, or who would have been so employed if he had not been dismissed in the circumstances described in regulation 7(1), including, where the transfer is effected by a series of two or more transactions, a person so employed and assigned or who would have been so employed or assigned immediately before any of those transactions.

Regulation 4(3) clearly applies to all employees employed by the transferor immediately before the transfer. Where there is a gap between exchange of contracts and completion, it is the date of completion which is the date of transfer for the purposes of reg 4.

However, reg 4(3) also applies to employees who would have been so employed had they not been unfairly dismissed in the circumstances described in reg 7(1) (see **8.3.1.4**). Regulation 7(1) provides that the dismissal is automatically unfair where the dismissal was by reason of the transfer or for a reason connected with the transfer, unless the employer can show that the dismissal was for an economic, technical or organisational reason ('ETO reason') entailing a change in the workforce. This statutory provision encapsulates the House of Lords' judgment in *Secretary of State for Employment v Litster* [1989] IRLR 161, in which the employees were dismissed one hour before the transfer. The House of Lords made it clear that a transferee may still be liable for a pre-transfer dismissal, and reg 4(3) preserves this rule. This means that a transferee cannot circumvent TUPE 2006 by insisting that the transferor dismisses employees prior to completion.

Regulation 4 therefore applies to two groups of employees:

(a)   to those employees actually employed by the transferor at the time of the transfer. Their contracts of employment transfer to the transferee and they will work for the transferee under the terms of those contracts; and

(b)   to those employees who were dismissed by reason of the transfer or for a reason connected with the transfer where no ETO reason exists. Any rights they may have had with regard to unfair or wrongful dismissal, together with any claim for a redundancy payment, will transfer to the transferee.

Employees whose contracts would 'otherwise be terminated by the transfer'

Those employees whose contracts would not be terminated by the transfer do not come within reg 4. This may, for example, apply to an employee who is retained by the transferor and redeployed in some other part of its operation within the terms of the employee's contract or with his consent. Such redeployment should take place before the transfer.

Where part of a business is transferred, employees will not be affected by reg 4 if they did not work in the part transferred. Even employees who perform duties in relation to the part transferred (eg administrative duties performed by a retained department) will not be covered unless they are assigned to the part transferred.

The question of whether an employee is assigned to the relevant part is a question of fact. Regard should be had to the test laid down in Case 186/83 *Botzen v Rotterdamsche Droogdok Maatschappij BV* [1986] 2 CMLR 50, ECJ. In summary, the test is whether there is a transfer of the part of the undertaking to which the employees 'were assigned and which formed the organisational framework within which their employment relationship took effect'.

Useful guidance on the *Botzen* test was given by the EAT in *Duncan Webb Offset (Maidstone) Ltd v Cooper* [1995] IRLR 633. In determining to which part of the employer's business the employee was assigned, a tribunal may consider matters such as:

(a)   the amount of time spent on one part of the business or the other;

(b)   the amount of value given to each part by the employee;

(c)   the terms of the contract of employment showing what the employee could be required to do; and

(d)   how the cost to the employer of the employee's services was allocated between different parts of the business.

In essence, then, the correct test is simply whether a person was assigned to an undertaking or a part. Note, however, that in *Carsway Cleaning Contracts Ltd v Richards* (EAT/629/97, 19 June 1998) the EAT held that an employer could not 'off-load' an unwanted employee by deliberately moving him to a part of the undertaking that the employer knew was about to be transferred. They held that such an act was fraudulent and, accordingly, void. The employee was not 'employed in the part of the undertaking' being transferred.

The employee's right of objection

The transfer of the contract of employment and rights, powers, duties and liabilities under and in connection with it will not occur if the employee informs the transferor or the transferee that he objects to becoming employed by the transferee (reg 4(7)). In that event, the transfer will terminate the employee's contract of employment with the transferor but he will not be treated for any purpose as having been dismissed by the transferor (reg 4(8)), that is, he will be regarded as having resigned.

The TUPE 2006 nevertheless include a provision in reg 4(9), whereby an employee whose contract of employment is or would have transferred under reg 4(1) may treat his contract as terminated and still be treated as having been dismissed by the employer, where the relevant transfer involves or would involve a substantial change in working conditions to his material detriment. This preserves the common law right of an employee to resign and claim constructive dismissal for a fundamental breach of contract by the employer. However, the provisions of reg 4(9) provide two further advantages, in that there is no need to prove the dismissal and the wording appears to cover a wider set of circumstances than just the employer's repudiatory breach. This provision does not create any automatic unfair dismissal rights (see **8.3.1.5**) but simply provides that in certain circumstances a employee will have the right to object to becoming employed by the transferee and yet still retain the right to bring a normal unfair dismissal claim. To determine whether the dismissal was fair, the tribunal must still be satisfied that the employer acted fairly, and there is no presumption that it is unfair for the employer to make the proposed changes. Interestingly, the Court of Appeal has held that, as the effect of the objection was that the contract of employment did not transfer to the transferee, then neither did the liability for any claim arising from the constructive dismissal.

Neither the general application of the automatic transfer principle, nor the existence of the employee's right to object is subject to a precondition that employees have knowledge of the fact of a transfer and/or the identity of the transferee (*Secretary of State for Trade and Industry v Cook* [1997] ICR 288, EAT). In addition, if the identity of the transferee is not known to the employee, he can object after a transfer, provided he does so promptly (see *New IDG Ltd v Vernon* [2007] EWHC B14 (Ch)).

8.3.1.4   What the transferee acquires

The transferee inherits those employees employed by the transferor immediately before the transfer on their existing terms and conditions, assuming that they do not object (reg 4(2)).

Changes to the employee's terms and conditions are possible only in limited circumstances (see **8.3.1.6** below), and the transferred employee has no right to insist that he be given the benefit of any superior terms enjoyed by the transferee's existing staff.

Rights transferring

The transferee inherits all accrued rights and liabilities connected with the contract of employment of the transferred employee, except for criminal liabilities and some benefits under an occupational pension scheme (see below). If, for example, the transferor was in arrears with wages at the time of the transfer, the employee can sue the transferee as if the original liability had been the transferee's. The transferor is relieved of its former obligations without any need for the employee's consent.

Equally, the transferee can sue an employee for a breach of contract committed against the transferor prior to transfer.

The transferee will also inherit all the statutory rights and liabilities which are connected with the individual contract of employment, for example to claims for unfair dismissal, redundancy and discrimination.

Regulations 11 and 12 contain provisions requiring the transferor to notify the transferee in writing of 'Employee Liability Information' for employees who are the subject of the relevant transfer. If a transferor fails to give this information in whole or in part, the transferee can complain to the employment tribunal which can award compensation.

The transferred employee's period of continuous employment will date from the beginning of his period of employment with the transferor, and the statutory particulars of terms and conditions of employment, which every employer is obliged to issue, must take account of any continuity enjoyed by virtue of TUPE 2006.

Restrictive covenants

In the case of restrictive covenants, these will normally be expressed in terms of protecting customers of the transferor. In essence, following the transfer of an undertaking a restrictive covenant should be read as being enforceable by the transferee, but only in respect of customers of the transferor who fall within the protection. It may be necessary for the transferee to consider redrafting restrictive covenants, but this will be subject to the limits on the transferor's rights to make changes to terms of the employees' contracts (see **8.3.1.6**).

Collective agreements

Under TUPE 2006, any collective agreements made with a trade union by the transferor are deemed to have been made by the transferee (reg 5). Further, the transferee is deemed to recognise the trade union to the same extent as did the transferor (reg 6). In effect, the transferee steps into the shoes of the transferor. Neither TUPE 2006 nor the general law, however, prevent the employer from seeking to derecognise the union entirely, or from amending the basis of the recognition.

Individually, however, there may be 'hangovers' from previous union recognition. Of course, all terms of the individuals' contracts, including those pursuant to any collective agreements, will be deemed to have been made between the transferee and the employee. It follows that, notwithstanding withdrawal from collective bargaining by the transferee, the right to have pay determined by collective bargaining can persist.

This was considered in *Whent v T Cartledge Limited* [1997] IRLR 153, where not only the rate of pay and general terms which existed at the time of the transfer, but also the terms providing for the collective bargaining mechanism itself, transferred as a result of the transfer. The fact that the employer had derecognised the union was irrelevant.

Rights and liabilities which are not assigned under the Regulations

The Regulations do not have the effect of assigning:

(a)   criminal liabilities; or

(b)   rights and liabilities relating to provisions of occupational pension schemes which relate to benefits for old age, invalidity or survivors (although the Pensions Act 2004 does require a transferee to offer transferring employees who are members of the transferor's occupational pension scheme membership of another such scheme that meets requirements prescribed by regulations made under that Act).

8.3.1.5   Dismissal of an employee resulting from a relevant transfer – reg 7

Where an employee is dismissed (whether actually or constructively and whether before or after the transfer), if the sole or principal reason for the dismissal is either the transfer or a reason connected with it that is not an ETO reason entailing a change in the workforce, the dismissal will automatically be unfair.

If the sole or principal reason for the dismissal is a reason connected with the transfer that is an ETO reason entailing changes to the workforce before or after the relevant transfer, there is no automatically unfair dismissal. The dismissal will be regarded as having been for redundancy where s 98(2)(c) of the ERA 1996 applies, or for some other substantial reason of a kind such as to justify the dismissal of an employee (reg 7(2) and (3)).

Regulation 7(4) states that reg 7 applies irrespective of whether the employee in question is 'assigned to the organised grouping of resources or employees that is or will be transferred'. This means that the protection of reg 7 on unfair dismissal is available to *all* employees. It is important, therefore, that transferees are aware that any remaining employees, as well as the transferring employees, are protected against TUPE-related dismissal. However, in order to bring a claim for unfair dismissal, an employee must have the usual minimum of one year's continuous employment.

When is a dismissal by reason of the transfer itself?

It will be a question of fact for the employment tribunal to determine whether a dismissal is by reason of the transfer itself or for a reason connected with it (see below). This is a new provision introduced by TUPE 2006. Guidance issued by the Department for Business Enterprise and Regulatory Reform (BERR) addresses the distinction only in the context of changes in terms and conditions, but it is useful by way of an analogy.

Q   What is the difference between an action that is by reason of the transfer itself and that which is for a reason which 'is connected with' the transfer?

A   Where an employer changes terms and conditions simply because of the transfer and there are no extenuating circumstances linked to the reason for that decision, then such change is prompted by reason of the transfer itself. However, where the reason for change is prompted by the knock-on effect of the transfer – say, the need to re-qualify staff to use different machinery used by the transferee – then the reason is 'connected to the transfer'.

It is thought that a dismissal following pre-transfer 'collusion' between the transferor and the transferee with regard to dismissals (ie the transferee had been involved in some way in the decision to dismiss) is likely to be regarded as a dismissal by reason of the transfer itself, although there is no authority, as yet, to support this view. In *Wheeler v Patel* [1987] IRLR 211, Mrs Wheeler was employed by the vendor of a shop in his business which he proposed to sell. Before transferring the shop to a prospective purchaser, Mrs Wheeler was dismissed in order to achieve an agreement for sale. The EAT held (under old law) that the dismissal was for a reason connected with the transfer, but it is likely to be seen under TUPE 2006 as a dismissal by reason of the transfer itself.

When is a dismissal for a reason connected with the transfer?

It is a question of fact whether or not a dismissal is for a reason connected with the transfer. Although dismissals which occur shortly before or after the transfer are likely to be found to be connected with it, if not necessarily by reason of it, an employee may have difficulty convincing the tribunal that a dismissal which took place weeks or even months before the transfer was by reason of the transfer or for a reason connected with the transfer. An employee dismissed prior to the transfer will come under reg 7 if he can prove that, at the time the dismissal took place, a transferee had been found and that the dismissal was connected to the transfer under negotiation.

Less clear is whether it is sufficient for the employee to show that his dismissal was in connection with transfers generally. There is a conflict of EAT decisions under the previous TUPE Regulations on this point.

In *Ibex Trading Co Ltd (in administration) v Walton* [1994] IRLR 564, the EAT held that the actual transferee had to be identified. Dismissal in respect of transfers generally was not sufficient. The employees were held to be dismissed by reason of 'a' transfer, rather than 'the' transfer.

However, in *Harrison Bowden Ltd v Bowden* [1994] ICR 186, and in *Morris v John Grose Group Ltd* [1998] IRLR 499, the EAT held that the words 'the transfer' in reg 7(1) did not necessarily have to refer to the particular transfer that had actually occurred.

The decision in *Morris* is to be preferred, because the ECJ has stated that the proper approach to the issue of whether dismissals have been made in connection with a transfer is to look back in time and consider what happened. On the basis of this method of analysis, the fact that no transferee can be identified at the moment of dismissal does not prevent employees' rights from being protected by the Acquired Rights Directive.

So, for example, if employees are dismissed because customers become aware of the transferor's plans to contract out part of the business and, in view of the uncertainty, they decide to take their business elsewhere, this is likely to be seen as a reason connected with the transfer.

Establishing an ETO reason if the dismissal was connected with the transfer

If there is a dismissal for a reason (which is not an ETO reason) connected with the transfer, the transferee (ie the buyer) will be liable for all claims by the dismissed employee (whether dismissed before or after the transfer – reg 4(3)). If the dismissal was for an ETO reason then liability for a pre-transfer dismissal will lie with the transferor (ie the seller).

If an ETO reason can be established, the dismissal will be deemed to be either for redundancy or for 'some other substantial reason' under s 98(1) of the ERA 1996 and s 135 of the ERA 1996. Even where the employer can show such a reason, the employment tribunal must still be satisfied that the employer has acted reasonably within s 98(4) of the ERA 1996.

The employer must show an ETO reason entailing a change in the workforce, otherwise the dismissal will be unfair.

There is no statutory definition of an ETO reason, but according to BERR guidance it is likely to include:

(a)   a reason relating to the profitability or market performance of the transferee's business (ie an economic reason);

(b)   a reason relating to the nature of the equipment or production process which the transferee operates (ie a technical reason); or

(c)   a reason relating to the management or organisational structure of the transferee's business (ie an organisational reason).

Likewise there is no statutory definition of the phrase 'entailing changes in the workforce'. Guidance issued by BERR refers to previous interpretations of the phrase by the courts under TUPE 1981, which restricted it to changes in the numbers of employees employed or to changes in their functions.

Two cases, in particular, have provided authoritative guidance on what the phrase means, as follows:

(a)   To be an ETO reason within reg 7, an 'economic' reason must relate to the conduct of the business as such, and does not include dismissing employees simply to obtain an enhanced price or to achieve an agreement for sale (*Wheeler v Patel* – see above on a dismissal by reason of the transfer). In *Hynd v Armstrong* [2007] IRLR 338, it was held that a transferor employer cannot rely on the transferee's reason in order to establish an 'economic, technical or organisational reason' so as to provide a potential defence under TUPE 2006. In this case a pre-transfer dismissal of a solicitor by the transferor because he was not required by the transferee was held to be automatically unfair. The Court of Session held that it is 'reasonably clear' that the Acquired Rights Directive would not 'permit dismissal in such circumstances'. A transferor can only rely on a reason of its own. In effect this means that where an employee is dismissed by the transferor prior to the transfer, the reason for the dismissal must relate to the transferor's future conduct of its business in order to be an ETO reason. That will never be the case where, as in *Hynd*, the transferor has no intention of continuing the business after the transfer. Although this was only a Court of Session case, and accordingly not binding on an EAT sitting in England, it is considered by practitioners that this approach is likely to be followed by the EAT in practice.

(b)   The ETO reason must entail a 'change in the workforce'. For a change in the workforce there has to be a change in the composition of the workforce, or possibly a substantial change in job descriptions (*Berriman v Delabole Slate Ltd* [1985] IRLR 305, CA). Effectively, therefore, an ETO reason entailing a change in the workforce will have to be a genuine redundancy situation. Although a real change in the functions of the workforce can satisfy the ETO requirement (*Green v Elan Care Ltd* [2002] All ER (D) 17), a mere change in the terms and conditions enjoyed by the workforce will not suffice. Consequently, a transferee who provokes an actual or a constructive dismissal by attempting to change the terms and conditions of the transferred employees to harmonise with those of his existing workforce, would be unable to rely on the defence.

Once an ETO reason has been established, the employer must still ensure that a dismissal for redundancy is fair within other legislative provisions, eg that the selection for redundancy is fair and not based simply on the fact that the person is a transferred employee. The employer must also follow the statutory procedures before actually dismissing an employee (see **Business Law and Practice**). In addition to any claim for unfair dismissal, dismissed employees may also be entitled to a redundancy payment if they have been employed for two years or more, and employers should ensure that any required periods of consultation with employees' representatives have been allowed (see **8.3.2.1**).

8.3.1.6   Changes to terms of employment

The 2006 Regulations provide that employees are entitled to retain the same terms and conditions post-transfer as they enjoyed pre-transfer, and that they are not penalised when they are transferred by being forced to accept inferior terms and conditions. This is achieved through two routes. First, TUPE 2006, reg 4(1) states that the contract of employment of any transferred employee 'shall have effect after the transfer as if originally made between the person so employed and the transferee', so effectively transferring the pre-existing terms and conditions (see **8.3.1.4**). Secondly, by way of reinforcement, the Regulations also impose limitations on the ability of the transferee and employee to agree variations to those terms and conditions. In particular, reg 4(4) confirms that any alteration in the employees' terms of employment is void if the sole or principal reason for the variation is the transfer itself, or a reason connected with it which is not an ETO reason entailing changes in the workforce. The wording of reg 4(4) mirrors the wording of reg 7 (see **8.3.1.5**) and, accordingly, there will be an ETO reason only if there is a change in the numbers or functions of the workforce. As far as the distinction is concerned between a 'reason relating to the transfer itself' and a 'reason connected with the transfer', BERR guidance suggests that where an employer changes terms and conditions because of the transfer and there are no extenuating circumstances linked to the reason for that decision, such a change is prompted by reason of the transfer itself. Therefore any decision to 'harmonise terms and conditions' will be seen as arising from the transfer itself and so void. However, where the reason for the change is prompted by a knock-on effect of the transfer, such as the need to re-train staff, then it is a reason connected with the transfer which will not be void if it can be shown as an ETO reason entailing changes in the workforce.

In *Power v Regent Security Ltd* [2007] UKEAT 499/06, the EAT held that this meant that the transferring employees could not be deprived of any rights that transferred with them but did not prevent the buyer being bound by favourable changes made to their terms of employment. This resulted in a change to the guidance given by BERR on TUPE 2006, which now provides that the Regulations do not prevent changes to terms and conditions agreed by the parties which are entirely positive.

Moreover, it is possible under reg 4(5) for a transferee or a transferor to agree to vary an employment contract with an employee where the sole or principal reason is either unconnected with the transfer or is a reason connected with the transfer but falls within the definition of an ETO reason. However, this ability to make such changes will be very limited in practice. There will be an ETO reason only if there is a change in the workforce, and as outlined above, this must involve a change in numbers or employees' functions.

There is additional flexibility to agree changes in the employees' terms where a transferor is subject to relevant insolvency proceedings (basically, administration) at the time of the transfer. Regulation 9 allows the transferor, transferee or administrator to agree permitted variations to employment terms with collective representatives of the employees (ie variations cannot be agreed on an individual basis). A 'permitted variation' is one for which the principal reason is the transfer itself, or a reason connected with it that is not an ETO reason, and one which is designed to safeguard employment opportunities by ensuring the survival of the transferred undertaking.

8.3.1.7   Summary of effect of TUPE 2006 on pre- and post-transfer dismissals

Pre-transfer dismissals

Reason unconnected with the transfer   Where the dismissal is not by reason of the transfer or for a reason connected with it (eg for misconduct), the normal rules on employment claims apply. In this situation, reg 4(3) does not apply (because the dismissal is not within the circumstances described in reg 7(1)), and therefore liability remains with the transferor.

The transferee will be liable to the dismissed employee only if that employee was employed immediately before the transfer (ie at the moment of the transfer).

Reason is the transfer itself or a reason connected with the transfer The effect of reg 4(3) is that a pre-transfer dismissal, however long before the transfer, which is automatically unfair under reg 7, will result in liability passing to the transferee (but this does not alter the fact that the dismissal remains effective to terminate the contract). Only where the dismissal has been for an ETO reason may the transferee escape liability, although this ETO reason must relate to the ongoing business as run by the transferor. Where the transferee does escape liability, liability will obviously fall on the transferor, who will have to make a redundancy payment if the employee has at least two years' continuous employment and, if the dismissal was not handled fairly and in accordance with the statutory procedures, an unfair dismissal payment. Any wrongful dismissal claim would also be against the transferor.

So, in the context of a pre-transfer dismissal for a reason connected with the transfer, the existence of an ETO reason for the transferor is essential to determine whether liability rests with the transferor or the transferee.

A genuine redundancy dismissal before the transfer should be for an ETO reason entailing a change in the workforce, provided it relates to the ongoing business of the transferor, and should not therefore involve the transferee in liability. However, where the transferee is identified and gets involved in the dismissal, the dismissal will be by reason of the transfer itself and the ETO reason will not be available, so liability will fall on the transferee.

Post-transfer dismissals

The liability for a post-transfer dismissal will obviously fall only on the transferee.

After the transfer, the transferee may wish to bring the contracts of the transferred employees into line with those of his existing workforce. An employer who expressly or constructively dismisses employees who refuse to accept new terms will encounter difficulty with reg 7. In addition, a purported variation of the terms and conditions enjoyed by the workforce will be void under reg 4(4) if the reason for the variation is the transfer itself, which would appear to be the case when changes are made to harmonise terms and conditions. Where the employer is able to show that the change is either unconnected to the transfer, or for an ETO reason connected with the transfer, the transferee and the employee may agree a variation to that contract (reg 4(5)). If the agreed variation is an entirely positive change for the employees, the Regulations will not prevent it taking effect.

Allocation of liability between transferor and transferee

Pursuant to regs 13 to 15, the transferor and transferee are jointly and severally liable in relation to any failure to comply with their duties to inform and consult employees under TUPE 2006 (see **8.3.2.1**). In other areas, joint liability is not possible: *Stirling District Council v Allan* [1995] IRLR 301. If the parties wish to allocate liability differently between themselves, they must do so by the inclusion of appropriate indemnities in the sale and purchase agreement. Where it may be unclear whether a claim should be made against the transferor or the transferee, an employee may bring a claim against both.

8.3.2 Consultation and allocation of risk

Regulations 11–16 of TUPE 2006 impose duties upon both the transferor and the transferee to provide information to each other, and to provide information to and consult with representatives of employees who may be affected by the transfer.

8.3.2.1   The duty to inform and consult trade unions

Regulation 13 obliges both the transferor and the transferee to provide information to recognised trade unions or elected employee representatives in respect of any 'affected employee', ie any employee of the seller or buyer who may be affected by the transfer or measures taken in relation to it. The employer must supply specified information long enough before the transfer to enable consultation to take place. The information to be given includes the legal, social and economic implications for the employees, and the measures which the employer is proposing to take in relation to them (if there are no measures proposed, this should be stated). The seller must also inform the union or elected representative of any measures which it understands the buyer intends to take in relation to affected employees. 'Measures' in this context would appear to include proposed changes in the workforce or in their terms and conditions.

The employer is under an obligation to consult where it envisages taking measures in relation to the affected employees, with a view to reaching agreement on the measures to be taken. The employer must consider any representations made, respond to them and indicate the reasons for rejecting any of them.

Failure to comply with reg 13 may lead to the tribunal, on the application of the union or elected representative, awarding up to 13 weeks' pay in respect of each affected employee (reg 15). The employer has a defence if it can show that it was not reasonably practicable to perform the duties due to special circumstances, but that it took all such steps towards performance as were reasonably practicable in those circumstances.

Collective agreements and union recognition agreements will generally be transferred to the buyer (regs 5 and 6).

8.3.2.2   Obligation to provide information

Under reg 11, the transferor must provide the transferee with employee liability information about:

(a)   the identity and age of the employees who will transfer;

(b)   details contained in those employees' written statements of employment under s 1 of the ERA 1996;

(c)   any collective agreements affecting those employees which will continue to have effect after the transfer;

(d)   any disciplinary proceedings taken against, or grievance brought by, an employee in the preceding two years, to which the Employment Act 2002 (Dispute Resolution) Regulations 2004 (SI 2004/752) apply;

(e)   any legal action brought by an employee against the transferor in the previous two years, and any such action that the transferor has reasonable grounds to believe may be brought against it.

The aim of this obligation is to help the transferee to prepare for the arrival of the transferred employees and to ensure that the transferee is fully aware of all its inherited obligations.

The information must be provided not less than 14 days before the transfer, or, if special circumstances mean this is not reasonably practicable, as soon as reasonably practicable (reg 11(6)). Once the information has been provided, the transferor is also obliged to notify the transferee in writing of any changes to it (reg 11(5)).

If the information is not provided, the transferee may bring a claim against the transferor in the tribunal (reg 12), and will receive compensation (subject to a minimum award of £500 per employee transferred) reflecting the losses sustained.

8.3.2.3 Allocation of risk

Although the parties cannot contract out of TUPE 2006, the buyer and seller will usually want to agree an allocation between themselves of liability for matters arising from the Regulations.

Due diligence

The parties will carry out the due diligence exercise in relation to the employees with the statutory obligations under reg 11 in mind. Since the buyer will inherit all liabilities in relation to the target's employees, arising under their contracts or otherwise, it is vital that full details of employment matters are obtained. The buyer must carefully examine the transferring employees' contractual terms in particular, as there will be little opportunity to vary those terms even with the employees' consent unless such variations are entirely positive.

The buyer will also want to ascertain which employees are working in or assigned to the undertaking being transferred. These employees will usually be specified in a schedule, although who is actually transferred is still a matter of fact for the EAT to determine.

The buyer will review this information to determine any likely costs it may incur in integrating these employees into its own business operations. This may involve the dismissal costs in relation to any surplus employees, or additional costs relating to more advantageous terms and conditions enjoyed by the transferring employees.

Warranties

The buyer should support the due diligence review with warranties in the sale and purchase agreement to the effect that:

(a)   the persons listed in the schedule of employees are the only employees working in or assigned to the undertaking being transferred and that all relevant terms and conditions of such persons have been disclosed to the buyer;

(b)   details of any collective agreements and whether there are any actual or threatened industrial disputes have been fully disclosed;

(c)   there are no outstanding or pending claims that have not been disclosed;

(d)   the seller has complied with its obligations to inform and consult with employee representatives and provided the required employee liability information; and

(e)   the information concerning the transferring employees provided in the disclosure letter is true and accurate.

In addition the buyer may also seek warranties relating to the operation of TUPE 2006. In particular, the buyer will seek a warranty that there have been no dismissals where the sole or principal reason for the dismissal is the transfer itself or a reason connected with the transfer which is not an ETO reason, since liability in these circumstances will transfer to the buyer. For the same reason, the buyer will also require the seller to warrant that it has not made any changes to the transferring employees' terms of employment where the sole or principal reason for the changes is the transfer itself or a reason connected with the transfer which is not an ETO reason. Such changes in terms would be void and the buyer bound by previous terms. Ideally the buyer will want both of these warranties to be supported by appropriate indemnities.

Indemnities

The buyer will usually also seek various indemnities from the seller, for example an indemnity against any costs or liabilities arising out of all outgoings in respect of the employees (eg salary, commissions, bonuses and holiday pay) up to the date of completion (an apportionment will be made to the date of completion). The buyer may also insist on an indemnity against any claims which are attributable to any breach by the seller of its employment obligations prior to completion (including claims arising on termination of any employee's employment) for which the buyer becomes liable through the operation of TUPE 2006.

Indemnities may also be appropriate in respect of any measures which may be taken in relation to the transferring employees both before and after the transfer date. For example, if redundancies are to take place before the transfer, the buyer may agree to indemnify the seller in respect of any claims arising out of such redundancies, although as discussed above it is more likely that liability will transfer to the buyer in any event through the operation of TUPE 2006. If employees are to be made redundant after the transfer, the parties may agree as part of the commercial transaction to provide a fund for redundancy costs rather than a straight adjustment of the price. This will usually be on the understanding that the dismissals will be for an ETO reason and that the buyer will follow the correct statutory procedure and act fairly in making the redundancies.

8.3.3 Pensions

Where the transferring employees are members of a pension scheme, the parties will need to give careful thought to the pension aspects of the acquisition. This is a complex area, which often gives rise to more discussion and negotiation between the parties and their advisers than any other aspect of the transaction; this is understandable, since the value of the pension fund may even exceed the consideration for the acquisition itself. It may be necessary to have a specialist pensions lawyer as part of the legal team involved in an acquisition. It is not intended to deal with pension considerations in detail but merely to highlight a number of general points which may be relevant on an asset acquisition.

8.3.3.1 Money purchase or final salary scheme?

The buyer will require full details of any pension scheme benefiting the transferring employees; in particular, pre-contract enquiries will include requests for copies of the trust deed and rules under which the pension fund is administered, a list of the members of the scheme, and confirmation that the scheme is 'exempt approved', ie that it enjoys a privileged tax status. There are two main types of pension scheme: money purchase schemes and final salary schemes.

Money purchase

In a money purchase scheme, the employer and employee make fixed contributions into the fund which are invested and used to purchase benefits for the employee on his retirement. Employees are not guaranteed any particular level of benefit on retirement; the amount they receive will depend entirely on the return on the contributions made by them and by the employer on their behalf. This is the most common type of pensions scheme.

Final salary

In a final salary scheme, the members are guaranteed a particular level of benefit on retirement; this will usually be on the basis of a fraction of their salary at the date of retirement for each year of completed service with the employer. Unlike money purchase schemes, there is no direct correlation between the contributions made to the fund (by employer and employee) and the benefits received by the employee. A final salary scheme may, consequently, be in surplus or deficit at the time of the acquisition; much will depend on the prevailing economic conditions which, of course, have an effect on investment performance. Whether the fund is in surplus or deficit and the amounts involved can be ascertained only by making a host of assumptions about future events. Such an exercise should be carried out by an actuary.

8.3.3.2 Is there a discrete pension scheme for the transferring employees or do they participate in a group scheme?

The pension implications of an asset acquisition are simplified if the transferring employees are members of a separate, self-contained pension scheme (a discrete scheme). However, it is often the case that they are members of a larger scheme involving other employees. For example, on an asset sale by a company, the selling company may be part of a group pension scheme.

8.3.3.3 Transferring the pension benefits

Discrete scheme

The assets in the pension fund do not form part of the assets of the business which are being acquired; the pension fund is a separate entity administered by the trustees. Where the transferring employees are members of a discrete pension scheme, they will remain in the scheme following the acquisition (usually, at least initially, even if the buyer has an existing scheme covering its own employees). If it is a final salary scheme, it is important for the parties to determine whether it is adequately funded or over-funded at the date of completion. The buyer will often commission an actuary to value the fund for this purpose.

If the scheme is revealed to be in surplus, the seller may seek an increase in the purchase price to reflect this. Although the buyer does not benefit directly from the surplus, it may enable a 'contributions holiday' to be taken, ie a period in which no contributions are made. If, on the other hand, there is a deficit, the buyer may seek a reduction in the price or require the seller to 'top up' the fund. If the actuarial valuation is not ready on completion, the agreement may provide for an adjustment of the price when it is to hand.

The sale and purchase agreement will usually contain a schedule setting out details of the scheme. Warranties relating to the scheme will include confirmation by the seller that all contributions have been paid to the date of completion and that there are no outstanding claims against the trustees.

Group scheme

Where the transferring employees are members of a group scheme, a transfer payment must be made from the group scheme to the buyer's scheme (whether an existing scheme or one established for the purpose). The amount of this payment is usually the subject of much argument and negotiation between the parties and their respective actuaries. The discussion often centres around who should have the benefit of any surplus in a final salary scheme. The different bases for calculating the transfer payment can produce vastly differing results. The calculation may, for example, be based on the benefits which the employees would receive on leaving employment, or on an apportionment of the fund between those leaving the scheme and those remaining (if the scheme is in surplus, the latter method will be more beneficial for the transferring employees).

The provisions relating to the transfer payment are normally contained in a pension schedule to the sale and purchase agreement. The parties' actuaries may not have agreed the amount of the payment by the date of completion, but the basis for calculating the payment is usually included in an 'actuary's letter' attached to the schedule.

It is important to appreciate that the trustees of the scheme will not be parties to the sale and purchase agreement, and can act only in accordance with the trust deed and rules. Since the seller cannot, therefore, force the trustees to make the transfer, the buyer is wise to insist on a guarantee by the seller to make up any shortfall if it is unable to procure the transfer of the full amount. Finally, if the buyer needs to establish a new scheme, the parties may agree that the target's employees should remain with the group scheme for a specified period after completion.

8.3.4   Flowcharts: unfair dismissal claims on transfer of an undertaking

8.3.4.1   Dismissals before the transfer

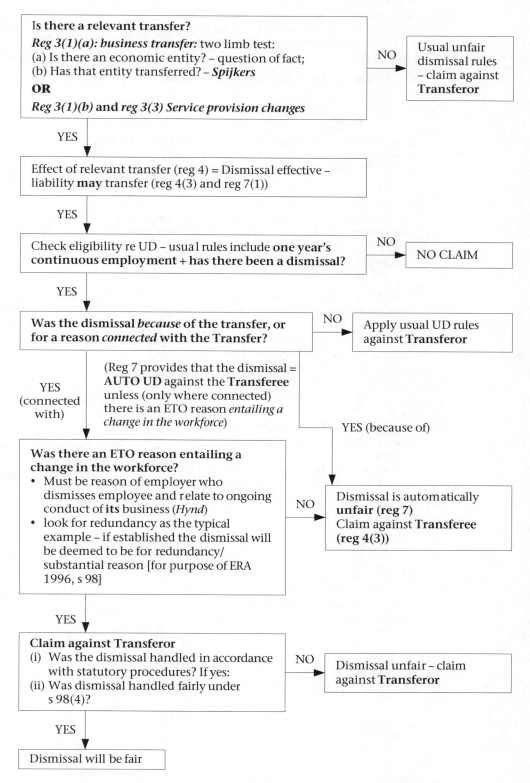

NB – ALSO check for redundancy payment claims and/or WD claims. Claim will be against the same party as the claim for UD.

8.3.4.2   Dismissals on or after the transfer

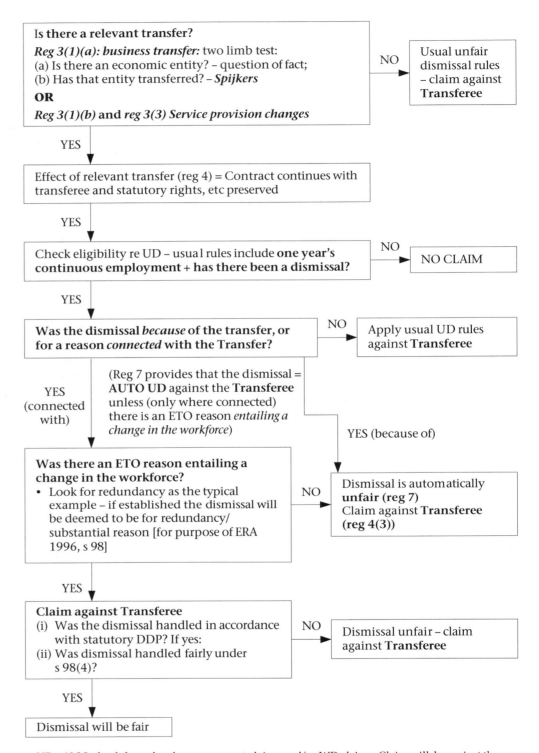

Is there a relevant transfer?

Reg 3(1)(a): business transfer: two limb test:
(a) Is there an economic entity? – question of fact;
(b) Has that entity transferred? – *Spijkers*

OR

Reg 3(1)(b) and *reg 3(3) Service provision changes*

→ NO → Usual unfair dismissal rules – claim against **Transferee**

↓ YES

Effect of relevant transfer (reg 4) = Contract continues with transferee and statutory rights, etc preserved

↓ YES

Check eligibility re UD – usual rules include **one year's continuous employment + has there been a dismissal?**

→ NO → NO CLAIM

↓ YES

Was the dismissal *because* of the transfer, or for a reason *connected* with the Transfer?

→ NO → Apply usual UD rules against **Transferee**

(Reg 7 provides that the dismissal = **AUTO UD** against the **Transferee** unless (only where connected) there is an ETO reason *entailing a change in the workforce*)

YES (connected with) ↓   YES (because of) ↓

Dismissal is automatically **unfair (reg 7)** Claim against **Transferee (reg 4(3))**

Was there an ETO reason entailing a change in the workforce?
• Look for redundancy as the typical example – if established the dismissal will be deemed to be for redundancy/ substantial reason [for purpose of ERA 1996, s 98]

→ NO → Dismissal is automatically **unfair (reg 7)** Claim against **Transferee (reg 4(3))**

↓ YES

Claim against Transferee
(i) Was the dismissal handled in accordance with statutory DDP? If yes:
(ii) Was dismissal handled fairly under s 98(4)?

→ NO → Dismissal unfair – claim against **Transferee**

↓ YES

Dismissal will be fair

NB – ALSO check for redundancy payment claims and/or WD claims. Claim will be against the Transferee.

8.4 Taxation

8.4.1 Introduction

The sale and purchase agreement for an asset acquisition will usually provide for the total purchase price for all the assets. However, an asset acquisition is a series of separate disposals, and for tax purposes the amount of the consideration which is attributable to each separate asset must be specified in the agreement (the apportionment is often contained in a schedule). The parties have some flexibility in making this apportionment and are usually influenced heavily by taxation and stamp duty implications.

This section outlines the tax consequences (including VAT and stamp duty) of an asset acquisition. It deals with the implications for a sole trader or partnership disposing of an unincorporated business, and for a company selling a continuing business. The tax position of the buyer is also considered.

It is not intended to explain in detail basic tax principles which are explored in full in *Business Law and Practice* and *Legal Foundations*, such as the nature of the charges to income tax, CGT and corporation tax, and the main relieving provisions, but to deal with these in the context of an asset acquisition where the intention is to continue a business in succession to the seller.

8.4.2 Implications for the seller of an unincorporated business

It is assumed here that a sole trader or partnership is selling the whole of his or its business to an unconnected person at full market value; the buyer may be an individual, a partnership or a company. We are not concerned with the gift of a business or, indeed, with the incorporation of a business, ie where the proprietors sell their business to a company which they have formed or acquired specifically for this purpose.

8.4.2.1 Sales for cash

A sole trader or partnership disposing of the business in an arm's length deal must consider the income tax and CGT implications of the transaction.

Income tax

The closing year rules The sale results in the discontinuance of the business carried on by the seller, so he will be assessed to income tax on the profits made from the end of the latest accounting period to be assessed until the date of the sale, less a deduction for overlap profit (ie any profit that has been charged to tax in two successive tax years).

Stock The value at which trading stock is sold will affect the final profits of the business assessable to income tax. It will be seen at **8.4.4.5** that the parties have some flexibility in apportioning the global consideration for the business between individual assets. Clearly, the higher the value attributed to stock, the higher the final income tax assessment.

Balancing charges The sale of the business may result in balancing charges arising in relation to assets on which capital allowances have been claimed (eg, items of plant and machinery or (until 1 April 2011, when this allowance will be withdrawn) industrial buildings). Most items of plant and machinery are 'pooled' together for the purpose of obtaining capital allowances, and it is only when the business is sold that HMRC calculates whether too much or too little income tax relief has been given on all the assets in the 'pool'. On the basis of the sale price attributable to those assets qualifying for capital allowances, HMRC will either make an income tax balancing allowance (where the pool is sold for less than its tax written-down value) or an income tax balancing charge (where the pool is sold for more than its tax written-down value). Once again, the apportionment of the global purchase price of the business between individual assets may have a significant effect on the tax position of the seller (and also the buyer, see **8.4.4.5**).

Relief for losses   The sale of the business will prevent any unrelieved losses from being carried forward under s 83 of the Income Tax Act 2007 (ITA 2007), since the provision only allows trading losses to be set against future profits of the trade. However, terminal loss relief under s 89 can be claimed if the taxpayer suffers a trading loss in the final 12 months in which he carries on the trade; unrelieved capital allowances in this period may be included for this purpose. The loss can be carried across against profits made in the final tax year and then carried back and deducted from profits of the same trade for the three years prior to the final tax year, taking the most recent years first. This may generate a repayment of tax.

The seller can also set a trading loss made in the year in which the sale takes place against any income or chargeable gains which he has in that year or the previous year under ss 64 to 71 of the ITA 2007. A loss relieved under ss 64 to 71 cannot form part of the terminal loss claim under s 89.

Capital gains tax

The seller will be liable to CGT at the rate of 18% for the tax year 2008/09 on any gain which arises on the disposal of chargeable assets of the business, such as land, buildings and goodwill. On a sale of the business by a partnership, each partner is separately assessed to CGT and is treated as disposing of his fractional share of each chargeable asset (this is determined by the partner's capital profit sharing ratio).

The gain on the sale of a business may be considerable, particularly where the seller has built up the goodwill of the business. For a long-established business, rebasing to 31 March 1982 (ie substituting market value on this date for actual cost in calculating the gain) may reduce the gain significantly. However, it should be noted that for a business established since 31 March 1982, the goodwill will have no base cost, resulting in virtually the whole of its value becoming chargeable.

Entrepreneurs' relief   Introduced in the Finance Bill 2008, entrepreneurs' relief is designed to remove part of the gain realised on certain business disposals from the charge to tax, thereby reducing the overall amount of CGT payable. It is a partial replacement for taper relief, which had applied to disposals between 6 April 1998 and 5 April 2008.

The relief will apply where there is a 'qualifying business disposal', the definition of which includes:

(a)   the disposal of the whole or part of a business (whether by a sole trader or an individual partner), where the business (or part of it) is sold as a going concern; and the seller has owned the interest in the business as a whole throughout the period of one year ending with the date of disposal; and

(b)   the disposal of company shares by an employee or officer of the company (such as a director), if the company is a trading company and is the seller's personal company (ie he holds at least 5% of the ordinary share capital giving at least 5% of the voting rights), and the seller has satisfied these requirements throughout the period of one year ending with the date of disposal.

If the conditions for the relief are met, the relief operates to reduce the amount of the capital gain chargeable to tax in two stages:

(1)   the gains arising from the qualifying business disposal are reduced by any losses made as part of the disposal; and

(2)   any net gain that remains after taking losses into account is reduced by 4/9ths. The relief is, however, subject to a maximum reduction of £1 million of qualifying net gains realised on or after 6 April 2008, and this represents a lifetime restriction so that only £1 million of net gains can qualify for the relief for each individual, whether those gains arise from a single disposal or several disposals spread over time.

Annual exemption   A sole trader, or in the case of a partnership each partner, will have the benefit of the CGT annual exemption (£9,600 for tax year 2008/09) if this has not otherwise been used up in the tax year.

Roll-over relief on replacement of business assets (TCGA 1992, ss 152–158)   A sole trader or partner who reinvests the proceeds of sale of his business or partnership share in another business venture may be able to defer the charge to CGT if he fulfils the conditions for roll-over relief. This relief is considered in **Business Law and Practice**. The main features of the relief are set out below.

(a)   Where the business or partnership share comprises qualifying assets (or an interest in such assets), the sole trader or partner can elect to roll any gain on such assets into replacement qualifying assets acquired within one year before or three years after the sale of the business or partnership share (it is sufficient that an unconditional contract is entered into within these time limits). Capital gains tax is deferred until the replacement assets are disposed of (without themselves being replaced).

(b)   It is not necessary for the replacement asset to be of the same kind as the original asset. It is sufficient if both the 'old' and the 'new' assets come within the list of qualifying assets, which includes land or buildings occupied and used for the trade, goodwill, and fixed plant and machinery. Thus, an individual who sells one unincorporated business and then invests in another will be able to take advantage of this relief. However, shares are not qualifying assets for the purposes of this relief.

(c)   Relief is restricted if the old assets have not been used in the seller's trade (or trades which he carried on successively) throughout his period of ownership, or if the whole of the proceeds of sale are not reinvested in new assets.

(d)   A partner who allows his firm to use the asset can claim relief on selling the asset if he reinvests in replacement assets.

(e)   Note that the seller cannot use his annual exemption to reduce the gain rolled over.

Deferral relief on reinvestment in EIS shares   An individual will be able to claim unlimited deferral of capital gains arising on the disposal, by sale or gift, of any asset when he invests the chargeable gain by subscribing for shares which qualify under the EIS. The individual's chargeable gain on the disposal of the asset (up to the subscription cost) is deferred until he disposes of the shares. The relief is available where the EIS shares are acquired for cash within one year before or three years after the disposal. An individual may apply entrepreneurs' relief (above) before deferring any remaining gain by investing in EIS shares.

8.4.2.2   Sales in consideration for shares

On an arm's length sale of an unincorporated business (whether a sole trade or a partnership) to an existing company, the proprietors of the business may agree to take shares in the buyer company as consideration for the sale. Two special reliefs may be available to individual sellers in these circumstances.

Carry forward of unrelieved trading losses

Where a business is sold to a company wholly or mainly for shares, s 86 of the ITA 2007 allows the seller to carry forward any unrelieved trading losses and deduct them from income received from the company. Initially, the deduction is from any salary paid to him as an employee of the company and then from any dividends paid to him as a shareholder. The set off is available in any year in which the seller retains beneficial ownership of the shares. For the sale to be 'wholly or mainly' in return for shares, at least 80% of the consideration should be in shares.

CGT roll-over into shares

Section 162 of the TCGA 1992 enables the seller to roll any chargeable gains on the sale of the business into the shares issued by the company in consideration, thus reducing the CGT acquisition cost of the shares by the amount of the gain. The effect of the relief is to postpone the CGT until the former proprietor of the business disposes of his shares in the company.

For the relief to operate, all the assets of the business (although cash can be ignored for this purpose) must be transferred to the company; it is not necessary, however, to transfer all the liabilities. Since the nature of the relief is to roll the gain into shares, to the extent that the seller receives cash or debentures in part satisfaction of the purchase price, an immediate potential liability to CGT will arise. This may suit a seller if, for example, he has capital losses brought forward from previous years which he can use to offset the gain.

8.4.3   Implications on the sale of a business by a company

8.4.3.1   Corporation tax

A company is charged to corporation tax on both its income profits and its capital gains. Thus, on an asset sale by a company, the following will give rise to a corporation tax charge:

(a)   capital gains (calculated in the same way as for CGT, save that companies are entitled to an indexation allowance to remove inflationary gains from the capital gains calculation) arising on chargeable assets of the business (profit on intangible fixed assets such as goodwill and intellectual property rights will generally be treated as income receipts in the hands of a corporate seller);

(b)   income profits on the sale of trading stock and intangible fixed assets (see above);

(c)   balancing charges. A company is entitled to capital allowances on plant and machinery and (until 1 April 2011) industrial buildings in much the same way as an unincorporated business. The disposal of its business will entail an adjustment to the corporation tax relief given on those assets in the form of either a balancing allowance or a balancing charge.

A company which has been accustomed to paying corporation tax at the small companies rate may find that the asset sale pushes its profits for the accounting period over the £300,000 threshold at which the higher rates of corporation tax (on income and capital profits) apply. The company does not have the benefit of an annual exemption to reduce its capital profits. However, if the selling company reinvests the proceeds of the asset sale in a new business, roll-over relief from corporation tax on replacement of business assets is available in much the same way as already described in relation to CGT.

The right for the company to carry forward trading losses under s 393 of the ICTA 1988 is lost on the sale of its business, since the provision only allows such losses to be set against subsequent profits which the trade produces. However, when a company ceases to trade, a trading loss sustained in its final 12 months may be set against profits of any description (income or capital) of the same accounting period, or, if the loss is not fully relieved, it can be carried back for up to three years, provided the company was then carrying on the same trade.

The reliefs discussed in **8.4.2.2**, entrepreneurs' relief and deferral relief on reinvestment in EIS shares are not available to a corporate seller.

8.4.3.2   Extracting the cash from the company

One of the attractions of selling a company by way of share transfer is that the sale price is received directly by the owners of the company, whether they are individual or corporate shareholders. Where, on the other hand, the assets of the company are sold, it is the company itself, rather than the owners of the company, which receives the price. Consider, for example, a company (A Ltd) with a single business which has two individual shareholders (Bob and Charlie). D Ltd, which is aware that Bob and Charlie wish to sell A Ltd, agrees to buy its business as a going concern. On completion of the sale of its business to D Ltd, A Ltd will be a mere 'cash shell' in which the net proceeds of sale (ie after deduction of corporation tax) are deposited (see **Figure 8.1** below). Further steps involving an additional tax charge must be taken for this money to end up in the hands of Bob and Charlie (see below). If, instead, D Ltd acquired A Ltd's shares, Bob and Charlie would receive the consideration direct, subject only to paying CGT (see **Figure 8.2** below and **9.4**).

Figure 8.1   Business sale

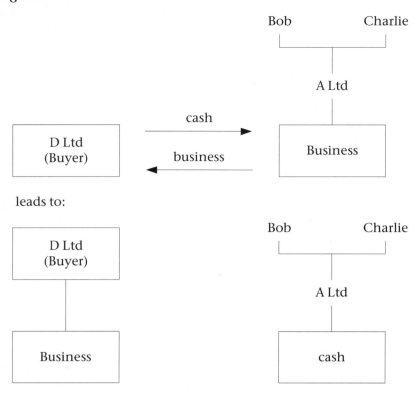

leads to:

Figure 8.2   Share sale

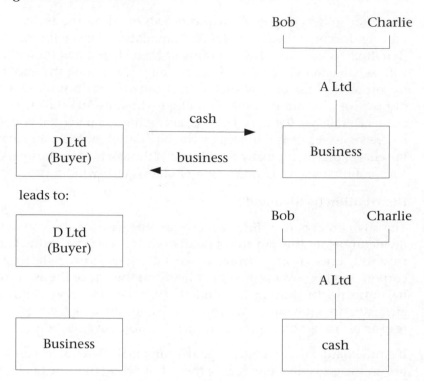

leads to:

Liquidating the company

The shareholders may extract the proceeds of sale of the assets of the business by putting the company into voluntary liquidation. On a winding up, however, the shareholders are treated as disposing of their shares, and individual shareholders will be liable to CGT on any resultant gain. A corporate shareholder will be liable to corporation tax on any such gain if the disposal is not exempt from tax as a disposal of a substantial shareholding (ie broadly 10% or more of the ordinary share capital – see **9.4.2.4**). There is, accordingly, a potential double charge to tax where an asset sale is followed by the liquidation of the company: a corporation tax charge on the company on the sale of the assets of the business, and a CGT (or corporation tax) charge on the shareholder on the winding up.

Distribution by dividend

The shareholders may find it more tax efficient for the company to declare a dividend before it is put into liquidation. However, for individual shareholders, this will, once again, involve a second charge to tax (ie in addition to the corporation tax payable by the company on the sale of the assets of the business). It is also worth bearing in mind that a pre-liquidation dividend may be less attractive to individuals, as their available reliefs (eg entrepreneurs relief) in respect of chargeable capital gains may be more advantageous.

If a pre-liquidation dividend is paid, individual shareholders are liable to income tax on the gross dividend (being the net dividend plus the tax credit), albeit with the benefit of a tax credit.

Corporate shareholders will not pay corporation tax on the receipt of a dividend from a subsidiary. Where a shareholding will not qualify on disposal for exemption from tax as a substantial shareholding, a pre-liquidation dividend will be the most tax-efficient method of distributing the proceeds of sale, provided there are genuine distributable profits (see **9.4**).

Where the shareholders have extracted cash from the company in the form of a pre-liquidation dividend, the ensuing liquidation is less likely to give rise to a charge to CGT (or corporation tax) since the distribution by the company will have reduced the value of the shares.

8.4.4   Implications for the buyer of a business

The great advantage to the buyer of acquiring the business of a company rather than its shares is that it does not assume responsibility for all the hidden liabilities of the company. It can therefore save the cost and time involved in carrying out an in-depth investigation into the tax affairs of the company, and in negotiating extensive warranties and indemnities.

The tax consequences of acquiring the assets of a business are similar whether the buyer is an individual or a company.

8.4.4.1   Capital allowances

Capital allowances are not restricted to the purchase of brand new assets. The buyer will be able to claim capital allowances on, for example, plant and machinery which it acquires from the seller. The allowances are calculated on the price the buyer pays for them and not their tax written-down value in the seller's hands. Assume, for example, that the seller originally acquired an item of plant and machinery for £8,000 and has received writing-down allowances totalling £6,000 up to the date of the sale. On an asset sale of the business, £4,000 is attributed to this item (ignore the effect of pooling for this purpose). As the seller has sold the asset for more than its tax written-down value (ie £2,000), a balancing charge will be levied on it. In the year of the sale, the buyer will receive an allowance based on the purchase price of £4,000.

8.4.4.2   Trading stock

The amount which the buyer pays for stock or work in progress will be a deductible expense in working out income profits liable to income tax or corporation tax as appropriate.

8.4.4.3   Base cost for capital tax

The price paid by the buyer for chargeable assets of the business will form its base cost for CGT or corporation tax purposes. This contrasts with a share acquisition, where the base cost of the chargeable assets of the target company for capital gains purposes will be their original cost to the target. This may be relevant if the buyer is proposing to dispose of certain unwanted assets soon after the acquisition.

8.4.4.4   Roll-over relief from CGT (or corporation tax) on replacement of qualifying assets

If the buyer has disposed of qualifying assets in the previous three years, or is intending to do so in the next 12 months, it will be able to roll any chargeable gain arising on such a disposal into those assets of the acquired business which are themselves qualifying assets.

8.4.4.5   Apportioning the purchase price

The parties will usually agree initially upon a global consideration for the assets of the business. For tax and stamp duty purposes, however, they will need to negotiate the apportionment of this overall figure between the various assets transferred. Although s 52(4) of the TCGA 1992 requires that any method adopted for this apportionment must be 'just and reasonable', in practice the parties have some flexibility as to the figures upon which they settle.

It will be clear from what has been said above that the seller and buyer may be pulling in different directions on this issue. For example, the buyer may prefer the consideration to be balanced in favour of goodwill, which will not attract stamp duty, and also stock, which will form a deduction from its income profits, and plant and machinery, on which capital allowances will be available. By contrast, the seller may prefer the apportionment to be weighted more in favour of qualifying assets for roll-over relief if it is proposing to reinvest the sale proceeds. Much will depend, of course, on the individual circumstances of the parties. If, for example, the seller has unrelieved trading losses which it would not otherwise be able to use, it may be happy for a relatively high value to be attributed to stock and plant and machinery. The carried forward losses would then be available to absorb some or all of the resulting trading profit.

8.4.4.6   Value added tax

Is VAT chargeable?

A taxable person must charge VAT on taxable supplies of goods and services made in the UK in the course or furtherance of a business carried on by him (Value Added Tax Act 1994 (VATA 1994), s 4(1)). Prima facie, therefore, on the sale of a business, VAT is chargeable on the stock and capital assets (including goodwill) of the business.

There is, however, a special exemption contained in Art 5 of the Value Added Tax (Special Provisions) Order 1995 (SI 1995/1268). This treats the transfer of the whole or part of a business as a going concern as being outside the scope of VAT. See further below.

Transfer as a going concern

For the Art 5 exemption to apply, the following two important conditions must be satisfied:

(a)   the assets must be used by the buyer in the same kind of business as that carried on by the seller with no significant break; and

(b)   the buyer must be a taxable person, or become a taxable person as a result of the transfer.

In determining whether the sale is of a business as a going concern or merely assets in the business, regard must be had to all the circumstances, including, for example, the following:

(a)   the wording of the acquisition agreement (however, the label which the parties put on the transaction is not conclusive);

(b)   whether goodwill (and the right to use the business name), contracts and customer lists are transferred;

(c)   whether the workforce is transferred;

(d)   whether the buyer can carry on the same type of activities without interruption;

(e)   where part of a business is transferred, whether it is a severable unit, capable of standing on its own.

It is very important to distinguish between the sale of a business as a going concern and a mere transfer of assets for VAT purposes (see **1.2.2**). It used to be common practice where there was any doubt (and particularly in the case of a sale of part of a business) for the parties to a transaction to seek a ruling from HMRC as to whether the proposed sale would come within Art 5. Recently, however, HMRC has stated that routine clearance applications will no longer be considered. In future, HMRC will give an opinion only when the transaction has unusual features, to which attention should be drawn in the application. This strict approach requires solicitors to take even greater care than before.

Provision in the sale and purchase agreement

The seller's solicitor should ensure that in the sale and purchase agreement the consideration is stated to be exclusive of VAT. Otherwise, if HMRC argues successfully that VAT is chargeable because the Art 5 conditions have not been satisfied, the purchase price will be deemed to be inclusive of VAT (VATA 1994, s 19(2)). The unfortunate result will be that the seller must account for the VAT to HMRC but is unable to recover this from the buyer. In the absence of advance clearance from HMRC, even if the seller believes that the sale comes within Art 5, the seller should seek an indemnity from the buyer against any VAT charge arising from the sale (plus any penalty or interest payable).

If the seller wrongly charges VAT on a sale in respect of which Art 5 applies, the buyer may be unable to recover the tax from HMRC by claiming an offset against input tax (although he should have a right of recovery from the seller).

8.4.4.7 Stamp duty land tax

Stamp duty is a tax which is payable by the buyer on transactions involving the transfer of land or interests in partnerships.

Rate of duty

Stamp duty land tax is payable by the buyer on commercial property at the following rates:

(a) nil where the consideration does not exceed £150,000;

(b) 1% where the consideration is more than £150,000 but does not exceed £250,000;

(c) 3% where the consideration is more than £250,000 but does not exceed £500,000;

(d) 4% where the consideration exceeds £500,000.

Where the consideration does not exceed £150,000, £250,000, or £500,000, the relevant instrument (ie the contract and the subsequent conveyance or transfer) must contain a certificate of value to this effect for the buyer to claim the nil, 1% or 3% rates respectively. On the acquisition of a business, the relevant consideration for stamp duty land tax is the aggregate consideration for all of the properties transferred. The Finance Act 2006 provides that where partnership property includes land, there will be no stamp duty land tax charged on the transfer of an interest in that partnership where the partnership's main activity is the carrying on of a profession or a trade (other than a trade of dealing in or developing land).

8.4.4.8 Financing the acquisition by borrowing: is tax relief available?

Individual buyer

If an individual borrows money to purchase a share in a partnership, he can obtain relief for interest payments he makes under the loan by treating the interest payments as an income tax deduction. This enables the interest payments to be set off against the total income of the individual. Alternatively, the interest payments can be treated as a deductible expense in arriving at the profits of the partnership (ITA 2007, s 383).

Corporate buyer

Tax relief on interest payable by a company on a loan to acquire a business will normally be available as a deductible expense under the loan relationship legislation contained in the Finance Act 1996.

8.4.5 Warranties

Since the buyer does not 'inherit' any of the tax liabilities of the seller of the business (whether the seller is an individual or a company), it does not need the protection of extensive warranties and indemnities in the acquisition agreement. Any warranties that are included are likely to be aimed at eliciting disclosures from the seller, particularly with regard to any concessions or dispensations agreed between the seller and HMRC (eg in relation to benefits provided to employees). The buyer will usually also seek assurances that PAYE, National Insurance and VAT records are complete and up to date.

Chapter 9

Share Acquisitions

9.1 The transfer of shares

In a share acquisition the only asset being transferred is the shares of the target company, the effect of the transfer being to transfer ownership of the company. The buyer usually seeks to acquire the entire issued share capital of the target company, thus making it the sole owner of the company, though the buyer can acquire effective control by acquiring a majority holding of the target's shares.

In a share sale and purchase agreement the buyer will seek reassurances both about the actual shares being transferred and about the company over which it will acquire ownership.

9.1.1 Shares

The share sale and purchase agreement will provide for the sale and purchase of the shares within its operative terms (**4.3.3**). The shares to be acquired will be specified, and if there are a number of sellers, details of their relative shareholdings will normally be contained in a schedule.

The shares will be expressed as being transferred free from all charges, encumbrances, liens, etc. If the shares of the target are owned by a holding company, it is likely that they will be subject to a charge, and accordingly arrangements should be put in place to ensure their release from the charge prior to the sale.

Shares in a private company are likely to be subject to restrictions on transfer contained in the company's articles. It is common for the articles of a private company to oblige a member proposing to transfer its shares to offer them pro rata to the existing members. Although the articles invariably allow for the pre-emption provisions to be overridden by special resolution, it is usually easier for the sellers to waive their rights. The sale and purchase agreement will often contain a clause whereby the sellers agree to waive any pre-emption rights they may have, whether conferred by the articles or otherwise (the rights may be incorporated in a shareholders' agreement rather than in the articles).

9.1.2 The company

In taking ownership of the target company, the buyer will indirectly be acquiring all the assets and liabilities in that company. As considered in **Chapter 5**, the buyer will want to seek reassurances about the target company through the provision of warranty statements. Although many of the warranties considered in the context of an asset acquisition will be equally appropriate on a share acquisition, the list of warranties in a share sale and purchase agreement is likely to be longer due to the greater degree of risk which the buyer of shares assumes.

Set out below are some of the areas where the buyer will wish to have warranty cover, together with, in each case, the typical warranties sought.

9.1.2.1 Constitution of the company

The buyer will seek to include the following warranties in relation to the constitution of the company:

(a)   that the statutory books of the company have been properly kept and are accurate and up to date;

(b)   that the memorandum and articles (attached to the disclosure letter) are true and complete;

(c)   that all documents and returns required to be filed with the Registrar of Companies have been duly filed and were correct;

(d)   that the directors listed in the agreement (usually in a schedule) are the only directors of the company.

9.1.2.2 Accounts

The buyer may seek to include the following warranties in relation to the most recent set of audited accounts:

(a)   that they have been prepared using the same bases and policies of accounting as were used in preparing the accounts for the previous three accounting periods;

(b)   that they comply with the CA 2006 and with all relevant standards set by the accountancy profession and contained in Financial Reporting Standards and Statements of Standard Accounting Practice, and are not affected by any exceptional or non-recurring item;

(c)   that they give a true and fair view of the assets and liabilities (including contingent, unquantified or disputed liabilities) of the company at the date of the balance sheet and of its profits for the relevant accounting period.

The seller is advised to be wary of the scope of warranties relating to the accounts. For example, the seller will often resist the inclusion of a warranty that management accounts are accurate or give a true and fair view. It is arguable that the buyer is not justified in placing much reliance on management accounts, which will have been drawn up for a specific management purpose and will not have been audited.

9.1.2.3 Financial matters

The buyer may seek assurances from the seller that the company has not done any of the following, for example, since the last accounts date:

(a)   incurred any liabilities except in the ordinary course of business;

(b)   incurred or agreed to incur any capital expenditure or disposed of any capital assets;

(c)   paid or declared any dividend or made any other distribution.

The buyer may also seek warranties in relation to the debtors and creditors revealed in the accounts, for example, that the company has paid its creditors in accordance with their credit terms and that the debtors have paid their debts in full. It may also ask for assurances that any amounts owing to the company on completion will be fully recoverable in the ordinary course of business (possibly with a long-stop date of, say, three months) and that no amounts owing by the company on completion have been due for more than a specified period (eg two months).

9.1.2.4 Trading

The buyer may seek warranties in relation to the trading position of the company, for example:

(a)   that the business of the company has been carried on in the ordinary course and that its turnover, financial position or trading position has not deteriorated since the date of the last accounts (the seller should resist the extension of this warranty to include 'trading prospects');

(b)   that the company is not engaged in any litigation or arbitration proceedings as claimant or defendant, and that no such proceedings are pending, threatened or, to the seller's knowledge, likely to arise;

(c)   that the sellers have no knowledge, information or belief that any supplier will cease to supply the company (or substantially reduce supplies) after completion;

(d)   that the sellers have no knowledge, information or belief that any customer will cease to deal with the company (or substantially reduce the level of business) after completion;

(e)   that compliance with the terms of the agreement will not result in a breach of any agreement to which the company is a party, relieve any person from any obligation to the company, or enable any person to determine any right or benefit enjoyed by the company or to exercise any right;

(f)   that the company has obtained all licences and consents required to carry on its business properly and is not in breach of their terms;

(g)   that the company is not a party to any contract or arrangement of an unusual or loss-making nature or which it cannot terminate on 60 days' notice or less;

(h)   that the company has not supplied or manufactured products which, in any material respect, are defective or do not comply with any warranties or representations made by it (whether express or implied);

(i)   that the company has conducted its business in accordance with all applicable laws and regulations.

9.1.2.5 Assets other than land

The buyer may seek warranties in relation to the underlying assets of the company other than land, for example:

(a)   that the company still owns and has good title to all the assets included in the latest audited accounts (except for current assets subsequently sold in the ordinary course of business) and has good title to all assets which it has since acquired;

(b)   that plant, machinery, vehicles, etc are in a good state of repair, and have been properly and regularly maintained;

(c)   that the stock-in-trade of the company is in good condition and capable of being sold in the ordinary course of business by the company at prices contained in its current price list;

(d)   that the stock of raw materials and finished goods held by the company is adequate (and not excessive) in relation to the trading requirements of the business on completion.

The particular warranties that are sought will take into account the nature of the target business and any specific concerns of the buyer.

9.1.2.6   Insurance

The buyer will usually require warranties that full particulars of the company's insurances are included in the disclosure letter, that they are in full force and effect, and that they contain adequate cover against such risks as prudent companies carrying on the same type of business would normally cover by insurance. The buyer will also seek a warranty that no insurance claims are outstanding or pending, and that the seller is not aware of any circumstances likely to give rise to a claim.

9.1.2.7   Intellectual property

Details of patents, trademarks, service marks, design rights and copyrights owned or used by the company will often be contained in the disclosure letter (with copies of agreements relating to these intellectual property rights attached). Warranties will be included that there are no outstanding claims against the company for breach of the intellectual property rights of any other person and that, to the seller's knowledge, the company is not in breach of any such rights in operating the business. The buyer may also require the seller to warrant that it is not aware of any infringement of the intellectual property rights of the company by any third party.

9.1.2.8   Land

The scope of the warranties in relation to land will depend on the extent of the buyer's property investigation and on whether the seller's solicitor is prepared to give certificates of title (see **3.5.6**). The following are some examples of the warranties that may be sought by a buyer in this area:

(a)   the company has good title to the each of the properties and has possession or control of all deeds and documents necessary to prove title;

(b)   each property is free from any mortgage, charge, lien or other encumbrance;

(c)   the current use of each property complies with town and country planning legislation, and all necessary planning and building regulation consents have been obtained;

(d)   all obligations, restrictions, conditions and covenants affecting any of the properties (leasehold or freehold) have been observed and performed, and no notice of breach has been received;

(e)   the company has vacant possession of each of the properties;

(f)   there are no outstanding disputes affecting any of the properties and no outstanding orders, notices or demands have been made by local or other authorities;

(g)   each of the properties is in good and substantial repair and fit for the purposes for which it is presently used;

(h)   each of the properties is free from any notice, inhibition, caution, land charge, or local land charge not of general application to the area.

9.1.2.9   Employees

When control of a company is acquired by share transfer, this has no direct effect on the employees of the target company. There is no change of employer in these circumstances and the employees retain exactly the same rights against their employer company, even though ownership of its shares has changed hands. The fact of the share acquisition will not of itself give rise to any employment claims as there is no dismissal either at common law or within the statutory definition. All the contractual rights of the employees are therefore preserved, TUPE 2006 do not apply and, unlike on an asset acquisition, there is no obligation for either the buyer or the seller to inform and consult with trade unions.

As the buyer will indirectly assume liability for the target's workforce, it will require confirmation of the particulars of all directors and employees, including dates of commencement of employment and remuneration (including bonuses, etc).The buyer will normally insist on a warranty that the particulars provided by the seller (either in a schedule to the agreement or in the disclosure letter) are true and complete.

The buyer may also seek warranties as to the following:

(a)   that all subsisting contracts of service can be determined at any time by the company on three months' notice or less (this warranty should prompt disclosures of any fixed-term or 'evergreen' contracts, or contracts with a substantial notice requirement);

(b)   that the company has not given notice terminating the employment of any employee;

(c)   that no employee of the company is entitled to give notice terminating his employment as a result of the agreement (this warranty should 'flush out' any 'golden parachute' clauses);

(d)   that there are no outstanding claims against the company by any current or former employee;

(e)   that no changes have been made to the terms and conditions of employment of any employee over a specified period (eg within three or six months of completion).

Lastly, the sale and purchase agreement may provide for new directors to be appointed, or for existing directors to enter into fresh service contracts on completion (the terms will usually be agreed prior to completion and annexed to the contract).

9.1.2.10   Pensions

Many of the pension considerations discussed in **Chapter 8** in the context of an asset acquisition are equally applicable to a share acquisition. The buyer of shares will similarly seek reassurances about the pension arrangements for the employees of the target company, the precise warranties sought being dependent upon how the company has organised its pension provision.

The pension fund is a separate entity from the target company, and is administered by trustees who are obliged to act in accordance with the trust deed and rules. The trustees will not be parties to the sale and purchase agreement, so suitable arrangements must be made to notify them of the change in ownership of the company. The buyer will acquire the target company with its inherent obligations in relation to payments into its pension scheme. Therefore, the buyer will seek appropriate reassurances about the current state of the pension scheme, including, for example (if the scheme is a final salary scheme), whether there is a deficit or a surplus in the fund. If there is a significant deficit, the buyer may ask the seller to make a payment into the fund, or, alternatively, seek to reduce the purchase price of the target. Where the scheme is in surplus, on the other hand, the seller may seek an increase in the purchase price to reflect this.

If the target company does not have its own discrete pension scheme but is a member of a group scheme (see **8.3.3.3**), the sale and purchase agreement must also provide for the transfer of the target company employees' pension entitlement. The parties must agree a basis for making a transfer payment from the group scheme to the buyer's scheme. The buyer should insist on a guarantee from the seller to make up any shortfall if the seller cannot procure that the trustees transfer the agreed amount.

Details of a discrete pension scheme or provisions relating to a transfer payment out of a group scheme are normally included in schedules to the sale and purchase agreement.

9.1.2.11   Taxation

Most tax matters will be dealt with separately, either in a deed of tax indemnity or by means of tax covenants. Whichever method is employed, the seller will often be obliged to compensate the buyer for any breaches on an indemnity basis (see **9.3**).

Where, however, the buyer is keen to elicit disclosures from the seller, it will include some tax warranties; problems may then be revealed which it is able to use as a lever to renegotiate the purchase price (or which may even prompt it to withdraw from the acquisition). In particular, the buyer will want confirmation that the company is not in dispute with HMRC and has complied with obligations, inter alia, to file returns, make payments and operate the PAYE system. The buyer may also require a warranty that the latest accounts make full provision or reserve for all taxation which could be assessed on the company in respect of the period covered by the accounts.

9.1.2.12   Information disclosed

Two controversial warranties that a buyer may seek relate to information disclosed by the seller to the buyer. First, the buyer may include in the initial draft of the agreement a warranty that all information about the target company provided to the buyer or its advisers prior to the parties entering into the contract is true and accurate in all material respects. This is clearly a wide-ranging warranty which would involve the difficulty of identifying the information which the seller and its advisers have passed to the buyer. A compromise might be for the warranty to be restricted to information contained in the disclosure letter.

Secondly, the buyer may seek to impose a warranty that the seller has disclosed everything which might materially affect the value of the shares, or which might influence a buyer in deciding whether to proceed with the acquisition. This 'catch-all' warranty should be resisted by the seller on the basis that it would cover matters which the buyer can be expected to find out for itself (eg information in the public domain) and information which the seller may not realise is significant.

9.1.3   Directors and senior managers

Directors of the target company who are also employees, and senior managers, are subject to the same regime as all other employees; however, their important position in the company requires that the buyer gives them careful consideration. The strengths and weaknesses of the management team should be analysed, and the buyer should identify those managers and directors it considers important to the future success of the company and those whom it does not wish to retain. Where the buyer is a company, part of its strategy for 'turning the company around' may be to introduce some of its own managers or managers from other parts of the group. Similarly, individual buyers may insist on becoming directors on completion. As early as possible in negotiating the acquisition deal, the buyer should consider how the key managers will be retained and what will be the costs and consequences of dispensing with others.

9.1.3.1 Removing 'surplus' directors and managers

The buyer should check whether the articles of the target company give weighted voting rights to directors on any resolution to remove them as directors or to change the article conferring those rights. Such provisions may, of course, have the effect of entrenching the directors by preventing their removal by ordinary resolution under s 168 of the CA 2006.

The buyer will often be concerned about the cost to the target company (and, therefore, indirectly, to itself) of removing directors and managers, and the possibility that those dismissed may damage the company by their activities after leaving.

Cost to the target company

The target company may face substantial claims for wrongful dismissal from directors or managers who are removed prior to the end of a fixed term or without proper notice. The cost of removing a director who is, for example, in the early stages of a five-year fixed-term contract which entitles him to a lucrative package of salary and benefits, may be prohibitive. Similarly, it may prove expensive to remove a director or manager who has a so-called 'evergreen' or 'rolling' contract. This is a contract for a fixed term which, on each anniversary of the commencement date, is automatically renewed for a further fixed term; automatic renewal will be avoided only if the employer gives notice before the anniversary of the commencement date that the contract will determine at the end of the current period.

In the case of directors who have been granted (before 1 October 2007) service contracts for over five years, or (from 1 October 2007) service contracts for over two years, the buyer should check that the term was authorised by ordinary resolution of the members in accordance with either s 319 of the CA 1985, in the case of the pre-October 2007 contracts, or s 188 of the CA 2006, in the case of those contracts entered into on or after 1 October 2007. In the absence of such approval, the contract can be terminated by the company at any time on reasonable notice.

To the extent that damages exceed £30,000, they are taxable in the hands of the employee and, consequently, in order to compensate for his actual loss, the award will be 'grossed up' to take account of this liability. Damages may be reduced significantly, on the other hand, to take account of accelerated receipt and the duty on the employee to mitigate his loss by seeking suitable alternative employment.

Restrictive covenants

The buyer should check whether the service contracts of the directors and managers of the target contain effective restraints on their activities after termination of their contracts. Typical clauses include covenants by the employee not to work in a competing business and not to solicit or entice away customers of the target company. The employee may also be prohibited from using or disclosing confidential information about the business of the target. In the absence of express terms, few post-termination restraints are implied into an employment contract (there is an implied term, however, that the employee will not reveal highly confidential information).

Restraints of this nature are valid and enforceable at common law only if they protect a legitimate trade interest of the employer (eg they protect the goodwill of the business), are not against the public interest and are reasonable between the parties. A non-competition covenant, for example, is likely to be considered void as being in restraint of trade unless its scope is limited in terms of duration and the geographical area which it covers. Similarly, a non-solicitation clause should be limited to customers who have recently dealt with the target (eg within the previous 12 months). It is now well established that clauses preventing the disclosure of information after termination can be effective only in relation to highly confidential information or trade secrets (*Faccenda Chicken Ltd v Fowler* [1986] IRLR 69, CA).

If any of the directors who are leaving are also selling shares in the target, the buyer should ensure that they agree to restrictive covenants in the acquisition agreement (see **5.10**). The courts will more readily uphold restraints which have been freely negotiated between parties to an acquisition than those included in employment contracts.

Even if restrictive covenants are prima facie valid, they will not survive a repudiatory breach of contract by the employer. This is on the basis that, by committing such a breach, the employer is indicating that it no longer considers itself to be bound by the contract and cannot, therefore, hold the other party to obligations contained within it. There is a danger here for buyers proposing that the target dismisses some of the management team; if dismissals are carried out in breach of contract, this may discharge the former employees from compliance with restrictive covenants (*General Billposting Co Ltd v Atkinson* [1909] AC 118, HL). Even if the covenant purports to enable the employer to enforce the covenant whatever the reason for the termination of the contract, this will not be effective (*Briggs v Oates* [1991] 1 All ER 411). Some directors' service contracts, however, permit the company to pay them salary in lieu of notice. Since, in this event, the company is not in breach of contract in terminating the contract without notice, it should be able to rely on post-termination covenants.

9.1.3.2   Retaining directors and managers

The buyer should consult with those directors and managers whom it is keen to retain as early as possible in the negotiations for the acquisition of the target company (subject to considerations of confidentiality). It may be able to negotiate a term in the sale and purchase agreement that certain key personnel enter into new service contracts on completion. If a director or manager chooses to leave, however, the rights of the parties will, inter alia, depend on the terms of any existing contract.

'Golden parachute' clauses

A director's service contract may include a so-called 'golden parachute' clause, entitling him to treat himself as dismissed without notice on a change of control of his employer company and to receive a specified payment from the company in this event.

A disadvantage for the director of receiving a contractual payment is that it is taxable in full as income. The first £30,000 of a claim for damages for breach of contract or a settlement of such a claim would, in contrast, be tax free within s 403 of the Income Tax (Earnings and Pensions) Act 2003.

'Garden leave' clauses

A 'garden leave' clause is intended to enable the employer to hold an employee to his contract if, for example, the employee attempts to resign in breach of contract. Although the employer must continue to pay the employee for the notice period, he will not usually intend to provide him with work. The advantage to the employer is that the employee is unable to work for anyone else during the notice period and must comply with all obligations of confidentiality, etc which apply during the contract, which can be more extensive than those imposed after termination of the contract. However, the enforceability of clauses of this nature is still open to question, particularly where the employer refuses to provide work for the employee.

9.2 Regulatory provisions

On a share acquisition, consideration has to be given to relevant provisions of the Financial Services and Markets Act 2000 (FSMA 2000) and the Companies Act 2006 (CA 2006).

9.2.1 Compliance with the Financial Services and Markets Act 2000

The Financial Services Act 1986 (FSA 1986) introduced a regime of consumer protection to regulate persons carrying on investment business through a system of self-regulation. In 1997, the Government decided that the system of regulation required an overhaul. The solution was to create a single regulator (the Financial Services Authority) to oversee all financial and banking services, and to provide framework legislation for the new system, in the shape of the FSMA 2000.

Solicitors must be aware of the effect of the FSMA 2000, and in particular of when they need authorisation and when they should seek the help of others with the requisite authorisation, in order to carry out acquisitions work.

9.2.1.1 Financial promotions and unsolicited calls

The proposal to acquire the shares of a private company may arise in a number of ways: the seller may, for example, have a particular buyer in contemplation, or the initial approach may come from the buyer. It may be, however, that the seller is searching for potential buyers for the company and wishes to bring the possibility of a sale to their attention. In these circumstances, the seller and its advisers must be careful not to contravene the provisions of the FSMA 2000 relating to financial promotions and unsolicited calls.

The basic restriction

Section 21 of the FSMA 2000 makes it a criminal offence for any person other than an authorised person to 'communicate an invitation or inducement to engage in investment activity' unless its contents have been approved by an authorised person. Any investment agreement entered into as a result of the breach is rendered unenforceable (although the court has discretion to permit enforcement in certain circumstances).

What sort of activities are covered by the restriction?

The restriction would seem to include approaches by a seller to potential buyers in the hope of inducing them to enter into negotiations for the acquisition of shares in the target company. The consequences of breach are serious, so the seller should seek the approval of an authorised person if there is any possibility of the section applying. An example of an authorised person used in these circumstances would be a merchant banker.

It is worth noting, however, that where there is a sale of a body corporate, an exemption from the restrictions on financial promotions is provided by Art 62 of the FSMA 2000 (Financial Promotion) Order 2005 (SI 2005/1529). The conditions under which this exemption applies are the same as those mentioned at **9.2.1.2** below in relation to the exclusion from regulated activities under Art 70 of the FSMA 2000 (Regulated Activities) Order 2001 (SI 2001/544).

9.2.1.2   Regulated activities

If a firm finds that it is involving itself in 'regulated activities', it must obtain authorisation, direct from the Financial Services Authority, for each specific type of activity with which it is involved.

'Regulated activities' are activities involving defined financial matters as a stand-alone service. Although advising on and arranging a share purchase would constitute 'regulated activities' as defined by s 22 of the FSMA 2000, there are a number of helpful exclusions under the FSMA 2000 (Regulated Activities) Order 2001. The most significant exclusion in the acquisitions context is provided by Art 70. This excludes from regulation activities carried on in connection with the sale of a body corporate if that sale will result in the buyer owning 50% or more of the company's voting shares, or if the transaction is designed to enable the buyer to obtain day-to-day control of the company's affairs. Most company acquisitions will clearly fall within the parameters of this exclusion.

In any event, the practical effect of the legislation is that most solicitors firms will be exempt from the requirement to be authorised, as they are unlikely to be providing regulated activities as a stand-alone service. However, if they are involving themselves in 'exempt regulated activities' as an incidental part of their legal services, The Solicitors Regulation Authority will supervise the provision of such services, and the Financial Services Authority will in turn monitor the effectiveness of such supervision.

The FSMA 2000 is considered in more detail in *Public Companies and Equity Finance*.

9.2.2   Compliance with the Companies Act 2006

9.2.2.1   The financial assistance rules

Under s 151 of the Companies Act 1985, all companies were prohibited from giving financial assistance for the purchase of their own shares. The rules were complex in their application and extended to financial assistance given before, at the same time as, and after the acquisition. The application of these financial assistance rules meant that arrangements such as the target company's assets being offered as security for loans to buy shares in the target, or parts of the purchase price being left outstanding at completion, could have serious consequences, including rendering the agreement for the purchase of shares void. As such provisions are often an integral part of a private company acquisition, a special relaxation procedure (known as 'the whitewash procedure') was available to authorise financial assistance for the acquisition of shares in the context of a private company. The prohibition on private companies giving financial assistance for the purchase of their shares, and the associated whitewash procedure, were abolished by Ch 2 of Pt 18 of the CA 2006.

However, the prohibition on giving financial assistance is retained for public companies under s 678 of the CA 2006, and s 679(1) restates the previous prohibition on the provision of financial assistance by a public company subsidiary for the purpose of an acquisition of shares in its private holding company. The exceptions from the prohibition are set out in s 678(2) (the principal purpose exceptions), s 681 (unconditional exceptions) and s 682 (conditional exceptions) of the CA 2006. For details on the rules of financial assistance for public companies, see *Public Companies and Equity Finance*.

9.2.2.2   Directors' interests

A director who is directly or indirectly interested in a contract or proposed contract with the company should declare his interest to the board in accordance with s 177 of the CA 2006 and comply with any relevant provisions of the company's articles (eg restricting him from voting or counting in the quorum of a board meeting discussing the contract).

On completion of a share acquisition, the target company must hold a board meeting in order effectively to transfer control of the newly-acquired company (see **7.3.3.2**). If a director has any interest in the proposed acquisition, this may give rise to a requirement to declare his interest (unless a general notice has already been given or the directors ought to have already have been aware of the interest – CA 2006, s 177). This may arise where a director of the target company (or of its holding company) is also a party to the sale and purchase agreement or connected with such a party.

Where a director is a party to any share or asset acquisition, consideration should also be given to the wider considerations of directors' duties (see *Business Law and Practice*).

If a director, or a person 'connected' with a director (this includes families and companies with which the director is associated), is buying a substantial non-cash asset from or selling such an asset to the company, the approval of the members by ordinary resolution is required (CA 2006, s 190) (see **7.3.1.1**). The requirement for authorisation under s 190 of the CA 2006 applies to both asset and share acquisitions but is often hard to identify on a share acquisition. Consider, for example, the following transactions:

Example 1

A Ltd is acquiring the entire share capital of Target Ltd. B is a shareholder in Target Limited and a director of A Ltd.

A Ltd is acquiring a non-cash asset (the shares) from one of its directors. If B's shares in Target Ltd are 'substantial', an ordinary resolution of the shareholders of A Ltd is required to authorise the transaction.

Example 2

A Ltd is acquiring the entire share capital of Target Limited. B is a director of A Ltd. C, who is B's son, is a shareholder in Target Limited.

Consent of the shareholders of A Ltd may again be required because A Ltd is acquiring a non-cash asset from a person 'connected' with one of its directors (the definition of 'connected persons' for this purpose is contained in s 253(2)(c) of the CA 2006).

Example 3

D Ltd sells shares in Target Limited to E Ltd. F is a director of D Ltd and is also a 30% shareholder in E Ltd.

D Ltd is disposing of a non-cash asset (the shares) to a person 'connected' with one of its directors. The definition of 'connected persons' for this purpose is contained in s 253(2)(c) of the CA 2006 and includes a company 'associated' with the director. E Ltd is an associated company of F by virtue of F's 30% shareholding, and is therefore a person connected with F. If D Ltd's shares in Target Limited are 'substantial', consent of the shareholders of D Ltd is required by s 190.

9.2.2.3 Payments to directors in connection with the transfer of shares by way of compensation for loss of office

Payments made to a director in connection with a transfer of the company's shares by way of compensation for loss of office may be governed by s 219 of the CA 2006. Any proposed payment for loss of office in connection with a transfer of shares in the company (or its subsidiary) which results from an acquisition must first be approved by an ordinary resolution of the holders of the shares to which the purchase relates.

A director who receives a sum in breach of these requirements holds it on trust for the shareholders who have sold their shares as a result of the offer. Section 219 does not apply to bona fide payments by way of damages for breach of contract.

It is also provided (s 216(2)) that if the price which is offered to the director for his shares is in excess of the price obtainable by other holders of like shares, the excess is deemed to be compensation for loss of office or consideration for or in connection with his retirement from office. This provision is designed to prevent compensation to a director being 'dressed up' as part of the purchase price of his shares.

9.2.2.4 Service contracts for directors

After a target company has been acquired, or as part of the completion arrangements, new directors may be appointed and granted service contracts, or existing directors may be awarded fresh contracts. If these contracts are to last for more than two years, consent of the members by ordinary resolution is required under s 188 of the CA 2006.

9.2.2.5 Interests of employees

Section 172 of the CA 2006 obliges directors to have regard to the interests of the company's employees in general. The directors of a target company should therefore try to strike a balance between the interests of the members and those of the employees when taking decisions relating to the share acquisition (eg at the completion board meeting). The directors owe this duty to the company and not to the employees, who are unable, therefore, to take any direct action to enforce it.

9.3 Acquiring tax liabilities

On a share acquisition, the buyer is acquiring an entity with a tax history and with all its tax liabilities intact. This obliges the buyer to carry out a more detailed investigation into the tax affairs of the target than on an asset acquisition (when tax liabilities remain with the seller) and to seek protection in the sale and purchase agreement by negotiating numerous warranties and indemnities. In some cases, the buyer may be attracted to a particular company because of its tax status; the target company may, for example, have unrelieved trading losses which the buyer intends to use to shelter future profits. In these circumstances, the buyer would wish to ensure that nothing has happened in the past which would mean that anticipated reliefs are prejudiced by the change in control of the company.

9.3.1 Warranties

Warranties are appropriate to deal with compliance requirements of the target, such as the proper submission of returns and the correct implementation of the PAYE system.

Tax warranties will also be used to obtain as much information as possible about the tax history of the company. This tax history may be relevant to potential future liabilities of the target. For example, the buyer will want to know the base cost of chargeable assets owned by the target, particularly if it is intended that the target will sell assets after completion.

9.3.2 Indemnities

The buyer will be keen to ensure that the target company has accounted for all outstanding taxes and has no hidden tax liabilities. Appropriate indemnities will be included in the sale and purchase agreement to cover specific tax charges which may arise over and above those provided for in the accounts and which are referable to the seller's period of ownership. Tax indemnities may be incorporated in a separate deed (often referred to as the 'Tax Deed' or 'Tax Covenant'), or embodied in a schedule to the sale and purchase agreement. It is helpful if the tax warranties are in a separate part of the sale and purchase agreement as a different (longer) limitation period will apply for claims brought by the buyer under these warranties.

It used to be the practice that indemnities were given in favour of the target company itself, not the buyer, as it is the target company upon which the tax liability would fall. The case of *Zim Properties Ltd v Procter (Inspector of Taxes); Procter (Inspector of Taxes) v Zim Properties Ltd* [1985] STC 90, however, threw considerable doubt on the tax efficiency of this practice (see **5.7.2**). Now, tax indemnities, whether in the body of the agreement or in a separate deed, should be expressed to be in favour of the buyer and not the target company. This avoids the target being assessed to tax on an indemnity payment under the *Zim* principle; instead, the price of the target will be adjusted for capital tax purposes if the liability crystallises.

9.3.3 Redress for loss of reliefs

The buyer may also negotiate an indemnity provision to enable it to obtain redress from the seller if expected reliefs, such as the target's ability to carry forward unrelieved losses, are forfeited on the change in ownership of the target as a result of events prior to completion.

9.3.3.1 Carry forward of trading losses

The target company may have unused trading losses which the buyer intends to offset against future profits of the company. Although s 393(1) of ICTA 1988 normally allows trading losses of a company to be set against future profits of the same trade, s 768 restricts this right if there is a major change in the nature or conduct of the target company's trade within a three-year period which includes a change of ownership.

The buyer should seek assurances from the seller that there has been no such major change in the nature and conduct of the trade before the acquisition, and must keep an eye on the position after the acquisition. What, then, amounts to a 'major change in the nature and conduct of the trade'? Section 768(4) states that it would include a major change in the type of property dealt in, or services or facilities provided, in the trade, or a major change in customers, outlets or markets of the trade.

9.4 Taxation on a share acquisition

The tax position on a share acquisition is relatively straightforward as the transaction involves the sale and purchase of only one type of asset – the shares.

9.4.1 Liability of the seller on the sale of shares

9.4.1.1 Individuals

Subject to available reliefs and exemptions, an individual shareholder pays CGT on the gain arising from the disposal of his shares at the rate of 18% for the tax year 2008/09. The date of the disposal for CGT purposes is the date that the parties enter into the acquisition agreement (or, if the agreement is conditional, the time when the condition is fulfilled) and not, if later, the date of completion.

9.4.1.2 Companies

A company which sells a shareholding, the disposal of which does not qualify for exemption from tax as a disposal of a substantial shareholding, pays corporation tax on any chargeable gain which arises on the disposal of the shares. The rate of tax depends on whether the total profits of the company's accounting period exceed the 'small company' threshold. The company pays the tax nine months after the end of the accounting period, unless it is a large company.

For large companies (those with taxable profit of at least £1,500,000), corporation tax will be paid in instalments, calculated according to the anticipated final tax bill for the accounting period. The first instalment is payable six months and 14 days into the accounting period. There are provisions for HMRC to repay tax to a company that believes it has over-estimated the instalments that become due. Interest will be payable on late paid instalments and HMRC will pay interest on overpaid tax.

9.4.2 Reducing the charge

There are a number of provisions in the TCGA 1992 enabling shareholders selling shares to exempt either the whole or part of the gain, or at least to postpone the occasion of the charge. There may also be scope for corporate sellers to take steps prior to entering into the contract which have the effect of reducing liability on the disposal.

9.4.2.1 Entrepreneurs' relief

Entrepreneurs' relief (see **8.4.2.1**) may be available where the share sale represents a 'qualifying business disposal' for an *individual* seller. That is, the target company must be a trading company, the seller's personal company (ie he must hold at least 5% of the ordinary share capital giving at least 5% of the voting rights), and the seller must be an employee or officer (such as a director) of the company. All these conditions must have been satisfied throughout the period of one year ending with the date of disposal.

If the conditions for the relief are met, the seller's gains on the sale of the target's shares are reduced by any losses made as part of the disposal, and any net gain is reduced by 4/9ths. The relief is subject to a lifetime restriction, however, of £1 million of qualifying net gains realised on or after 6 April 2008, so the seller can claim only £1 million of net relief from CGT, whether the gains arise from a single disposal or several disposals spread over time.

Deferral relief on reinvestment in EIS shares

This relief, will avail an *individual* who, for example, disposes of shares of any kind and reinvests the chargeable gain by subscribing for shares which qualify under the EIS. The individual's chargeable gain on the disposal of the original shares (up to the subscription cost) is deferred until he disposes of the EIS-qualifying shares. The EIS shares must be acquired within one year before or three years after the original disposal. The seller can apply any available entrepreneurs' relief before deferring any remaining gain by investing in the EIS shares.

The relief will not avail a corporate shareholder, though a corporate shareholder may obtain tax relief if selling shares in circumstances which qualify under the Corporate Venturing Scheme (see *Legal Foundations*). The detail of the Corporate Venturing Scheme is beyond the scope of this book.

9.4.2.2 Emigration

An *individual* seller who sells shares whilst neither resident nor ordinarily resident in the UK can avoid a charge to CGT. However, the requirements for an individual to establish that he is neither resident nor ordinarily resident have always been stringent. The detailed rules on what constitutes residence are outside the scope of this book and readers are referred to *Private Client: Wills, Trusts and Estate Planning* for a fuller discussion.

The basic rules on whether an individual is resident in the UK are set out in s 10A of the TCGA 1992 (as inserted by the Finance Act 1998). Individuals who fulfil the following criteria will be liable to CGT on any chargeable gains on assets disposed of after their departure from the UK. Individuals will be subject to CGT if they:

(a) have been resident in the UK for any part of at least four out of the seven tax years immediately preceding the tax year in which they left the UK; and

(b) have been not resident and not ordinarily resident for a period of less than five full tax years between the year of departure and the year of return; and

(c) own the assets disposed of before they leave the UK.

A gain made in the tax year of departure will be assessed in that tax year. A gain made after the date of departure will be assessed in the tax year of return to the UK. The scope for tax planning in this area is very limited.

9.4.2.3 Share for share exchanges (TCGA 1992, s 135)

Section 135 of the TCGA 1992 provides another form of roll-over type relief where the seller of shares (*individual or corporate*) receives shares issued by an acquiring company as consideration for the sale.

Nature of the relief

The effect of the relief is to roll any gain on the target company's shares into the shares in the acquiring company which are issued in consideration. The seller pays no capital tax on the sale of the target company's shares as it is treated as not making a disposal at this stage; it is deemed, however, to have acquired the consideration shares at the same time and for the same price as the original shares. The effect is to postpone any CGT or, in the case of a corporate seller, corporation tax until the disposal of the new shares.

This relief cannot be used in conjunction with the annual exemption.

Conditions for the relief

The buyer must hold a minimum stake in the target   For the relief to operate, the buyer must hold over 25% of the ordinary shares of the target company, either before or in consequence of the share exchange. Alternatively, the exchange must result from a general offer made to the shareholders of the target conditional on the buyer obtaining control of the target.

The exchange must be effected for bona fide commercial reasons   Section 137 of the TCGA 1992 provides that, for s 135 relief to be available, the exchange must be effected for 'bona fide commercial reasons' and must not form part of a scheme or arrangement of which the main purpose, or one of the main purposes, is to avoid CGT or corporation tax. This provision does not, however, affect the availability of the relief to a shareholder who holds 5% or less of the shares or debentures (or any class of shares or debentures) in the target company (s 137(2)).

A clearance procedure is contained in s 138, under which HMRC can be asked to confirm that it is satisfied that the exchange is effected for bona fide commercial reasons and not for a tax avoidance motive. It must notify its decision within 30 days of the application for clearance, unless it requires further information. Although it is clearly in the seller's interest to obtain a clearance, the section provides that the application for clearance must be made either by the target company or by the acquiring company. Another curious feature of the procedure is that clearance from HMRC does not guarantee that relief will be granted; it confirms that s 137 will not prevent the relief, but not that the conditions for the relief are met.

Other paper-for-paper exchanges

Relief is generally available in the same way if the shares in the target company are exchanged for debentures or loan notes issued by the acquiring company. There are two caveats, however: first, special rules apply to certain debentures which come within the definition of 'qualifying corporate bonds' (these rules, which are contained in s 116 of the TCGA 1992, are outside the scope of this book); secondly, HMRC is unlikely to give advance clearance where loan notes issued in exchange can be redeemed by the holder within six months of issue. Subject to this, it may suit a seller to receive staggered payments (loan notes will often be redeemable at six-monthly intervals, see **8.4.2.3**), thereby effectively enabling it to pay the CGT or corporation tax in instalments.

9.4.2.4   Exemption for company gains on substantial shareholdings

The Finance Act 2002 introduced legislation to facilitate corporate restructuring. The effect of the legislation is to exempt from tax capital gains arising on the disposal by corporate shareholders of substantial shareholdings in trading companies. The main conditions attached to the provisions are as follows:

(a)   The vendor company must have held at least 10% of the ordinary share capital of the company being disposed of for at least 12 consecutive months in the two years prior to the sale.

(b)   The vendor company must be a trading company or a member of a trading group throughout the shareholding period (referred to in (a) above) and immediately after the disposal. A trading company or trading group is essentially a company or group the activities of which do not include 'to any substantial extent' activities other than 'trading activities'. Broadly, 'trading activities' are activities carried out in the course of a trade, or in preparation to carry on or acquire a trade.

(c)   The company whose shares are being disposed of must be a trading company or qualifying holding company throughout the shareholding period and immediately after the disposal. (The provision does, however, extend to cover gains only (ie losses are not allowable) on shares in a company which is not a qualifying trading or holding company immediately after the disposal by reason only of it ceasing to trade/being put into liquidation at the date of disposal.)

A qualifying holding company is a company the activities of which, together with those of its 51% subsidiaries, do not to any substantial extent include non-trading activities.

It should be noted that although the test for 'substantial shareholding' is measured by reference to ordinary shares only, if the test is satisfied, relief will be available in relation to disposals of any class of, or interest in, shares.

9.4.3   How is the seller taxed when the consideration is deferred?

It is common for some part of the purchase price to be left outstanding on completion. The seller may have agreed to receive payment by instalments, or to the buyer retaining a specified amount as security for breaches of warranty. The price may even be determinable by reference to future profits (an 'earn out', see **4.3.4.2**). What, then, are the tax implications of such arrangements?

9.4.3.1   The general rule

The general rule, stated in s 48 of the TCGA 1992, is that even if some part of the consideration is deferred, CGT (or corporation tax) is payable on the total consideration by reference to the date of the sale. This applies even if the seller has only a contingent right to receive part of the price (although, if the amount is uncertain, special rules apply, see **9.4.3.3**). The section does provide, however, that if the seller does not in fact receive the full amount of the deferred consideration, an appropriate adjustment will be made to the tax payable, thus entitling the seller to a tax refund.

The contingent liability which the seller has to the buyer in respect of warranties and indemnities will not affect the calculation of the gain. However, any payment which the seller makes to the buyer after completion under a warranty or indemnity will have the effect of reducing the proceeds of sale and, consequently, the gain for capital tax purposes (see **5.7.3**).

9.4.3.2   Payment of the consideration by instalments

Where the consideration is payable in instalments over a period exceeding 18 months, the tax may be paid by instalments at the option of the taxpayer, who must agree the instalment schedule with HMRC.

9.4.3.3   Where the amount of deferred consideration is uncertain

The tax position is complicated if the amount of the deferred consideration cannot be determined on completion; the most obvious example is on an 'earn out', where the total amount payable by the buyer depends on the profits earned by the target company in the two or three years following completion.

Following the case of *Marren (Inspector of Taxes) v Ingles* [1980] 3 All ER 95, HMRC charges tax on the basis of the consideration actually received at the time of the disposal plus the current value of the right to receive the future consideration. It regards this contingent right to future consideration as a *chose in action* (ie a future right to something which may be recovered, if necessary, by court action) which is itself a chargeable asset. Thus, when the seller receives the deferred consideration, it is treated as disposing of the chose in action and may face a further charge to CGT (or corporation tax).

Although no HMRC guidance has yet been published on the point, it is thought that the disposal of the chose in action will not constitute a qualifying business disposal for the purposes of entrepreneurs' relief, so an individual seller will only be able to claim this relief, if available, to reduce the charge to CGT on the gain made as at the date of completion of the acquisition.

Consider, for example, an individual seller who disposes of his shares in 2008 and who has agreed to receive £250,000 on completion plus 20% of profits (as defined) of the target for the next two years; the base cost of his shares is £30,000.

In calculating the capital gain on the disposal of shares, HMRC will deduct the base cost of the shares (£30,000) from the consideration received on completion (£250,000) plus its valuation of the seller's right to the deferred consideration.

The 20% of profits of the target for the next two years is treated as the seller's right to the deferred consideration. HMRC will estimate the value of this right as, say, £200,000. In this example, this would produce a gain of £420,000, which may be reduced by applicable reliefs, such as entrepreneurs' relief.

When the individual seller receives the deferred consideration (at the end of the two-year period), he is treated as making a chargeable disposal of a chose in action (ie his right to receive that deferred consideration). A further gain may arise, resulting in a subsequent CGT payment being made.

Let us assume that the consideration received at the end of the two-year period is, in fact, £350,000. The individual seller's gain is arrived at by deducting from this figure the base cost of the chose in action (ie £200,000) to produce a gain of £150,000. Again, this gain may be reduced by available reliefs, though as mentioned above this will not be a qualifying business disposal for entrepreneurs' relief.

A number of problems may arise out of this treatment. If the amount of deferred consideration received by the seller is less than the value placed on it by HMRC, a loss will accrue to the seller on the disposal of the chose in action. A capital loss can, of course, be relieved if the seller makes gains in the future against which the loss can be set. In addition, a recent measure allows an individual seller to elect for a loss arising in these circumstances to be treated for CGT purposes as though it arose in an earlier year (in practice, the seller will generally elect for the loss to be treated as having arisen in the year of the original disposal of shares).

The rule in *Marren (Inspector of Taxes) v Ingles* applies where the consideration is unascertainable at the time of completion. It would not apply if, for example, some part of the consideration is left outstanding pending the drawing up of completion accounts. In this case, although the consideration is not known on completion, the information is available for it to be ascertained.

9.4.3.4   Deferred consideration satisfied in shares

Where the deferred consideration is to be satisfied by the acquiring company issuing shares to the seller, the seller can elect to treat the chose in action as a security for capital tax purposes, with the result that it should not be charged to tax in respect of the deferred consideration until disposal of the shares issued in satisfaction of this deferred element. Instead, roll-over relief on a share for share exchange is available, provided the seller does not have the option to take cash instead.

9.4.4   Tax implications for the buyer

The immediate tax consequences for the buyer of acquiring shares are uncomplicated; the buyer pays stamp duty on the price paid which also forms his base cost for CGT (or, in the case of a company, corporation tax) purposes.

9.4.4.1   Stamp duty

The buyer pays stamp duty at the rate of 0.5% of the consideration, rounded up to the nearest £5, and should present the stock transfer forms for stamping within 30 days of completion. Where completion accounts are to be drawn up, the buyer should present the stock transfer forms to the Stamp Office within 30 days but undertake to pay the duty when the price has been determined. Stamp duty reserve tax (SDRT) is chargeable (at the rate of 0.5% of the consideration) on an agreement to sell shares. The tax is payable on the seventh day of the month following that in which the agreement was made or became unconditional. Any SDRT charge will, however, be cancelled (and any SDRT paid refunded) if the transfer is executed and stamped within six years of the agreement.

9.4.4.2   Financing the acquisition by borrowing: is tax relief available?

Close companies

An individual who takes out a loan to buy ordinary shares in a close trading company will obtain tax relief on the interest as a charge on income if he either controls more than 5% of the ordinary share capital (shares acquired as a result of the borrowing are included), or works for the greater part of his time in the management of the company (ITA 2007, s 383).

Enterprise Investment Scheme (FA 1994, s 137 and Sch 5)

The Finance Act 1994 introduced the Enterprise Investment Scheme to encourage individuals to invest in shares issued on or after 1 January 1994 by a qualifying unquoted trading company. If certain conditions are fulfilled (eg the shares must be held for three years), income tax relief (at 20%) is available on up to £500,000-worth of investment for any tax year (ie a maximum of £100,000 of income tax relief). In addition, any gains on disposal of the shares are exempt from CGT and relief is given for any losses. Shares traded on the Alternative Investment Market are treated as 'unquoted' for this and other tax purposes.

Corporate buyer

A company will generally receive tax relief as a debit under the loan relationship rules contained in the Finance Act 1996 on the interest which it pays on a loan to acquire shares.

Chapter 10

Private Equity Acquisitions

10.1 Private equity overview

Private equity transactions are full of terminology such as 'sweet equity' and 'subordination'; it is easy to become bewildered as you try to learn the language of the private equity world. However, the basic premise of private equity is actually very straightforward. It is simply an investment in the share capital of a private company.

By acquiring shares and thereby ownership rights in a company, the investor (the private equity provider) hopes to receive income from the profits generated by that company (often through dividends) and to make a capital gain from the onward sale of those shares.

Making an investment in a private company is an inherently risky venture, but one where the potentially high risks may be matched with potentially high returns. Shares in a private company cannot readily be sold if the venture does not prove to be successful, so an investment of this nature should be based on expert advice and the use of appropriate strategies to try to minimise the possible risks. Over recent years expertise has developed in this type of investment and, as a result, many investors have seen great success.

The development of private equity began with the provision of finance to new developing businesses, and in particular with business managers seeking to finance the purchase (or 'buyout') of the business in which they worked (**10.2**). The provision of such finance was often referred to as 'venture capital' and usually involved the investor taking a minority stake in the developing company. This type of financing is still made available by private equity providers in the form of start-up or developmental funds and traditional management buyouts.

However, as the private equity market has developed, some private equity providers have become interested in seeking wider investment opportunities by acquiring a majority stake in an underperforming company, in the hope that the investor's involvement will turn the company's fortunes around and it can then be sold on for a profit. In these circumstances, the private equity provider is actively seeking a company whose performance it believes can be improved either through the introduction of new management, or through the use of the existing management in a restructured company. Once the company has returned to optimum performance, the investor can realise its investment at a profit. This has proved to be a very successful strategy, with private equity providers seeking out bigger and better investments. The expansion of the private equity market has even led to 'public to private transactions', where private equity providers consider underperforming listed companies as potential acquisition targets. In recent years there have been increasing concerns about the development of the private equity markets, and there has been some regulation through the Financial Services Authority of these large acquisitions to try to address some of the concerns regarding possible conflicts of interest and extreme levels of debt within the acquired business (excessive leverage). Changes in the economic climate (eg in 2008, the so-called 'credit crunch') are also likely to lead to the development of further constraints on the private equity market.

10.1.1   The private equity provider

So what are a private equity fund and a private equity provider? The private equity fund is the money that is to be invested. The fund may come from a variety of sources, such as particular individuals or companies, or from institutional investors like pension funds, banks and insurance companies. Specialist funds are created whereby these investors agree, usually (primarily for tax reasons) through the form of a Limited Partnership, to provide funds to be invested in particular types of private companies. The private equity fund will usually have a statement as to the type of investments for which the fund may be used. The investment of the money within the fund will be made by a private equity provider (sometimes referred to as the private equity house). The private equity provider makes its profit by the successful investment of private equity funds (often through the imposition of fees based on percentage profits of successful investment returns). It is vital for the private equity provider to undertake successful investments since, if the funds it invests do not generate acceptable returns, the investors are unlikely to put money into funds run by that provider again. A private equity provider will try to maximise profit for the investors whilst at the same time minimising the risks of the investment in order to grow its own business successfully and develop a good reputation in the private equity market.

10.1.2   The decision to invest

Before undertaking an investment, the private equity provider will usually follow an agreed internal procedure for the approval of the investment. As an acquisitions lawyer working on a private equity transaction, it is important to appreciate any requirements there may be for such internal approvals before funds are placed, as this can have a significant impact on the timetable of a proposed acquisition. The internal procedure will usually involve the production of an investment paper which will then be presented to an investment committee of the private equity provider. This paper will set out the proposed structure for the transaction and the anticipated rate of return on the investment. Where the funds to be provided are for a buyout (**10.1.3**), an offer for the acquisition will be made on the basis of this initial approval, and final approval of the investment committee may also be required when the detail of the proposed acquisition has been agreed. The investment of the funds will often be provided through particular corporate investment structures. If the transaction is large this may involve the use of a number of corporate entities in order to layer the input of the required finances (a method known as 'structural subordination') and may also involve the use of overseas holding companies (for tax and investment planning purposes).

10.1.3   Types of investments

Private equity investments broadly fall into three categories: start-up capital (providing financing at the outset of a business); development capital (providing finance for expansion); and buyouts (where finance is provided for the acquisition of a business). For both start-up capital and development capital, the investment will usually take the form of a subscription for shares in the existing company. Where funds are to be provided for a buyout, the investment may take a variety of forms depending of the nature of the buyout that is proposed. This chapter covers two different types of buyout that are common in practice: a traditional management buyout, and an institutional leveraged buyout.

On a buyout, the method by which the investment is made will vary depending on both the type and size of the buyout. For a small management buyout, a direct subscription for shares may be made in the company undertaking the target business. In the case of a large management buyout, it is likely that there will be a substantial amount of debt finance as well, so a corporate structure may be created in order to undertake the acquisition; and on large institutional leveraged buyouts it is likely that a fairly complex corporate structure will be used to cope with the numerous layers of investment and debt finance.

10.2 Management buyout

A management buyout ('MBO') is a transaction by which the target is acquired by some or all of its management, usually through the vehicle of a new company established for this purpose ('Newco'). Management buyouts may proceed as share or asset acquisitions. The prospective management team is unlikely to be able to generate sufficient capital itself to finance the acquisition and will therefore usually seek funding elsewhere. The management team draws up a business plan designed to attract investment by a private equity provider. Often, several private equity providers will be invited to bid for the opportunity to be involved in the deal.

The financing for the acquisition will comprise a combination of equity finance provided by the management team and the private equity provider, and debt finance to be secured on the assets of the target company. In a management buyout that has been instigated by the existing management team, the private equity provider will expect the management team to provide a substantial investment, primarily to ensure that the team is heavily committed financially as well as commercially to the success of the venture. The private equity provider will usually prefer to take a majority·shareholding in the venture, but may be prepared to accept a minority shareholding on certain MBOs provided it can also negotiate measures to allow it more control if it becomes concerned that the venture is failing.

10.2.1 The investment

As indicated above, the investment by the private equity provider will often be made through a new corporate vehicle established for the purpose ('Newco'). Both the private equity provider and the management team will subscribe for ordinary shares in Newco, although each party will have carefully negotiated the rights attaching to those shares. The private equity provider will also make a large proportion of its investment in return for redeemable preference shares that carry preferential rights to receive income by way of dividends and to the return of capital on a winding up of Newco (to try to minimise its exposure should the venture prove to be unsuccessful).

In addition to requiring particular class rights in relation to the issued shares, the parties to the venture will expect to enter into an 'investment agreement' (see **10.4.1** below). This agreement will set out the basis on which the investment has been made, any required restrictions on the running of the acquired company and relevant provisions governing the realisation of the investment through an onward sale or listing. On a traditional MBO the investment agreement will also include extensive warranties given by the management team about the target business and also the business plan drawn up by the team to attract the investment. Where a company is being sold to its own management, the seller will often be able to resist giving extensive warranties (see **10.2.3**). However, the private equity provider will not be satisfied with the seller's limited warranties and will require the management team itself to provide comfort by warranting all key information about the target business.

10.2.2   Conflict of interest

When a management team is contemplating a buyout, it must take great care to ensure that its actions do not breach any obligations of good faith or confidentiality owed to the target company. The management team, in negotiations for the purchase of the target, will inevitably try to achieve the best price possible, and this may place them in a position of conflict with their duties to the company, its shareholders and employees. If a management team member is also a director, consideration should be given to his statutory duties. As soon as a director has decided to initiate a MBO an approach should be made to the board to declare his interest and to seek consent to proceed. Even where the management team member is not a director, an approach to the board is still advisable as the MBO process is otherwise likely to involve breaches in the terms of his employment contract, in particular any terms as to confidentiality.

Management buyouts may also give rise to consideration of s 190 of the CA 2006 and the need for shareholders' approval where a company buys an asset from or sells an asset to a director (see **9.2.2.2**). If the director will hold shares in the corporate vehicle created for the purpose of the buyout (Newco) then this could fall within the classification of an associated company and so be deemed to be 'connected' with the director under s 234 of the CA 2006. Although a single director is unlikely to hold the relevant 20% holding required for Newco to be his associated company under s 254(2), the legislation refers to a 20% holding by a director and/or his connected persons. Where the management team will have a shareholding of 20% or more in Newco, a detailed review should be undertaken to ascertain whether or not shareholders' approval under s 190 of the CA 2006 will be required for the sale.

10.2.3   Warranties

As indicated above, another feature of MBO transactions is the issue of warranty provision, which may involve more negotiation than on a traditional asset or share sale. The seller is likely to resist extensive warranties being included in the sale and purchase agreement on the basis that the managers who are buying the target are likely to have more knowledge about the business than the seller. On the other hand, warranties are designed to allocate risk between the seller and the buyer, as well as to elicit information about the business. The seller will, of course, be receiving full consideration whether or not the buyers are part of the management team, and should arguably, therefore, be prepared to give full warranties.

10.3   Institutional leveraged buyout

On an institutional leveraged buyout, the private equity provider will hope to acquire a majority shareholding in a private company (or even an underperforming public company that could be converted into a private company) that has the potential to generate substantial profits. The private equity provider will be managing funds created by institutional investors such as pension funds, banks and insurance companies. These institutional fund holders will be seeking to achieve good returns whilst trying to minimise potential risks. Having identified a possible target company as the proposed investment opportunity, the private equity provider will follow its internal procedures for approval of the proposed investment. In recent years many companies have been sold through the auction process (2.4.2), and on some such transactions there may be a number of private equity providers who are bidding for the right to acquire the company.

10.3.1   Debt/equity ratio

In arranging the structure of a leveraged buyout, consideration will be given to the overall arrangement for financing the acquisition. The private equity provider will try to achieve the best debt to equity mix in order to maximise its profit. As part of its investment decision, it will consider its internal rate of return (how much gain will be achieved on the sale based on projections for the increase in value of the target company). This will be dependent on how much equity needs to be provided: the lower the amount of equity, the greater the gains per share.

A feature of such private equity-led acquisitions is a very high level of debt funding. The key advantage of private company investments is that they are not subject to prohibitions on the provision of financial assistance (see 9.2.2). This means that any borrowing for the acquisition of the target company's shares can be secured on the assets of the target company. Provision of security in this way is not possible on the acquisition of a public company, so where a public company is to be acquired through a private equity-led investment, the public target will immediately be converted into a private company.

10.3.2   The management team

On a leveraged buyout, the management team will not be the driving force behind the acquisition but will still be instrumental in that it will usually have the expertise necessary to maximise the investment potential of the target company. The management team selected may be the existing managers, external managers brought in by the private equity provider or a combination of the two. The managers will usually be provided with some form of financial incentive in order to achieve a successful exit from the target company. This will usually be in the form of a class of equity shares (often called 'sweet equity') that the management team will be able to sell when the target company is sold. As with a traditional MBO, the management team will be expected to give warranties in relation to its business plan and information provided by it about the target. The provision of warranties in this case, though, is usually driven more by a concern to establish the management team's full commitment to the process rather than as a risk allocation exercise. Unlike on a traditional MBO, the seller will usually provide full warranties, and any claims will be made by the buyer under those warranties rather than by pursuing the management team.

10.3.3   Common structures on leveraged buyout

In order to accommodate the varying interests of the parties involved in a leveraged buyout and to maximise the security and tax planning opportunities, the private equity provider will not invest directly into the company to be acquired. Instead, a corporate structure will be put together to receive the investment initially, the complexity of which will vary according to the particular circumstances of the transaction.

At its most straightforward the structure will consist of a holding or 'top' company which will act as the investment vehicle for all the equity funds (ie those provided by the private equity provider and any provided by the management team). This top company will usually then have a wholly-owned subsidiary that will undertake the bank borrowing needed to provide the balance of the acquisition cost. The actual purchase of the target company may be made by this wholly-owned subsidiary, or by the subsidiary of that wholly-owned company if that suits the tax and other circumstances of the transaction.

The layering of the corporate structure used for the acquisition relates primarily to considerations of tax and structural subordination which are outside the scope of this book. The companies undertaking the debt finance and the purchase of the target company will be wholly-owned subsidiaries of the top company. The equity investment is placed in the top company, which will be responsible for overseeing the operation of the investment, as governed by the terms of the investment agreement and by appropriate provisions in its articles.

10.4   Key documentation

On any buyout there will essentially be three key parties: the private equity provider; the debt financiers (there may be several); and the management team. Each of these parties will have its own aims and objectives in the transaction, though they will all seek to manage the risks that they agree to take on as part of the buyout arrangement. This will be achieved in part by the corporate buyout structures discussed above, but also by the terms of the documentation governing the investment (the investment agreement) and the rights attaching to the equity shares that are acquired.

10.4.1   The investment agreement

The investment agreement is a contractual document that will set out the agreed terms of the proposed investment, the ongoing management of the target company and the terms of any proposed realisation of the investment. The agreement will usually expressly state that its terms take precedence over any other documentation that may be required to govern individual relationships between the various parties to the transaction, such as loan agreements, constitutional documents or service contracts.

Although the investment agreement is intended primarily to cover the terms of the equity investment (it is sometimes referred to as the subscription and shareholders' agreement), the providers of the debt finance will often also be a party to it. The providers of the debt finance will enter into facility agreements setting out the terms on which they are prepared to lend the required funds and the terms of any charges or other security that will be taken over the assets of the target company. The debt financiers will want to ensure that any relevant provisions in the investment agreement are not inconsistent with the agreed security provisions.

The terms of the investment agreement will cover three key areas, as set out below.

10.4.1.1   The terms of the investment

The investment agreement will specify how the money required for the proposed purchase will be raised. This will include how much money is being invested by the private equity provider and the management team, as well as the proportion of funds to be raised by borrowing. The investment by the private equity investor will often take the form of different classes of shares. A relatively small proportion of the funds will be invested in ordinary shares, with the remainder invested in shares carrying particular rights in terms of dividend payments and the return of capital (often redeemable preference shares). The private equity provider may also provide some of its investment in return for debt securities such as loan notes or payment in kind notes (PIK notes – see *Banking and Capital Markets*).

The agreement will also provide details of the proposed acquisition. The acquisition will proceed only if all elements of the proposed investment proceed. The terms of each separate investment will usually be described as 'conditions precedent' to the transaction. This means that the various parties will all sign the investment agreement but each party will become committed to making its investment and proceeding with the acquisition only once all the other parties have also made their respective investments. On a traditional MBO, the management will also be required to give the specified management warranties (**10.2.1**). Management warranties will also be expected on an institutional leveraged buyout if the existing management team are being given the opportunity to take an equity stake in the venture.

10.4.1.2 Governance of the investment

The investment agreement will set out the agreed structures for the ongoing management of the target business. This structure will vary depending on whether the private equity provider has taken a minority or a majority stake in the venture. If the private equity provider has taken a minority stake, directly into the target company itself or a corporate vehicle created for the purpose of the acquisition in a traditional MBO (see **10.2**), then that provider will want very strict restrictions on the activities of the target company in order to protect its investment. If the provider has a majority stake it is likely to be more relaxed about restrictions, as it should be able to take over effective control of the company if necessary. On an institutional leveraged buyout the provider will usually require a majority stake, but will still require provisions to be put in place to monitor the investment and enable it to step into place if it needs to quick take control of the top company or any of its subsidiaries.

The particular type of restrictions imposed will vary with each transaction. However, the agreement will usually provide for the right to appoint board members, the right to dismiss all board members (this will be a point of negotiation on a traditional MBO), the right to obtain information and the right to veto certain decisions. The restrictions provided for in the investment agreement will be reflected in the articles of the top company (or the target company on a direct investment) and will usually be expressed as rights attaching to the particular class of shares issued as part of the investment.

10.4.1.3 Realisation of the investment

The investment agreement will usually include provisions relating to the intended realisation of the investment. The private equity investor will want to realise its investment within a specified period of time, usually about five years. There are a number of ways in which the investment may be realised. A listing is usually the most desirable outcome for the private equity provider and the documentation will often provide for the conversion of particular classes of shares, such as preference shares, into ordinary shares, prior to those shares being admitted onto a public market such as the London Stock Exchange. If a listing is not possible the private equity provider will seek to realise the investment through a trade sale, or even a sale to another private equity provider. With these forms of sale the buyer will usually expect the seller to provide warranties about the company being sold.

However, a private equity provider will not be prepared to give such warranties, as the money it realises from the investment must be returned to the private equity funds and cannot be subject to a possible later charge. In the investment agreement, therefore, the private equity provider will include a statement as to the intended length of its investment and that it will not be prepared to give any warranties on any subsequent sale.

The investment agreement will usually include agreed forms of the articles of association of the company in which the investment is to take place. In particular, these articles will include extensive provisions governing the transfer rights of the different classes of shares. The articles will usually prohibit the transfer of any shares taken by the management team, but will also provide for the mandatory sale of those shares if a director leaves whether through dismissal, retirement or death. The price paid for the shares in those circumstances will usually depend on whether the manager is considered a good or a bad leaver, usually roughly correlating to whether he left under amicable circumstances or was dismissed for poor performance or behaviour. On a traditional MBO these provisions will be heavily negotiated, as a considerable amount of money may depend on whether the manager is classified as a good or a bad leaver.

The transfer articles will also usually include transfer provisions known as 'drag along' and 'tag along' provisions. A drag along provision will usually be imposed on any minority management shareholders. When the private equity provider is seeking to realise its investment through the onward sale of the company, it will want to ensure that it can force the minority shareholders to sell their shares at the same time. Drag along provisions in the articles mean that the company can act as agent for the minority shareholders by automatically offering their shares to a buyer who has made an offer for a majority shareholding in the company. However, the minority shareholder will also usually require a reciprocal arrangement whereby it is able to 'tag along' or join in any sale of shares where an offer has been made to the private equity provider.

10.4.2 Associated documentation

In addition to the investment agreement, the parties to a private equity-led acquisition will enter into a number of associated documents covering their individual relationships. This documentation will cover the three different aspects of the transaction: the investment; the debt finance; and the acquisition.

10.4.2.1 The investment

The parties to the transaction must agree the terms of the articles of association of the top company. These articles will usually be agreed between the parties and attached to the investment agreement. The articles will set out the agreed class rights of each type of share that is to be issued, including rights to income and return on capital, and any rights relating to the governance of the company. The articles will also include any agreed restrictions on the transfer of shares and provisions regarding mandatory sales where a manager is dismissed or an offer to purchase the shares is received.

If the private equity provider is also providing funds using loan or PIK notes, the form of these must also be agreed.

The managers will usually be employees of the top company, and the terms of their service contracts must be negotiated. These contracts will usually include detailed provisions governing confidentiality and restrictive covenants.

10.4.2.2   The debt finance

The bank will usually be a party to the investment agreement on an institutional buyout, but there will also be separate banking documentation to govern the provision of the debt finance. This documentation will usually include a bank facility agreement specifying the amount of money being lent, which usually covers both the balance of the purchase price for the acquisition and the provision of working capital for the new venture. The bank will also require a package of documentation detailing the security it will have over the assets of the target business. If there are a number of providers of debt finance, there will also be an inter-creditor agreement setting out an agreed order of priority between the debt financiers for the different security taken over the target company's assets.

10.4.2.3   The acquisition

The acquisition process will be exactly the same as on a trade acquisition; it is simply that the focus of the buyer on a private equity acquisition will be firmly on the investment potential of the target rather than on trade implications. The buyer will undertake the required due diligence (although if the management team comprises existing managers this can give rise to particular issues on warranty provision (**10.2.2**)). The buyer and seller will enter into a sale and purchase agreement in the usual way, together with any associated documentation that may be required such as the disclosure letter, tax covenant, pension transfer provisions, etc.

Chapter 11

Group Reorganisations

11.1 Introduction to group companies

Groups of companies involving a parent (or holding) company, one or more subsidiaries and, sometimes, sub-subsidiaries, are popular structures for the carrying on of business enterprises both in the UK and abroad. It is not only well-known public companies listed on The Stock Exchange which avail themselves of this structure, groups are also common among smaller concerns and private companies.

The attraction of operating through a group of companies rather than divisions of a single company has much to do with the fact that each company within the group is a separate legal entity with limited liability. The parent company, for example, is not liable for the debts of its subsidiaries unless it has agreed to assume responsibility for them or there are other special circumstances (see **11.1.3**).

The group structure enables risky businesses or activities to be packaged into separate subsidiaries so that their failure will not impact too heavily on the remainder of the group. The valuable, asset-rich parts of the enterprise can be isolated from more speculative and uncertain ventures.

A group arrangement will often prove less cumbersome than having all activities under the umbrella of one company. It may be convenient for separate businesses or parts of a business to be run as identifiable units with their own management teams. Another factor is that a group structure provides greater flexibility where acquisitions and disposals are contemplated, since it is usually easier to transfer a subsidiary than part of the business of a company.

11.1.1 How do groups come about?

A group can come into existence in a number of ways.

11.1.1.1 Enterprise formed as a group

The promoters of a business venture may decide from the start to incorporate a parent company and several subsidiaries (which may be wholly owned by the parent) to carry on different aspects of the enterprise.

11.1.1.2 Splitting up a large concern

A company may decide to transfer certain sectors of its business (eg manufacturing, retail, distribution, etc) to subsidiaries specifically formed for this purpose. Similarly, where a number of different businesses are being run under the umbrella of a single company, these may be separated out and hived down to subsidiaries (**1.4**).

11.1.1.3   Mergers and acquisitions

Where a company acquires control of another company by share acquisition, the relationship of parent and subsidiary is created between the acquiring company and the target company; if the entire issued share capital of the target changes hands, it becomes a wholly-owned subsidiary of the acquiring company. Where the target company itself has subsidiaries, the acquisition brings into existence a group with three levels (and so on). The buyer will often be content to maintain this structure rather than incur costs in transferring the businesses out of the subsidiaries. A group which expands in this way by making acquisitions rather than by achieving 'organic' growth of its core business may end up with an array of diverse activities under its wing (such a group is known as a conglomerate group).

11.1.2   Company law status of groups

Company law makes very little specific provision for groups of companies. Each company within the group is treated as a separate entity with its own assets and liabilities. Generally, a company (even the parent company of a wholly-owned subsidiary) does not have any additional liabilities or obligations imposed on it, or benefits granted to it, through being a member of a group. Some provisions of the CA 2006 do, however, make specific reference to groups.

11.1.2.1   Extension of restrictions to group companies

Membership of holding company prohibited

Section 136 of the CA 2006 prohibits a subsidiary or its nominee from being a member of its holding company and renders any transfer or issue of the holding company's shares to a subsidiary or its nominee void, except where the subsidiary is acting as a trustee or as an authorised dealer in securities.

Substantial property transactions involving directors

Section 190 of the CA 2006 requires the passing of an ordinary resolution of the members of a company where a director of the company or its holding company acquires an asset from the company or disposes of an asset to the company which is 'substantial' (see **9.2.2.2**). If the director is a director of its holding company, an ordinary resolution of the holding company is also necessary to approve the transaction. No approval is required under s 190, however, by any company which is a wholly-owned subsidiary.

Loans to directors

Under s 197 of the CA 2006, shareholder approval is required for a company to make loans to its directors; and similarly, if a loan is to be made to a director of the company's holding company, the approval of the members of the holding company must also be sought.

11.1.2.2   Definition of group

Section 1159 of the CA 2006 defines the terms 'holding company' and 'subsidiary' used in the provisions outlined above. A company is a 'subsidiary' of another company, its 'holding company', if that other company:

(a)   holds a majority of the voting rights in it; or

(b)   is a member of it and has the right to appoint or remove a majority of its board of directors; or

(c)   is a member of it and controls alone, pursuant to an agreement with other members, a majority of the voting rights in it,

or if it is a subsidiary of a company that is itself a subsidiary of that other company.

In determining the voting rights for this definition, indirect holdings are taken into account, so this may include voting rights held through other subsidiaries, certain nominees and trustees.

11.1.3 Group indebtedness

One of the consequences of treating each member of the group as a completely separate entity is that a parent company is not liable for the debts of an insolvent subsidiary; the parent may even take priority to other creditors if, for example, it has loaned money to the subsidiary and taken security over its assets. Intra-group loans are common within groups of companies, as are group banking arrangements. In the event that a company is sold out of the group, steps must be taken to settle any intra-group debts and release the company to be sold from any forms of security that have been given in relation to the group finances.

11.1.3.1 Guarantees

Often, when a subsidiary company is entering into an agreement, a creditor may seek some form of guarantee or security from the parent company or other company in the group which has a stronger financial standing. This may extend to a guarantee of provisions in a sale and purchase agreement. For example, if part of the purchase price is to be left outstanding at completion, the seller may want to make the buyer's parent company a party to the agreement in order to guarantee the payment (**4.3.5.2**).

11.1.4 Group accounts

One area where the CA 2006 does impose additional obligations on group companies is in the preparation of accounts.

11.1.4.1 Definition for accounting purposes (CA 2006, s 1162)

A slightly different definition of a group is used for accounting purposes from that used for other purposes. Broadly, the differences are as follows:

(a)   the terms 'parent undertaking' and 'subsidiary undertakings' are employed. The definition of 'undertaking' includes companies, partnerships and unincorporated associations;

(b)   a parent/subsidiary relationship arises in a similar way to a holding company/subsidiary relationship as described at **11.1.2.2** above. In addition, a company will be a parent undertaking for accounting purposes if:

    (i)   it has the right to exercise a dominant influence over the 'subsidiary undertaking', or

    (ii)   it is managed on a unified basis with the 'subsidiary undertaking'.

11.1.4.2 Obligation to prepare accounts

A parent company is obliged to prepare consolidated annual accounts for the group, ie a profit and loss account and balance sheet incorporating the results, assets and liabilities of the parent and all the subsidiary undertakings in the group; this is in addition to preparing its own annual accounts. Group accounts must be approved by the directors of the parent company and audited by its auditors; they must be laid before the members of the parent company and filed with the Registrar of Companies (at the same time as the parent company's own accounts). The purpose of these provisions is to enable the members of the parent company to obtain an overall impression of the prosperity (or otherwise) and prospects of the group as a whole.

There is no obligation to produce group accounts where the group comes within the definition of a 'small' group. Also, an intermediate parent company which is itself included in consolidated accounts does not generally have to produce group accounts; it must, however, file a copy of these consolidated accounts with the Registrar of Companies together with its own accounts.

Lastly, certain information must be included in notes to the accounts. For example, parent companies must list their subsidiary undertakings and give details of their shareholdings, whilst subsidiaries are obliged to reveal the name of their ultimate parent company.

11.1.5   Taxation

Although each company in a group is a separate legal entity, the group is treated as a single entity for certain tax purposes. This has the advantage of avoiding a plethora of tax charges on intra-group transactions and enables the group as a whole to take greater advantage of reliefs (**11.4**). Indeed, if each member of the group were treated as independent for tax purposes, the group structure, which has proved so popular commercially, would compare very unfavourably with the divisional structure. Inevitably, the legislation is complex and the companies within a 'group' must meet the specific definitions in the tax legislation.

11.1.5.1   Small companies rate of corporation tax

Although each group company is responsible for its own taxation, the tax legislation does recognise that the income generated by each group company contributes to the overall profit of the group. Each member of a group does not have the full benefit of the small companies rate of corporation tax, where profits do not exceed £300,000, or the marginal rate of tax where profits are between £300,000 and £1,500,000. Where companies are 'associated', the upper limit of each tax band is divided by the number of companies in the association. Two companies are associated if one has control (broadly, a majority of the issued share capital or voting power: ICTA 1988, s 416) of the other, or if they are under common control (ICTA 1988, s 13).

Example 1

D Ltd has four wholly-owned subsidiaries. The upper limit for the small companies rate for each company will be £60,000, and the threshold for the full corporation tax rate will be £300,000 (limits divided by five, as there are five companies in the association – D Ltd plus four subsidiaries). In other words, if the profits of one of the subsidiaries are £59,000 then, for the tax year 2008/09, it will pay corporation tax at 21%. Similarly, if another subsidiary makes profits for the same tax year of £400,000, it will pay corporation tax at 28%, and so on.

11.1.5.2   VAT group registration

Tax legislation also recognises that group companies will supply goods and services to each other, or even on behalf of each other. Two or more companies which are UK resident can apply to HMRC for a group VAT registration if, inter alia, one controls each of the others (VATA 1994, s 43). Broadly, control is defined as holding a majority of the voting rights or controlling the composition of the board of directors.

Group registration is in the name of a 'representative member'. Any supply made by a group member to a person outside the group is deemed made by the representative member. Equally, any supply made to a group member by a person outside the group is deemed made to the representative member. This does not mean that other group members escape liability; all members of the group registration are jointly and severally liable for VAT due from the representative member.

The other main consequence of registration is that supplies between members of a group registration are disregarded for VAT purposes.

Once a group registration is in place, other companies may be included, or existing companies may be excluded from the group on application to HMRC. This will be a relevant factor if a subsidiary which is a member of a group registration is transferred outside the group. The buyer of a subsidiary should always check its VAT status and seek warranties that VAT has been properly accounted for (whether or not the subsidiary is part of a group registration).

In the Finance Act 1996, HMRC was given wide discretionary powers to counter avoidance schemes. These include, for example, the power to direct that supplies between group companies are to be subject to VAT.

11.2 Overview of group reorganisations

Group reorganisation is a generic term that can be used to describe anything from the transfer of a couple of assets to a complete restructuring of an entire group of companies. On an initial consideration it may be thought that if a transfer is between companies under common ownership there is no need for a formal acquisition process. However, each company is a separate legal entity and should enter into an agreement for the transfer of assets only after due consideration. Any such transfer should be properly documented and any tax considerations carefully examined. Although there may be no need for lengthy negotiations on the allocation of risk in the transaction, other concerns may need to be addressed. This is the case particularly if the intra-group transfer of assets is to be followed by a sale to an external third party. The third party buyer should investigate the terms of the intra-group transfer in its due diligence investigations in case there are any latent tax liabilities or breaches of company law provisions.

11.2.1 Why companies transfer assets intra-group

Many businesses develop through a series of acquisitions or internal expansion and so are not necessarily well-organised, self-contained units. Within a group, assets may be used by a number of different group companies and a variety of services may be provided across the group. This situation may not be regularised until a restructuring of the group becomes necessary, whether to improve efficiency, to prepare a group company or division for sale to an external third party, or to accommodate a new acquisition.

11.2.1.1 Transfers before a sale to third party

A transfer of assets between group companies may be required if a prospective buyer has indentified that a particular asset or service that it requires is actually held by another company within the group.

A transfer may also be required in order to create a packaged unit for sale to an external third party. For example, the buyer may want to acquire a division but the parties prefer the transaction to proceed as a share acquisition. The seller may undertake a hive-down (**1.4.2**) by which it transfers the assets of the division into a newly-created subsidiary, the shares of which are then sold on to the buyer.

11.2.2   Documenting the transfer

As with a sale to an external third party, an intra-group transfer should be properly documented with details of the assets being transferred. This is relatively straightforward where the transfer is of a shareholding in a subsidiary from one group company to another. However, contracts held by that subsidiary company should still be checked to confirm that they will not be affected by clauses that may enable termination in the event of a change of control of the company (although such clauses usually exclude transfers within the same group of companies). Where the transfer is of other assets, the details of those assets should be specified in the contract and the appropriate individual transfers undertaken. This may involve obtaining consents from third parties as in an asset acquisition with a third party (see **8.2**).

11.3   Regulatory issues on intra-group transfers

On transfers between group companies, consideration has to be given to the potential company law issues that may arise on the transfer. Although these are unlikely to be of practical significance whilst the companies involved are under the same ownership, these issues will be the subject of careful scrutiny in the event that any company is subsequently sold out of the group or becomes subject to insolvency proceedings.

11.3.1   Directors' duties

11.3.1.1   Duty owed to own company

The board of directors of every company involved in an intra-group transfer should give formal approval for the transfer in the same manner as required for an acquisition with a third party. The directors of each company owe a duty to their own company, so the intra-group transfer should be considered to be in the best interests of the companies involved. Each company must be treated as a separate legal entity, and the directors of a particular company are not entitled to sacrifice the interests of that company for the interests of other members of the group (*Charterbridge Corporation v Lloyds Bank Limited* [1970] Ch 62).

As with any other acquisition, the directors must ensure that in approving the transfer they are complying with their statutory duties and that consideration of the interests of the company is recorded in the minutes. However, even if the transfer does give rise to a potential breach of duty, if it is in the interests of other companies within the group, the breach may be ratified by the shareholders (*Rolled Steel Products (Holdings) Ltd v British Steel Corporation* [1986] 1 Ch 246), provided that the transaction is lawful (**11.3.2**), within the objects of the company and that the company is solvent at the time of the transfer (**11.3.1.2**).

11.3.1.2   Transfer at book value

Intra-group transfers have traditionally been undertaken on the basis of the value of the assets as specified in the company's accounts ('book value'). This avoids the need for any separate valuation to ascertain the actual value; however, it does mean that the company may well transfer the assets at less than their market value.

A transfer at book value is potentially a breach of duty and the directors should, for their own protection, seek confirmation from the holding company that the reorganisation is in the best interests of the group. This confirmation will act as a ratification by shareholders of any potential breach of duty, including a transfer at undervalue. However, it should be noted that such ratification will not be effective if the company is insolvent at the time of the breach, because in these circumstances the duty to the company would also extend to the creditors (*West Mercia Safetywear Ltd v Dodds* [1988] BCLC 250). There may also be specific problems with transfers at an undervalue under insolvency law and therefore, if there are any concerns about the solvency of the transferring company, the assets should either be transferred at market value or evidence of the solvency of the transferring company should be obtained.

11.3.2 Distributions in kind

An intra-group transfer at an undervalue can also give rise to company law issues as a distribution in kind. A transfer of an asset at an undervalue from a subsidiary to its holding company will be treated as a distribution in kind, as will a transfer between two subsidiaries that have the same holding company.

For this deemed distribution in kind to be lawful, it must be made in accordance with the statutory provisions governing distributions, ie there must be sufficient distributable profits available for the distribution to be made. A distribution will usually be declared by the company, but a deemed distribution in kind can be ratified by the shareholders, thereby rendering the distribution lawful. However, if the amount of the distribution exceeds distributable profits then the amount of the excess will be regarded as an unlawful reduction of the transferor's capital and this will not be capable of ratification (*Aveling Barford* [1989] BCLC 626).

In order to determine whether a distribution in kind can lawfully be made, the amount of that distribution has to be established.

How the amount of the distribution in kind is determined will depend on the distributable profits of the transferring company. Section 845 of the CA 2006 provides that the amount of the distribution is calculated by reference to the book value of the asset. The amount of the distribution will be zero if the asset was transferred at book value, or, if transferred for less than book value, the distribution will be of the amount by which the book value exceeds the consideration actually received for the asset. However, this section applies only if the transferring company has distributable profits at the time the asset is transferred and could lawfully make a distribution of the amount calculated under the provisions of the section.

If the company had no, or insufficient, distributable profit available, the distribution will be unlawful and the amount of the unlawful distribution will be the full difference between the market value of the asset and the consideration actually received by the company (s 846). This is significant, because any member of the company who knows or has reasonable grounds for believing that the distribution is unlawful is liable to repay the distribution (s 847(2)(a)). Where both companies had common directors (as is often the case with group companies) the requisite awareness might be implied. Such a request for payment would not usually arise between group companies, but if one of the companies is sold out of the group, the new shareholders may make a request for repayment.

11.4   Tax implications of intra-group transfers

A transfer of assets between group companies is subject to the same general taxation principle as a sale to an external third party. A transfer of assets is taxed according to the nature of the asset transferred. For example, a transfer of shares in a subsidiary company will be the transfer of a capital asset and the transfer of a division may involve the transfer of a number of different types of assets, each taxed according to the nature of that asset, such as land (capital), intellectual property rights (intangible) and stock (income). However, as highlighted earlier, a group of companies may be treated as a single entity and such transfers may be treated as 'tax neutral' if they are within a particular tax group. Unfortunately there is no single universal definition of a 'group' for tax purposes. Whether the relationship between the transferring companies is sufficient for them to obtain, or indeed be subject to, group provisions will vary depending on the tax legislation in question. However, in determining these relationships, a common system of classification of subsidiaries is employed within tax legislation.

11.4.1   Classification of subsidiaries for tax groups

Groups are defined for tax purposes by reference to the percentage of ordinary share capital which companies hold in their subsidiaries. Subsidiaries are described, inter alia, as '51% subsidiaries', '75% subsidiaries', and '100% (or wholly-owned) subsidiaries' (ICTA 1988, s 838). For a company to have a 51% subsidiary, it must own, directly or indirectly, over 50% of the ordinary share capital of the company; for a 75% subsidiary, the holding must be not less than 75%. Clearly, a 75% subsidiary also qualifies as a 51% subsidiary. Certain 'economic ownership tests' must also be satisfied (see **11.4.1.4**).

11.4.1.1   'Ordinary share capital'

The definition of ordinary share capital is wide; it includes all the issued share capital of a company (whatever it is called), other than capital the holders of which have a right to a dividend at a fixed rate but no other right to share in the profits of the company (s 832(1)). Thus, shares with no voting rights or carrying no rights to a dividend may still be classed as ordinary shares for this purpose.

11.4.1.2   Owned 'directly or indirectly'

Ownership may be direct or indirect. Indirect ownership means ownership through another company. Consider the examples below (which assume that the relevant 'economic ownership tests', as discussed at **11.4.1.4**, are satisfied).

Example 2

B Ltd is a wholly-owned subsidiary of A Ltd (direct).

C Ltd is a 51% subsidiary of B Ltd (direct).

C Ltd is also a 51% subsidiary of A Ltd (indirect).

Example 3

D Ltd owns 80% of E Ltd. E Ltd is a 75% subsidiary of D Ltd.

E Ltd owns 80% of F Ltd. F Ltd is a 75% subsidiary of E Ltd.

D Ltd owns 80% × 80 = 64% of F Ltd. F Ltd is a 51% subsidiary of D Ltd (but not a 75% subsidiary).

Example 4

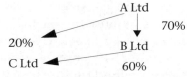

A Ltd owns 70% of B Ltd. B Ltd is a 51% subsidiary of A Ltd.

B Ltd owns 60% of C Ltd. C Ltd is a 51% subsidiary of B Ltd.

A Ltd owns 20% (directly) and 70% × 60 = 42% (indirectly) of C Ltd. C Ltd is a 51% subsidiary of A Ltd.

11.4.1.3 Beneficial ownership

The company must be the beneficial owner of the appropriate percentage of the share capital in the other company. A company which enters into an unconditional contract (or a conditional contract if the condition can be waived by the buyer) for the sale of the entire share capital of a subsidiary ceases to have beneficial ownership of the shares. It is important, therefore, that any intra-group transactions take place before this happens.

11.4.1.4 'Economic ownership tests'

In order to prevent the creation of artificial groups, 'economic ownership tests' must also be satisfied for a company to come within the definition of a 51% or 75% subsidiary (ICTA 1988, Sch 18). In addition to owning beneficially the required percentage of the ordinary shares of the subsidiary, the parent company must fulfil the following two requirements:

(a) be beneficially entitled to more than 50% (or, in the case of a 75% subsidiary, not less than 75%) of the profits available for distribution to equity holders of the subsidiary; and

(b) be beneficially entitled to more than 50% (or, in the case of a 75% subsidiary, not less than 75%) of any assets of the subsidiary available for distribution to its equity holders on a winding up.

Beneficial entitlement to profits and assets may arise directly or through intervening companies. Special rules for determining this entitlement are at ICTA 1988, Sch 18.

11.4.2 Transfer of income assets

The transfer of a division is likely to involve the transfer of income assets such as stock or work in progress. In a group reorganisation such assets will often be transferred at cost and so would not give rise to a taxable profit. However, it should be noted that for certain large corporations the transfer of goods will be deemed to have been at market value regardless of the actual price paid if the parties are deemed connected under the Transfer Pricing Rules (ICTA 1988, Sch 28AA), the details of which are outside the scope of this book. In the event that an income profit has been made, there is scope to offset this profit against any trading losses that may have been made in another company.

11.4.2.1   Group relief (ICTA 1988, s 402)

Group relief enables a company (the surrendering company) which has incurred a trading loss in an accounting period, or which has charges on income or loan relationship debits, such as interest payments, to surrender these to another member of the group (the claimant company). This enables the claimant company to set the loss or charges on income or debits against its own taxable profits (ie income profits and chargeable gains), thus reducing its liability to corporation tax. The claimant company must first deduct its own charges on income and any current or brought forward losses. The surrendering company can surrender only trading losses, etc, of its current accounting period. The claimant company must set them against profits of the corresponding accounting period and cannot carry them forward or back. There are special rules which regulate the amount of losses which can be surrendered and claimed by companies with different accounting periods.

The whole of the trading loss, etc does not need to be surrendered and partial surrenders may be made to different members of the group. If the claimant company pays the surrendering company for the use of the trading losses, etc, the payment itself does not affect the tax position of either company, provided it does not exceed the amount of losses surrendered.

11.4.2.2   Applicable groups

Two companies are members of a group for the purposes of this relief if one is a 75% subsidiary of the other, or if both are 75% subsidiaries of a third (ICTA 1988, s 413(3)). Generally, for the relief to apply, the surrendering and claimant companies should both be resident in the UK (though since April 2006, companies may, in limited circumstances, claim relief for losses incurred by subsidiaries resident in the European Economic Area – see *Marks & Spencer plc v Halsey (Inspector of Taxes)* [2007] EWCA Civ 117). Consider Example 5 below.

Example 5

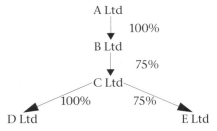

D Ltd is a 100% subsidiary of C Ltd and a 75% subsidiary of both B Ltd and A Ltd. A Ltd, B Ltd, C Ltd and D Ltd are members of a 75% group.

E Ltd does not form part of such a group since A Ltd and B Ltd own only 75% × 75 = 56.25% of E Ltd.

E Ltd is a 75% subsidiary of C Ltd. C Ltd, D Ltd and E Ltd form a 75% group.

11.4.2.3   Example of group relief

Example 6

A Ltd owns 100% of B Ltd. Both companies have the same accounting reference date of 30 September. In the accounting period ending 30 September 2007, B Ltd makes a trading loss of £50,000 (and no chargeable gains), whereas A Ltd makes total profits of £150,000.

B Ltd can carry the loss back against any profits of the preceding year, thus entitling B Ltd to reclaim tax (ICTA 1988, s 393A). Carry forward relief against trading profits is also available to B Ltd to reduce future corporation tax assessments (s 393). B Ltd may, however, choose to surrender all or part of the trading loss to A Ltd. If the whole of the loss is surrendered, A Ltd's profits liable to corporation tax for the year ended 30 September are reduced to £100,000.

11.4.2.4   Companies joining or leaving the group

As an anti-avoidance measure, s 410 of ICTA 1988 was designed to prevent the artificial manipulation of group relief by the forming of groups on a temporary basis in order to obtain relief. In other words, a company with a loss arising, or due to arise, cannot join an unconnected group, surrender its losses and then depart from the group afterwards.

A company will not be regarded as a member of the group if 'arrangements' are in existence for the transfer of that company to another group: relief is not available during any period when such arrangements are in force (*Shepherd (Inspector of Taxes) v Law Land plc* [1990] STC 795).

In the context of an acquisition, therefore, losses will generally be available for surrender between other members of the group only if they arose *before* 'arrangements' are in place for the sale of the target.

So, when do 'arrangements' come into existence for this purpose? It is clear that there does not have to be a binding contract for the acquisition of the shares; the signing of heads of agreement may, for example, be sufficient to prevent group relief. Although there is no statutory definition of 'arrangements', HMRC provides some guidance in a Statement of Practice (SP 3/93). The main points arising from the Statement are as follows:

(a)   arrangements will not normally come into existence in the case of a straightforward sale of a company before the date of the acceptance (subject to contract or on a similar conditional basis) of the offer;

(b)   where a disposal of shares requires approval of shareholders, no arrangement will come into existence until that approval has been given or the directors are aware that it will be given;

(c)   'arrangements' might exist if there is an 'understanding between the parties in the character of an option' for a potential buyer to acquire shares.

When a company joins or leaves the group, ss 403A–403C of ICTA 1988 provide for the group relief to be apportioned.

11.4.3   Transfer of capital assets

11.4.3.1   Tax neutral

If capital assets are transferred within a defined group then the transfer will be deemed as tax neutral (TCGA 1992, s 171). Such a disposal is treated as being for such a consideration (whatever the actual consideration passing) as not to give rise to either a capital gain or a loss. However, if that asset is transferred out of that defined group, or the company that received that asset leaves the defined group within six years of receiving that asset, then a tax charge will arise.

11.4.3.2   Definition of 'group'

The definition of a group for the purposes of the provisions on the transfer of capital assets is contained in s 170 of the TCGA 1992. The following rules apply:

(a)   a company (the 'principal company') forms a group with all its 75% subsidiaries;

(b)   the group also includes any 75% subsidiaries of those subsidiaries (and so on) if they are 'effective 51% subsidiaries' of the principal company;

(c)   for a subsidiary to be an 'effective 51% subsidiary', the principal company must be beneficially entitled to more than 50% of any profits available for distribution to equity holders of the subsidiary and more than 50% of any assets available for distribution to equity holders on a winding up;

(d)   a company which is a 75% subsidiary of another company cannot itself be a principal company unless it is prevented from being part of a group because it fails the 'effective 51% subsidiary' test.

All companies must be UK tax resident. See Example 7 below.

> **Example 7**

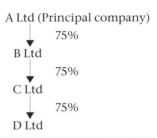

A Ltd, B Ltd and C Ltd form a group (C Ltd is a 75% × 75% = 56.25% subsidiary of A Ltd).

D Ltd is not part of the group as it is not a 51% subsidiary of A Ltd (A Ltd indirectly owns 75% × 75% × 75% = 42.18% of the shares in D Ltd).

As D Ltd cannot be part of the group it can be a principal company of its own group. Thus if D Ltd has a 75% subsidiary, E Ltd, D Ltd and E Ltd form a group.

Note that B Ltd and C Ltd cannot be principals of their own groups because they are 75% subsidiaries of other companies and do not fail the 51% subsidiary test.

11.4.3.3   Degrouping charge on company leaving the group

A corporation tax charge on the postponed capital gain will be triggered if the company leaves the group within six years of *receiving* the asset from another group member on a no gain/no loss basis. Section 179 of the TCGA 1992 provides that, on leaving a group, a company is treated as if it had sold and immediately re-acquired any asset which had been transferred to it from another member of the group within the previous six years. For the purpose of calculating the gain (or loss), this disposal and reacquisition is deemed to have taken place on the date the asset was last acquired intra-group. The gain or loss (often called a 'degrouping gain/loss') is, however, treated as arising immediately after the start of the accounting period of the company in which it ceases to be a member of the group. The buyer of a target company must therefore investigate whether his acquisition will trigger any such charges and obtain suitable warranties or indemnities from the seller.

Example 8

A Ltd buys some land for £100,000 in 2003. A Ltd transfers the land in 2004 to its wholly-owned subsidiary, B Ltd, for £150,000 (its market value). B Ltd then transfers the land to C Ltd (B Ltd's wholly-owned subsidiary) in 2006 for £250,000 (its market value).

In 2008, C Ltd leaves the group.

No corporation tax is paid on the transfer from A Ltd to B Ltd and on the transfer from B Ltd to C Ltd. These transfers are deemed to be on a no gain/no loss basis.

C Ltd's exit from the group in 2008 triggers a degrouping charge since it leaves the group within six years of acquiring the land. C Ltd is deemed to have sold the land for its market value in 2006 (£250,000) (and reacquired it at that value).

Ignoring indexation, the chargeable gain is £250,000 less the deemed acquisition cost of £100,000, ie £150,000. C Ltd is treated as making this gain in 2008.

Two reliefs are available in respect of a degrouping gain or loss which accrues to a company which ceases to be a member of a group:

(a)   The exiting company can make an election with another company in the seller group to treat all or part of the degrouping gain or loss as accruing to that other company (TCGA 1992, s 179A). Where the operation of s 179 gives rise to an allowable loss, such a loss can also be transferred to another company in the group.

(b)   If the exiting company reinvests in qualifying business assets, the degrouping gain can be rolled over into those new assets (TCGA 1992, s 179B). The usual conditions for business asset roll-over relief apply.

Claims for these reliefs must be made within two years of the end of the accounting period in which the exiting company leaves the group.

If shares are the asset being transferred then the substantial shareholdings exemption may be applied to the degrouping gain or loss, if the company owning the substantial shareholding at the time of the degrouping would have been entitled to the exemption. The company leaving the group will be treated as if it had sold and then reacquired the shareholding immediately before the degrouping and so would qualify for the exemption.

Example 9

A Ltd has two subsidiaries, B Ltd and C Ltd. B Ltd holds shares in another subsidiary, D Ltd. These companies all form a defined group under s170 of the TCGA 1992. In 2006, B Ltd transferred its entire shareholding in D Ltd to C Ltd for no gain/no loss. In 2008, the shares of C Ltd are sold by A Ltd and so C Ltd leaves the group. C Ltd is subject to a degrouping charge because it has left the group within six years of receiving a capital asset from another member of the group. However, as C Ltd is deemed to have sold and immediately reacquired the shareholding at the time it leaves the group, it will have held the shares for the length of time (12 months) required to qualify for the substantial shareholdings exemption and so will have no tax to pay.

Although this gives a flavour of the interaction between intra-group provisions and other corporation tax reliefs, in practice it will be important to take specialist advice.

11.4.3.4   Transferring an asset out of the group

When a company transfers an asset out of the group, there is a charge to corporation tax on any gain that results. Here, the gain is the consideration received on transferring the asset out of the group *less* the price paid by the member who first brought the asset into the group.

So, using the figures from Example 8 in **11.4.3.3**, if C Ltd were to sell the land in 2008 for £300,000 (instead of leaving the group), the gain would be £300,000 less £100,000 (the price paid by A Ltd), ie £200,000.

11.4.4   Intangible assets and loan relationships

Provisions similar to those in relation to the transfer of capital assets apply to assets which are subject to the intangible assets regime (ie intangible assets such as intellectual property rights that were created or acquired from an unrelated party after 1 April 2002) under paras 55 and 140 of Sch 29 to the Finance Act 2002. If such intangible assets are transferred within a defined group, the transfer will be deemed as tax neutral (ie so as to create neither a capital gain nor a capital loss). The defined group is substantially the same as that under s 170 of the TCGA 1992 for capital assets, and if the receiving company leaves the defined group it is subject to a degrouping charge based on the same criteria as those which relate to the transfer of a capital asset. However, there is one important distinction; rather than arising at the start of the accounting period in which it leaves the group, as for a capital asset, the resulting degrouping charge arises immediately before the transferee leaves the group.

It should also be noted that similar provisions apply in relation to the transfer of certain intra-group loans and debt securities, the details of which are outside the scope of this book.

11.4.5   Stamp duty and stamp duty land tax

Subject to certain anti-avoidance provisions, complete relief from stamp duty is available on a transfer of shares between companies where one company is a 75% subsidiary of the other or both are 75% subsidiaries of a third company (Finance Act 1930, s 42, as amended). In determining whether a company is a 75% subsidiary of another, direct or indirect shareholdings of ordinary shares are taken into account, and the economic ownership tests referred to at **11.4.1.4** must be satisfied.

For the purposes of stamp duty land tax, intra-group transactions are deemed to take place at market value regardless of the actual consideration given (Finance Act 2003, s 53). However, it is generally possible to claim group relief (subject to certain anti-avoidance provisions). The group relief for stamp duty land tax purposes is broadly the same as for stamp duty (Finance Act 2003, Sch 7). However, stamp duty land tax group relief can be clawed back if, within three years of the effective date of the intra-group land transaction, the transferee leaves the group of which it and the transferor were members and it, or a relevant associated company, holds the land that was transferred intra-group (Finance Act 2003, Sch 7, para 3).

The Finance Act 2008 introduced a further extension to the clawback rules. The Revenue had identified a number of schemes which allowed the transferor to leave the group first, thereby allowing the transferee company subsequently to leave the group without any clawback of group relief. The additional anti-avoidance provision will operate where the transferor company leaves the group and there is a subsequent change in control of the transferee within three years of the land being transferred.

Index